D0205662

The Founders of
Humanistic
Psychology

THE **FOUNDERS** OF **HUMANISTIC PSYCHOLOGY**

Roy José DeCarvalho

Foreword by Stanley Krippner

PRAEGER

New York
Westport, Connecticut
London

Library of Congress Cataloging-in-Publication Data

DeCarvalho, Roy José.
    The founders of humanistic psychology / Roy José DeCarvalho.
      p.   cm.
    Includes bibliographical references and index.
    ISBN 0–275–94008-X (alk. paper)
    1. Humanistic psychology. 2. Psychologists—United States—
Biography. I. Title.
  BF204.D4   1991
   150.19'8—dc20   91–444

British Library Cataloguing in Publication Data is available.

Library of Congress Catalog Card Number: 91–444
ISBN: 0–275–94008–X

First published in 1991

Praeger Publishers, One Madison Avenue, New York, NY 10010
An imprint of Greenwood Publishing Group, Inc.

Printed in the United States of America

The paper used in this book complies with the
Permanent Paper Standard issued by the National
Information Standards Organization (Z39.48–1984).

10 9 8 7 6 5 4 3 2 1

To Celiza

Contents

viii   Contents

Foreword

Psychological theories have reflected external and internal realities in various ways. Freudian psychoanalysis was influenced by "energy" models predominant at the time, and Freud's model of the psyche resembled a hydraulic pump supplying (or denying) libido for various human activities. Watsonian behaviorism presented a model resembling a slot machine; an external stimulus produced an output, and the inner workings of the machine were disregarded. It is not a simple matter to present a single model of humanistic psychology because each theory reflects the background and interests of its author. As a result, it is more appropriate to refer to the "humanistic psychologies" and consider each of them separately.

This is the procedure followed by Roy DeCarvalho in this book. His remarkable historical analysis reveals that humanistic psychology had no single founder. As a result, he focuses on five prominent individuals and traces the roots of their models, emphasizing such diverse origins as European existentialism and phenomenology, American pragmatism, and the Gestalt and organismic theorists. However, the humanistic psychologies have made unique contributions as well, emphasizing the importance of values, ethics, creativity, human potentials, and goal-direction or intent. Indeed, Charlotte Buhler once defined humanistic psychology as "the scientific study of behavior, experience, and intentionality."

The models of human nature discussed in this book can all be subsumed by Buhler's definition. However, there are unique emphases and distinctions. Gordon W. Allport opposed using natural science prototypes to describe human beings, preferring to study individuals and their differences in terms of traits. One can imagine a prism composed of these traits—but a prism that is constantly developing and changing, a prism different from all others in the world, a prism that constantly interacts with its environment—hence producing a continuing display of colors and hues, yet an array that manifests a stable structure (i.e., the "proprium").

Abraham H. Maslow's model resembles a terraced hillside, each hill's terrace representing a level of his "hierarchy of needs," working their way up from the physiological needs to those of safety, security, affiliation, esteem, and finally—as one approaches the crest of the hill—the self-actualization needs. Each hillside is a part of the entire terrain; Maslow's interest in human synergy enjoined him from seeing the hills as independent from each other.

Carl R. Rogers's model is one of two overlapping circles—one of the self's structure and one of experience. When the self is in touch with its experience, the circles are congruent; the absence of congruence reflects itself in poor adaptive skills and flawed communicative ability. However, there is an inner tendency toward harmony, and this inclination can be fostered by the internal or external endowment of self-regard.

Rollo May presents a model of the person beset by anxiety. Imagine a figure being pulled by two strong forces, a vulnerable entity torn between his or her expectations and realities, between the infinite and the finite, between being and non-being. But the denouement of this paradox can be accomplished through an appeal to myths—those perennial narratives that have always helped humankind deal with the dilemmas of existence.

James F. T. Bugental's model can be visualized as a spotlight which illuminates the "ever-flowing moment," the only point at which the experiencing person is actually alive. To provide vitality, insight, and life to this moment, an individual needs to adopt a "humanistic ethic" which stresses personal responsibility for one's actions. This ethic is in constant dialogue with one's society; when they clash, the person may become a social change agent. This ethic brings meaning to suffering, conflict, and grief, as well as to love, joy, and mutuality of relationships.

It has been my great fortune to have known each of these historical figures, each of them an inspiring thinker who has brought an important perspective to psychology. This humanistic perspective is able to incorporate insights and information from psychoanalysis, behaviorism, and all the other schools of psychology. In addition, the humanistic psychologies add something of their own to the brew—a recognition that human beings must be studied on their own terms. The paradigms of nature science, the data from the animal laboratories, and the dogmas inherent in religious, economic, and political theories can be of limited value in fathoming human behavior, experience, and intention. For this we must turn to the lived human adventure itself. And for this disciplined inquiry owes the humanistic psychologies—and the psychologists discussed in this book—a monumental debt.

—Stanley Krippner
Professor of Psychology, Saybrook Institute

Acknowledgments and Bibliographical Note

I wish to thank Professor Victor Hilts of the Department of the History of Science for his wisdom, guidance, and patience. His trust in my academic abilities was a major source of encouragement and inspiration without which this manuscript would have never been written—a debt I can never repay.

I am thankful to Stanley Krippner and Deborah Swachkamer, who were instrumental in arranging small grants when financial despair almost brought this project to a halt; to Carl Rogers, Rollo May, Jim Bugental, Mike Arons, and the staff of the Association for Humanistic Psychology for their assistance during the early stages of the project; and to my beloved students, who gave me a deeper insight into humanistic psychology. I am also indebted to Debra Rabin, who made graduate school and this academic achievement possible, and I gratefully acknowledge the indefatigable support of Stanley Kripper toward the completion of this project. I am, above all, thankful to my wife, Celiza, for preparation of the early version of the manuscript and constant reminder of the deadlines, as well as healthy distractions from what could otherwise be a manuscript obsession. The joint New York State/United University Professions, Dr. Nuala McGann Drescher Affirmative Action Leave Award supported the writing of the last three chapters and the final preparation of the manuscript for publication.

Because of extensive discussion of the writings of the five humanistic psychologists examined in this study, I developed a special reference format. Appended at the end of the manuscript are complete chronological bibliographies. The chapter notes referring to these bibliographies include the year of publication and item letter, followed by the page number. The codes used were: "A" for Allport, "M" for Maslow, "R" for Rogers, "MY" for May, and "B" for Bugental. For example, "A1923a:64," refers to Allport's chronological bibliography, year 1923, item "a" (e.g., "Germany's state of mind"), page 64.

The Founders of Humanistic Psychology

1

Introduction

Despite the growth of the psychoanalytical movement after World War II, the behavioristic orientation permeated mid–twentieth-century American psychology. Some psychologists, however, during the "golden age" of behaviorism following World War II, were discontented with behaviorism's view of human nature and method. They drew upon a long tradition linking psychology with the humanities and, in a rebellious manner, institutionally founded humanistic psychology. They regarded themselves as a "third force," alluding to the fact that they were an alternative to the dominant behavioristic and psychoanalytical orientation in psychology.

This book relates the formal organization of humanistic psychology and attempts to delineate the intellectual trends characteristic of the movement's beginning. More specifically, it discusses the place of humanistic psychology in the context of the main currents of post–World War II psychology. It explains the revolt of the humanistic psychologists against behaviorism and psychoanalysis, and the impact that the neo-Freudians, existentialism, Kurt Goldstein, personality psychology, and Gestalt psychology had on their thought.[1]

The eclectic melting pot of the founding members of the Association for Humanistic Psychology (AHP) and the absence of a single founder or humanistic orthodoxy in psychology make an intellectual account of the history of humanistic psychology an extremely difficult task. The 200 members of the AHP in 1963 and 500 in 1965 included psychologists sympathetic to the orientations of classical phenomenologists (Franz Brentano, Edmund Husserl, Maurice Merleau-Ponty), European theorists of Geisteswissenschaften (Wilhelm Dilthey, Duane Schultz); dialogical-religious (Gabriel Marcel, Martin Buber, Soren Kierkegaard), secular (Martin Heidegger, Jean-Paul Sartre, Albert Camus), and psychological (Karl Jaspers, Ludwig Binswanger, Medard Boss) emphases of existentialism; Gestalt psychology (Max Wertheimer, Kurt Koffka, Kurt Lewin), person-oriented neo-Freudians (Alfred Adler, Carl Jung, Otto Rank), organismic psychology of Kurt Goldstein; personality theorists who advocated an active and interactive self (William James, John Dewey, Margaret Mead, Harry Stack Sullivan), and the contributions of American personality psychologists (Henry Murray, Gardner Murphy, Hadley Cantril, George Kelly, Clark Moustakas). Finally, to make the picture more confusing, we find traces of the hippy counterculture of the 1960s, the human potential movement, and the Big Sur–Esalen phenomena, from which the more academically oriented humanistic psychologists sought to distance themselves. The only common ground the founding members of the AHP shared was a willingness to do something about their deep dissatisfaction with the domineering presence of behaviorism and psychoanalysis in mid-century American psychology.

When the movement came to maturity, however, affirmative statements replaced mere protest and few humanistic psychologists stood out either because of their leadership roles or because their writings were sought for intellectual inspiration and legitimization. In writing this intellectual history I refer to this group as the founders of humanistic psychology. They are Gordon Allport, Abraham Maslow, Carl Rogers, Rollo May, and James Bugental.

Intellectual histories are often vague because they focus on ideas as if they have an ontological reality and assign a vague, puppetlike role to their human protagonists. To avoid this pitfall I assumed that the original ideas of the five founders of humanistic psychology share crucial similarities, thus emphasizing people over the abstract synthesis of their thought. I focused on the individual nuances of the humanistic thought they shared, aiming to capture the uniqueness of each while writing an intellectual history. Each thinker is biographically introduced in Chapter 3.

The thoughts of individuals, however, are not the only forces involved in the organization of intellectual movements within the sciences; political institutions that bring the individuals together are also necessary. In order to advance their ideas and concerns as a movement they need grants, research facilities, and intellectual stimulation by means of seminars, conferences, and journals; they need, in other words, institutions. The institutionalization of humanistic psychology was primarily a product of the efforts of Abraham Maslow and Anthony Sutich; it is discussed in Chapter 2.

Although there was no melting pot of humanistic psychologies, in focusing on the selected five thinkers we learn that despite philosophical similarities between Continental existentialism, phenomenology, and humanistic psychology, humanistic psychology has unique American characteristics because it was primarily a pragmatic response to behaviorism. But since, in addition to existentialism and phenomenology, the other sources of inspiration in humanistic psychology (e.g., Kurt Goldstein, the neo-Freudians, Gestalt and personality psychologies) were also of European origin, the history of humanistic psychology should be included in the broad context of the history of Western psychology.

Two models, or paradigms, of human nature and scientific method have dominated modern psychology: the objective or experimental (whether in its behavioristic or psychoanalytical forms) and the subjective or experiential (whether in its phenomenological or existential forms). The objective-experimental paradigm views human nature as a natural phenomenon best studied by the methods of the natural sciences. The positivist philosophy of Auguste Comte at the beginning of the nineteenth century offered the first clear enunciation of this view. Working from the assumption that the physical, biological, human, and social phenomena were equal in principle, he argued that it was time to introduce the method of positivism to the human sciences, which he named "social physics."

A century later, experimental psychologists took up Comte's program seriously. They advocated the exclusive use of observation in the study of human behavior. Throughout the first half of the twentieth century, behaviorism perpetuated Comte's ideal. J. B. Watson, the American proponent of the science of behavior, thought that people and animals could be studied with equal success under the same experimental conditions, since no line divided them. He thus proposed a psychology that was to be a "purely objective experimental branch of natural sciences."[2]

During the first quarter of the century, Edmund Husserl criticized this positivistic attitude as "psychologism." He argued that humans have a subjective existence, the study of which requires the development of a unique science, not an imitation of the natural sciences. In 1925 he termed this unique science "phenomenological psychology," or "the science of inner-experience, subjectivity, and the mental."[3]

A decade later, reacting against Husserl's transcendental phenomenology and the concept of the transcendental ego, Martin Heidegger and Jean-Paul Sartre argued that Husserl had gone too far in the search for transcendental concepts within subjectivity, thus betraying his own phenomenological principles. By requesting a return to subjectivity, they created an existentialist wing in the phenomenological movement. Sartre proposed his own existential psychoanalysis, and Ludwig Binswanger and Medard Boss, elaborating on Heidegger's concept of Dasein, developed the Daseinsanalysis.[4]

Following Husserl's criticism of psychologism, phenomenological and existential psychologists have deemed the positivist ideal of experimental psychology to be philosophically immature. In return, experimental psychologists have considered their study of consciousness and subjectivity as the pursuit of an illusion. Proponents of both paradigms accused one another of naively misunderstanding human nature and the methodology of psychology. This philosophical antagonism has been such that, historically speaking, rapprochement has been impossible. In many ways this is the controversy between the Lockean and Leibnitzian philosophical traditions, according to Allport, and the Apollonian and Dionysian cultures, according to Frederick Nietzsche.

As an intellectual history, this study examines humanistic psychology in the context of the conflict between the objective or experimental and the subjective or experiential paradigms. This approach to the history of humanistic psychology is particularly suitable to clarification of the philosophical tension between the paradigms because the movement represented an attempt to introduce the understanding of phenomenology and existentialism into the heart of the behavioristic milieu that intellectually nurtured humanistic psychologists. Indeed, no one understood both paradigms better than they did—a rare occurrence in the history of psychology. Therefore, this history is more than a mere internal history of humanistic psychology; it is also a discussion of what is, in our understanding, the most dramatic issue in the history of psychology.

Chapter 4 examines the confrontation of humanistic psychology with behaviorism; Chapter 5 explores the encounter of humanistic psychology with psychoanalysis; Chapter 6 probes the relationship among humanistic psychology, phenomenology, and existentialism; and Chapter 7 discusses additional sources of intellectual influence in humanistic psychology.

The image of human nature is a striking feature of humanistic psychology. It underlines the thoughts of Allport, Maslow, Rogers, May, and Bugental on the nature of psychology and the critique of behaviorism and psychoanalysis. It forms the gravitational pole of their thinking and the unifying element of the humanistic movement in American psychology. They legitimated this feature by firmly asserting that any psychology deserving the name rests a priori on an image of human nature. There was no escape from dealing with the problem of human nature, since—consciously or not—such a view determines the questions of empirical research, the gathering and interpretation of evidence, and above all, the construction of theories. All five founders of humanistic psychology focused much effort in the delineation of their views on human nature. These views are examined in Chapter 8.

Another related theme discussed in Chapter 9 is the founders' views on ethics. No other current in the history and systems of psychology was as concerned with problems of values as were humanistic psychologists. Psychology, they thought, had a major role in clarifying and treating modern ethical dilemmas. It should study human values, guide the neutralism of science and technology with human values, and reintroduce the human perspective to psychology. Although the humanistic psychologists shared a humanistic philosophy, their thoughts on ethics were also heterogeneous: Rollo May advocated an existentialist ethics concerned with courage in the face of freedom and destiny; Maslow and Rogers emphasized a naturalistic ethics based on the growth hypothesis of human nature; and Gordon Allport supported ethical views that were phenomenologically based.

Chapter 10 examines the psychological systems of Allport, Maslow, Rogers, and May in the context of the tension between experimental and experiential methodologies in psychology. The chapter delineates their quantitative and phenomenological studies of the person and attempts to integrate both methodologies. It is argued that their proposal for a humanistic method in psychology was a unique occurrence in the history of Western psychology that clarifies the philosophical tension between the methodological poles.

In conclusion, this intellectual history of humanistic psychology examines the thoughts of five of the founders of the movement in the context of the history of psychology, with emphases on the philosophical encounter of humanistic psychology with behaviorism, psychoanalysis, and existentialism. It also examines the institutionalization, primary sources of intellectual inspiration, unique methodology, views on human nature, and ethics of humanistic psychology.

NOTES

1. There are two types of histories of psychology—those written by historians and those written by psychologists. Psychologists have always pursued historical interests primarily as hobbies. Their histories have pedagogical purposes and, often, are introductory textbooks addressed to psychology students. Authors express their positions on current controversies within the discipline and, in extreme cases, seek legitimacy for current activities and ideas. These histories concentrate almost exclusively on scientific contributions, but they do not place such achievements in the context of broad intellectual and social developments. "History" in this sense, as a historian of science pointed out, is almost synonymous with book review. (R. M. Young, "The Scholarship of the Historiography of the Behavioral Sciences," *J. Hist. Sci.*, 1966, 5:1–51) Written from this perspective, the traditional histories of psychology have ignored or misrepresented the history of humanistic psychology. Only recently have historians of psychology developed an ethos of writing history for its own sake, rather than for legitimizing or pedagogical purposes.

2. J. B. Watson, "Psychology as the Behaviorist Views It," *Psy. Rev.*, 1913, 20:158.

3. Edmund Husserl, *Phenomenological Psychology*, English trans. John Scanlon, The Hague: Nijhoff, 1977.

4. For an overview of the experimental or subjective paradigm, see Rollo May, Ernest Angel, Henri F. Ellenberger, eds., *Existence: A New Dimension in Psychiatry and Psychology*, New York: Basic Books, 1958; P. E. Craig, "Psychotherapy for Freedom," *The Humanistic Psychologist*, 16(1) (special issue).

2

The Institutionalization of Humanistic Psychology

Individual thinkers need social structures, such as associations, conferences, and journals, that bring them together to develop their shared beliefs into a coherent whole. In short, they need institutions. The institutionalization of humanistic psychology was the product of the work and reputation of key psychologists of the period—such as Rollo May, Carl Rogers, Clark Moustakas, Henry Murray, Sydney Jourard—and, primarily, the enthusiasm of Abraham Maslow and the organizational ability of Anthony Sutich.

By the late 1940s Maslow was recognized as a talented experimental psychologist, but as he began exploring "unconventional" subjects he was ostracized by the psychological community. At Brooklyn College, where he first taught, he was very popular among the students, although he had little appreciation within his department. Indeed, colleagues began avoiding him because of his unorthodox interests within the field of psychology. This situation improved somewhat when, in 1952, he was invited to chair the new psychology department at Brandeis University; nevertheless, in relationship to the psychology community at large, his feelings of isolation deepened. In a conversation with a friend, Maslow blamed this situation on the dominant behavioristic presence in psychology. He pointed out, for instance, that it was increasingly hard for him to publish in the mainstream journals of the American Psychological Association (APA). Maslow was, indeed, not alone in this regard; the same complaint was repeatedly voiced by the few in the early 1950s who had not joined the ranks of behaviorism.[1]

This chapter is adapted from an earlier work published by Roy J. DeCarvalho, "A History of the 'Third Force' in Psychology," *Journal of Humanistic Psychology* 30, no. 4, Fall 1990, pp. 22–44. Copyright © 1990 by Sage Publications, Inc.

Maslow began contacting other like-minded psychologists, and in 1954 he compiled a mailing list of about 125 names to provide a means of exchanging mimeographed copies of their respective writings. Over the years the mailing list grew. In the early 1960s the individuals on this list became the first subscribers to the *Journal of Humanistic Psychology* (*JHP*) and members of the American Association for Humanistic Psychology (AAHP). Discontented with the theory and practice of orthodox behavioristic science, Maslow's colleagues slowly emerged as a distinct group within psychology seeking the construction of a separate set of theories and research in psychology.[2]

Maslow's list was generated as a result of his personal relationships with other discontents. Betty W. Keane, one of the people on the list, was a typical case. Keane, who practiced psychotherapy in the 1960s in New York City, advocated an approach to self-discovery through sensory awareness or direct experiencing rather than through verbalization. She was fascinated by the writings of Julian Huxley, Viktor Frankl, the Zen and Gestalt psychologists, and, in particular, Kurt Goldstein. When she read Maslow's *Toward a Psychology of Being* in the early 1960s, she wrote him a letter reporting how impressed she was with the book. Maslow surprised her by calling long distance and expressing interest in learning from her about "sensory awareness." They eventually met and became friends, and Maslow entered her name on the list. For this, Keane wrote many years later, she was "extremely grateful and honored."[3]

Maslow's discontents also included Norma Rosenquist (later Lyman), once referred to as the "midwife of the AAHP" and its first secretary. In 1962 she attended a workshop conducted by May, Maslow, and Rogers at Sonoma State College in California. She was so deeply impressed with the presentations that her life took on a new direction. After the meeting, Maslow put her in touch with Sutich, who was instrumental in the founding of the *JHP* and AAHP. Maslow's organizational efforts were, indeed, quite effective. Jack Gibb, who joined the AAHP in its formative stages and was its president in 1968, wrote that he had joined the "third force" primarily "because of the contagious excitement in a letter from Abe Maslow."[4]

An outgrowth of Maslow's mailing list, which he named the "Eupsychian Network," was published as an addendum in his 1962 work *Toward A Psychology of Being*. He introduced the list by stating,

This is a mailing list that I made up for my own convenience. I call it the Eupsychian Network because all these groups, organizations and journals are interested in helping the individual grow toward fuller humaneness, the society grow toward synergy and health, and all societies and all peoples move toward becoming one world and one species. This list can be called a network because the memberships overlap considerably and because these organizations and individuals more or less share the humanistic and trans-humanistic outlook on life even prior to confirmation of that outlook.[5]

In the late 1950s one of those on Maslow's original list, Anthony Sutich, became Maslow's aide in the founding of two key institutions of humanistic psychology—the Journal and the American Association for Humanistic Psychology. Because of severe progressive arthritis that began in his childhood, Sutich was largely self-taught. His first publications, influenced by Alfred Adler and Carl Jung, were in semantics, ethics, and values. In the early 1940s he exchanged correspondence with Gordon Allport on the publication of a "Code of Ethics for Psychologists," and in the early 1950s he became involved with group therapy as an outgrowth of his interest in Rogers's concept of growth. Sutich first met Maslow in 1949 through a friend of Maslow's family. In this initial contact, they expressed a deep common anger over the dominating behavioristic attitude in psychology; during the next eight years they had additional informal contacts.[6]

After reading *Motivation and Personality* in 1954 and Maslow's studies of self-actualization, Sutich began to identify himself with a humanistic perspective. In the mid-1950s Maslow and Sutich corresponded about the inefficiency of the mailing list as a means of communication. Heinz L. Ansbacher, then the editor of the *American Journal of Individual Psychology*, in 1957 had addressed the individuals on Maslow's list with a mimeographed letter proposing to incorporate Maslow's growth-oriented perspective in his journal. Sutich and Maslow were not enthusiastic about Ansbacher's proposal, however, because they did not want the Adlerian label. Sutich wrote to have been "wary of associating with an orientation that was to be extended beyond its limits as I understood them."[7]

Sutich then wrote Maslow that many on the list had suggested the establishment of a journal. Maslow replied that "such a journal is very badly needed," and he suggested possible titles such as *Being and Becoming*, *Psychological Growth*, and *Personality Development*. In other correspondence Maslow advised Sutich on how he might proceed in organizing a journal and promised to "scout around as actively as I have time for help and money." He referred to Sutich thereafter as the "boss of the new enterprise."[8]

Soon Maslow and Sutich agreed upon the statement of purpose for the Journal and began the search for a title. The news spread quickly, and Sutich began receiving manuscripts and expressions of interest from unexpected sources including the U.S. Office of Vital Statistics. Moving quickly to organize the Journal, Maslow and Sutich assembled a board of editors that included Kurt Goldstein, Rollo May, Lewis Mumford, Erich Fromm, Andras Angyal, and Clark Moustakas. The main challenge was to ensure financial support and sponsorship for the new journal. Although at first the president of Brandeis University refused to offer any support, he eventually agreed to sponsor the venture—without any financial participation, however. The first badly needed money came from donations from friends and Sutich's own funds.[9]

The first choice for a title, *Journal of Ortho-psychology*, was opposed by the American Orthopsychiatric Association. Other names such as *Third Force*, *Self-Psychology*, and *Existence* were proposed. The eventual name, *Journal of Humanistic Psychology*, was suggested by Stephen Cohen, a senior psychology student at Brandeis who was also Maslow's son-in-law. With Sutich as the editor, the first issue of the *JHP* appeared in the spring of 1961. Its first subscribers were the individuals on Maslow's mailing list.[10]

As the *JHP* gathered momentum, psychologists other than those on the mailing list contacted Sutich. It soon became obvious to him that the subscribers to the Journal needed their own association. Sutich and Maslow exchanged notes on the issue and appointed James Bugental as president pro tem of the future association. With the help of a small grant arranged by Allport, the founding meeting of the AAHP (the first "A" standing for "American" was dropped a few years later) took place in Philadelphia in the summer of 1963. It was a high-spirited meeting with about seventy-five participants.

Maslow opened the meeting by commenting on the narrowness and exclusiveness of psychoanalysis and behaviorism, or what he called "low-ceiling psychology." Discussion went on into the night about the relationships among humanistic psychology, psychoanalysis, and behaviorism, and about methodological problems. The most frequently mentioned theme of the day was "the feeling of professional isolation, loneliness and its accompanying frustration in communication and research." An equally important theme was the place of values in our lives, psychology, and science. Radical views were expressed: Sydney Jourard, for example, asserted that psychology lacked imagination and needed more dreamers; S. I. Hayakawa called social scientists illiterate; and Rollo May suggested that psychology students should also study literature. "My primary impression of the Philadelphia meeting," wrote Sutich two years later, "was that of mutual discovery. Within a single day, a hundred or so like-minded individuals found that they constituted a 'belonging group.' The days of professional and intellectual isolation were over."[11]

The second annual meeting of the AAHP in Los Angeles in September 1964 convened twice as many members—about 200. By this time Bugental was becoming increasingly involved with the movement; his "Humanistic Psychology: A New Breakthrough" published in *The American Psychologist* (1963) was a milestone of the period. A quarter of a century later, Bugental pointed out that at the Los Angeles meeting four subgroups emerged that have ever since been evident and influential in the AHP: practitioners, social/political activists, academic/theoretical thinkers, and "touchy-feely" personal growth seekers.[12]

The emergence of humanistic psychology as a third force in American psychology was culminated by a conference held in November 1964 in a small country inn at Old Saybrook, Connecticut. Bugental appointed a "Theory Committee," and Robert Knapp of Wesleyan University chaired it. Allport and Rogers had been a little reluctant to participate in the AAHP and its journal, but their attendance at the Saybrook Conference finally made their support public. Allport, Bugental, Maslow, Rogers, and May were present, as well as other well-known discontents such as Jacques Barzun, Charlotte Buhler, George Kelly, Clark Moustakas, Gardner Murphy, and Henry Murray. The presentations dealt with the basic theoretical issues implied by the "new psychology" and were published in the *JHP* (in the 1980s the Humanistic Psychology Institute changed its name to "Saybrook Institute" partly in homage to this "founding conference.")[13]

Soon after the Saybrook Conference, the AAHP and the Journal disaffiliated from the Brandeis sponsorship and, in December 1965, incorporated as a non-profit educational institution. According to Sutich, the Association's independence occurred a year earlier than had been expected and was a result of the "rapidly accelerating speed of historical change in the field of psychology"; the rapid growth of membership during the first years, indeed, confirms Sutich's statement. In 1968 Sutich transferred the editorship of the *JHP* to Miles Vich, who had been co-editor since 1963.[14]

In 1968, Maslow was increasingly enthusiastic about the new developments and was convinced that humanistic psychology was "already established as a viable third alternative" in American psychology. He admitted to thinking that the humanistic trend was a revolution that would bring "new ways of perceiving and thinking, new images of man and of society, new conceptions of ethics and of values, new directions in which to move." It was, in his opinion, "one facet of a general weltanschauung, a new philosophy of life, a new conception of man, the beginning of a new century of work."[15]

At first, however, the AAHP was little more than a protest group. Its early organizational meetings were colored by a deep dissatisfaction with and rebellion against behaviorism. Recalling the early meetings, Bugental reported that there were two distinct groups. One group wanted to define humanistic psychology by merely stating what it did not stand for—namely, behaviorism and, to a certain extent, psychoanalysis. The second group advocated statements of a positive sort. They sought to identify the Association with the introduction of human meanings and values into mainstream psychology.[16]

The first policy statements of the new association represented a compromise between the two groups and were quite vague. Adopting Bugental's "Humanistic Psychology: A New Breakthrough" (1963) as "a good statement of the Association's aims and orientation," the members agreed that the AAHP did not deny the psychoanalytical and behavioristic orientations, but rather aimed to incorporate these views within a broader phenomenological orientation that would emphasize the validity of human experience and meaning. The statement contained five postulates: (1) that a person supersedes the sum of his or her parts; (2) that we are affected by our relationships with others; (3) that a person is aware, (4) has choice, and (5) is intentional. The "new member drive" published in the first number of the *AHP Newsletter* advertised:

If you are dissatisfied with a psychology that views man as a composite of part functions, a psychology whose model of science is taken over from physics, and whose model of a practitioner is taken over from medicine—and you want to do something to change this state of affairs, fill out this application.[17]

As membership in the Association grew from the seventy-five participants of the founding Philadelphia meeting in 1963 to 500 members in 1966, so, too, did the need for clearer statements of the policies, aims, and methods of humanistic psychology. In November 1965, Charlotte Buhler, the newly elected president of the AAHP, took on the challenge of confronting "the great deal of confusion regarding the objectives and methods of a humanistic psychology." But there was already a growing sense of what humanistic psychology stood for. In his recollection of the meeting, Sutich stated that "for those of us who may have been concerned about AAHP being merely a protest group, the Chicago meeting was most reassuring . . . there seemed to be more of a general sense of what we really are as a group. Protest was being transformed into exciting but tough-minded experimental projects." The 1969–1970 AAHP president, Floyd W. Matson, recalling this early phase with some nostalgia, described it in Eriksonian terminology as a "crisis of identity" and proudly stated that humanistic psychology was no longer a protest group but a firmly established "third force."[18]

In 1969 the AAHP dropped the "American" from its title because its activities had indeed become international in scope. The history of "American" in the Association's title is an interesting one. When Maslow and Sutich exchanged thoughts on the name of the future association, they decided to include "American" in anticipation of difficulties with the Internal Revenue Service in trying to establish a sponsoring organization for the journal. Many years later, Sutich referred to this choice as a means of protecting the association from any questioning of its patriotism during the "subversion" hysteria of communist suspicion during the post-McCarthy era. "American" was thus included in the name of the association as a "temporary device and until a more relaxed political climate would arrive." And, indeed, by the end of 1969 the climate was such that "American" was dropped from the title.[19]

Because of the influence and international prestige of Charlotte Buhler, the Association's president in 1965–1966 and the chair of the AHP International Advisory Board in 1970, international membership grew and activities were extended. Carmi Harari of the Committee for International Organization also provided a great stimulus. By the 1970s the AHP had international chapters in several European countries, as well as in Israel, India, and Central and South America. In 1972, for instance, the AHP either sponsored or was involved with humanistic conferences in London, Stockholm, Moscow, Hong Kong, Canton, Peking, Tokyo, and Hawaii. In a list of growth centers published in 1975, the *AHP Newsletter* listed fifty-two humanistic psychology–related centers in thirteen countries.[20]

One of the primary concerns of the early AHP was bringing humanistic psychology into mainstream psychology as represented by the American Psychological Association (APA). In this attempt, as early as 1964 the AHP cosponsored four symposia at the national APA meeting. Also, institutions advertised in the *AHP Newsletter* for humanistically oriented personnel. In the July 1966 issue, for example, the Comprehensive Community Mental Health Center of Lexington,

Kentucky, invited humanistically oriented social workers and psychologists to apply for its twenty-one positions.

An outcome of these efforts for professional acceptance was the creation of Division 32 on humanistic psychology within the APA. In 1971, 374 members of the APA requested the creation of a humanistic psychology division within the APA with the purpose of applying "the concepts, theories and philosophy of humanistic psychology to research, education, and professional applications of scientific psychology," and of ensuring "that humanistically oriented ideas and activities operate within APA and some of its divisions." Within the space of a decade, humanistic psychology had earned a small but official place within mainstream psychology.[21]

By the 1970s the AHP had become a network of networks, a system for information diffusion about humanistically oriented groups, practitioners, and growth centers. The *AHP Newsletter* often contained special sections with such listings. The first listing in July 1968 included 32 entries for growth centers in the United States. Only two years later there were 112 entries, and in 1975 there were 281 entries in the USA and 52 in 13 other countries. These entries ranged from academic and theoretical views; Gestalt, encounter, and human potential groups; psychodrama; and psychosynthesis to mystical and esoteric practicing groups.

Education became an important concern of the AHP. Educational topics received the greatest amount of space in the *AHP Newsletter* in the 1960s and early 1970s—in the form of articles, notices, and information about humanistically oriented education in general and psychology in particular. As early as 1965, the *Newsletter* contained reports on the teaching of humanistic psychology and requests from members for information on where to find humanistically oriented programs. It also listed schools and programs in humanistic psychology.[22]

The first master's program in humanistic psychology was established in the fall of 1966 in the psychology department of the Sonoma State College (SSC). Two other important centers were established at West Georgia College and the Humanistic Psychology Institute in San Francisco.[23]

The B.A. and M.A. programs at West Georgia College in Carrollton were established in 1969 by faculty members who were convinced that a completely new approach to psychology and university teaching was needed. Myrons Arons was instrumental in the founding of the department. Arons, who had been a graduate student of Maslow and had also studied with Paul Ricoeur in France, was interested in the psychology of creativity. Arons's colleagues established an original and innovative curriculum in which students' personal and intellectual growth and imaginative development were the main goals. The program flourished throughout the 1970s and is still popular.[24]

In 1970 the AHP created the Humanistic Psychology Institute (HPI) as an educational and research institute dedicated to Maslow's memory. It aimed to respond to the need for educational opportunities in humanistic psychology. The initial goal of the institute was to provide an alternative university model for higher education. Since the HPI was financially dependent on the AHP during its formative period, there was some discussion about whether the HPI was meant to be an "operating educational institution" or an "educational arm of the AHP."

The creation of the HPI was closely related to the Sonoma State College program in humanistic psychology. Its first graduate courses were offered through the Extension Division of the SSC, and only in the summer of the following year (1971) was a "branch" opened in San Francisco. The SSC first class had an enrollment of thirty students, but in the second year there were already 170 students from all over the nation, a much larger number than expected. In 1982 the HPI changed its name to the Saybrook Institute. Other institutions with programs on humanistic psychology today are Union Graduate School, Fielding Institute, Center for Humanistic Studies in Detroit, Walden University in Florida, and Duquesne University in Pittsburgh.[25]

NOTES

1. Anthony Sutich, *The Founding of Humanistic and Transpersonal Psychology: A Personal Account*, unpublished doctoral dissertation, Humanistic Psychology Institute (now Saybrook Institute), 1976, p. 30.

2. Thomas Kuhn, *The Structure of Scientific Revolutions*, 2d ed., Chicago: University of Chicago Press, 1970.

3. Letter of Betty W. Keane to the author dated April 15, 1985.

4. *AHP Newsletter*, April 1968, p. 1; April 1970, p. 9.

5. M1962b:237–40.

6. Sutich, *The Founding of Humanistic and Transpersonal Psychology*, pp. 7–51; *AHP Newsletter*, pp. 15–18.

7. Sutich, *The Founding of Humanistic and Transpersonal Psychology*, p. 52.

8. Ibid., pp 52–64.

9. Ibid., pp. 65–88.

10. Ibid.; Tom Greening, "The Origins of the Journal of Humanistic Psychology and the Association for Humanistic Psychology," *J. Hum. Psy.*, 1985, 25(2):7–11.

11. *AHP Newsletter*, December 1963, November 1965; Sutich, *The Founding of Humanistic and Transpersonal Psychology*, p. 118.

12. Ibid., pp. 89–126.

13. Ibid., pp. 127–39.

14. *AHP Newsletter*, November 1965, p. 4; May 1966, p. 5.

15. M1962b, preface to the second edition of 1968, p. iii; see also M1970a:ix–xi.

16. Interview by the author with Dr. Bugental in San Francisco on March 8, 1985; see also Jack Gibb's statements in *AHP Newsletter*, April 1968, p. 1.

17. *AHP Newsletter*, December 1963, p. 3.

18. *AHP Newsletter*, November 1965, p. 1; October 1969.

19. Sutich, *The Founding of Humanistic and Transpersonal Psychology*, pp. 94–95.

20. *AHP Newsletter*, October and December 1969; April, Summer, and November 1970.

21. *AHP Newsletter*, February 1973, p. 6; Summer 1972, p. 3; December 1971; p. 6.

22. See, for example, *AHP Newsletter*, October 1966; June and October 1967; April 1968; January and July 1969; February, April, and October 1970.

23. *AHP Newsletter*, July 1966, p. 4.

24. *AHP Newsletter*, April 1969; April 1970.

25. Throughout the 1970s, the *AHP Newsletter* had a special column on the HPI. See especially October 1970, p. 2; April, June, Summer, October, and December 1971, p. 9; February, March, June, and Summer 1972; February 1974. For references to graduate programs in humanistic psychology, see *The Humanistic Psychologist*, 17(1989):338.

3

Biographical Sketches

GORDON W. ALLPORT

Gordon Willard Allport was born on November 11, 1897, in Montezuma, Indiana, and spent his childhood in Cleveland, Ohio. He was the youngest of four children. His father was a country physician of English descent and his mother was a schoolteacher of German and Scottish background. He described his parental upbringing as colored by "plain Protestant piety," hard work, humanitarianism, trust, and affection. His intellectualism—already apparent in the early years of his education—had an isolating effect on him, although he was always appreciated by a small group of friends. He graduated second in a high school class of 100.[1]

In 1915, Allport enrolled at Harvard University, where with only minor interruptions he was to spend his entire academic career. As an undergraduate student he specialized in psychology and social ethics, two themes upon which most of his later research would focus. After graduation in 1919, he taught English and sociology for one year at Robert College in Constantinople, where he found teaching congenial to his interests. His Ph.D. degree from Harvard was awarded in 1922. His dissertation project was an experimental study of personality traits and their application to social diagnosis; the topic foreshadowed his two lifelong interests in personality and social psychologies.

Between 1922 and 1924, Allport studied in Germany and England on a post-doctoral fellowship. In Germany, his encounters with Carl Stumpf, Max Wertheimer, Wolfgang Kohler, Eduard Spranger, William Stern, and Heinz Werner had a profound impact upon the development of his psychology of personality. In his memoirs, he confessed that in Germany he found a psychology which "I had been longing for but did not know existed." The influence of German psychology helped him to conceptualize a structural view of personality and to focus on the organizational aspects of personality rather than upon the study of individual psychological profiles.[2]

By the time he returned to the United States, Allport realized that he had grown away from behaviorism and psychoanalysis, two approaches that he now regarded as simplistic. After a two-year lectureship in social ethics at Harvard, he taught social and personality psychology for four years at Dartmouth College. During summer sessions he taught at Harvard, where he returned full-time in 1930. The 1930s and 1940s were Allport's most creative decades. He was the editor of the *Journal of Abnormal and Social Psychology* (1937–1948), chairman of the new and independent psychology department at Harvard where he was tenured in 1937, and president of the American Psychological Association (1939). He published *Personality: A Psychological Interpretation* in 1937 and contributed to the World War II civilian effort. Allport died in 1967, shortly before his seventieth birthday.

Allport's lifework revolved around the search for a theoretical system that encompassed the interdependency of philosophy and psychology and supplied an adequate image of human nature. Such an image, he thought, was more than a mere intellectual statement; it had concrete applications for social service such as individual and social betterment, respected the essential uniqueness and integrity of every person, encompassed the totality of human experience, and utilized the human democratic potential. Allport also persistently sought to create what he named "morphogenic" or "idiographic" methods, in order to test his humanistic view of human nature and make psychology an experimental science. His emphasis throughout these studies was on normality rather than pathology.

Allport was an eclectic thinker; he believed that there was no single correct method in psychology. All avenues that contribute to the understanding of human nature were legitimate. He recognized that understanding human nature was a difficult task, and he believed that students of human nature had the right to delimit the variables under study and temporarily neglect other variables. But in doing so they should recognize that what they neglect is nonetheless an integral part of the person. Any statement about human nature was thus to be tentative, eclectic, and humble.

In the 1960s Allport adhered to the humanistic movement in American psychology. He funneled funds to Anthony Sutich, who was then, along with Abraham Maslow, instrumental in the institutionalization of the movement. In 1964, Allport's participation at the Saybrook Conference on the theory of humanistic psychology made public his support for the emerging humanistic movement in psychology.

Allport wrote three systematic expositions of his views on the place of the person in psychology. *Personality: A Psychological Interpretation* (1937) contained the first comprehensive exposition of his thought. *Becoming: Basic Considerations for a Psychology of Personality* (1955) was a refined statement of a more intellectually mature thinker. This work was revised in 1961 and retitled *Pattern and Growth in Personality*. Focusing on different facets of personhood in psychology, Allport also compiled selected papers under the titles *The Nature of Personality* (1950), *Personality and Social Encounter* (1960), and *The Person in Psychology* (1968).

Personality theory and social psychology permeated Allport's lifelong work in what he called "the humanistic pastures of psychology." His studies of the structural dynamism of the components of personality covered a broad variety of themes: human motivation, religious sentiments, ethics, and character traits. He also studied the purely social aspects of personality such as wartime rumors and morale, communication (the psychology of radio and newspaper), and group conflict and prejudice. Both in personality and in social psychologies he sought practical problem-solving applications: guidance, mental health, pedagogy, the World War II civilian effort, and the control of racial prejudice.[3]

Human personality, as Allport viewed it, was the unique pattern or agglomeration of generic attitudes, formations, or traits of the individual. He analyzed several of these attitudes and traits, always recognizing that a mere listing of them falls short of a complete picture of personality. The whole and integrative personality, he argued, is more than just the sum of its parts. Personality, according to Allport, also had "propriate functions" or "complex integrative processes," such as growth, becoming, maturity, learning, perception, and non-projective expressive behavior. He understood human motivation among healthy persons as future-oriented and determined by their changing values. He argued that human motivation is functionally autonomous in the sense that motives, goals, and attitudes—that is, the propelling forces present in the structure of personality—undergo an ongoing metamorphosis. Personality is thus a never-ending process of becoming.

In 1964, the American Psychological Association chose Allport for its Distinguished Scientific Contribution Award. The citation read as follows:

For reminding us that man is neither a beast nor a statistic, except as we choose to regard him so, and that human personality finds its greatest measure in the reaches of time. This is to say that, while life may have its crude beginnings, it has its noble endings too, and there is a line that leads from one to the other—a line that graphically portrays the character of the individual, and of mankind as well.[4]

ABRAHAM H. MASLOW

Abraham H. Maslow was born on April 1, 1908, in New York City, the first of seven children. Maslow's relationship with his parents, Russian-Jewish immigrants from Kiev, was neither intimate nor loving. In his memoirs, Maslow recalled that he had been surprised that he was not insane, given that his mother was schizophrenic. He attended New York City schools. At the age of nine he moved to a non-Jewish neighborhood and, since he looked quite Jewish, discovered anti-Semitism there. He described himself during his first twenty years as extremely neurotic, shy, nervous, depressed, lonely, and self-reflecting. He isolated himself at school, and since he could not stand being at home, he practically lived in the library. At school he was an achiever, enrolling in law school upon the advice of his father. Due to lack of interest, however, he did not finish the freshman year. At the end of 1928, then twenty years old, he married Bertha, a cousin whom he had courted for a long time. Both enrolled at the University of Wisconsin–Madison, where he received a B.A. (1930), M.A. (1931) and Ph.D. (1934) in psychology.[5]

In Madison, Maslow was still very shy and timid, but he was well liked by his teachers. Fascinated by J. B. Watson's behaviorism that was in vogue at the time, he concentrated on classical laboratory research with dogs and apes. His earliest papers focused on the emotion of disgust in dogs and the learning process in infra-human primates. His doctoral dissertation explored the role of dominance in the social and sexual behavior of apes, arguing that dominance among primates is usually established by visual contact rather than fighting.

From the time he received his doctorate until 1937, Maslow worked as a research assistant in social psychology for Edward L. Thorndike at Teachers College, Columbia University. His first teaching and academic position was with Brooklyn College between 1937 and 1951. During this post–World War II period, exiled German psychologists made New York an intellectual capital, and Maslow associated with the psychologists Max Wertheimer, Erich Fromm, Karen Horney, Kurt Goldstein, and the anthropologist Ruth Benedict.

In 1951 Maslow was invited to head the recently established Department of Psychology at Brandeis University, a position he was to hold for ten years. In 1969 he left Brandeis to take a fellowship at the Laughlin Foundation in Menlo Park, California.

Soon after leaving Madison, Maslow became convinced that most of modern psychological research and theory relied too much on subjects who had turned to psychologists for pathological reasons. The image of human nature delineated by studies of these patients was inevitably pessimistic and distorted. Trying to remedy the situation, Maslow began studying what he thought were the finest examples of healthy people. He called them "self-actualizing" individuals, since they showed a high degree of need for meaningful work, responsibility, creativity, fairness, and justice.

In his epoch-making article of 1943, "A Theory of Human Motivation," and more explicitly in *Motivation and Personality* (1954), Maslow argued that there are higher and lower needs in human motivation. Both are "instinctoid" and arranged in a hierarchy. These needs are, in order: physiological well-being, safety, love, esteem, and self-actualization. Each group of needs relies on the prior satisfaction of the previous group of needs. Thus, following Maslow's reasoning, human nature is the continuous fulfillment of inner needs, beginning with basic physiological needs and progressing to meta-needs. Self-actualizers had satisfied the lower needs and sought to fulfill higher reaches of human nature by becoming all they were capable of becoming.

In *Religion, Values and Peak-Experiences* (1964), Maslow argued that one could find in self-actualizing people the guiding or ultimate values by which humans should live. These values were meant to be the basis of a science of ethics. In the same work, Maslow also concluded that self-actualizing people have had simple and natural experiences of ecstasy or bliss, moments of great awe or intense experiences—"peak-experiences," as he named them.

In *Eupsychian Management* (1965), Maslow made an excursion into the then relatively new field of organizational psychology. In that work, under the assumption that he could not improve the world through individual psychotherapy, he presented the idea of a Eupsychia or good psychological management. He used the term "Eupsychia" originally to describe the culture that would be generated by a thousand or so self-actualizing people in a sheltered environment free from external interference. In *Eupsychian Management*, he maintained that workers could achieve the highest possible productivity if their "humanness" and potential for self-actualization were given the opportunity to grow so that their higher needs, or meta-needs, could be fulfilled. Toward the end of his life, mainly in the posthumously published *Farther Reaches of Human Nature* (1971), Maslow went a step farther and argued that there are needs beyond self-actualization—that is, transcendental or transpersonal needs centered on the cosmos, religion, and the mystical realms of being.

Throughout the 1960s, Maslow, with the cooperation of Anthony Sutich, was instrumental in the institutionalization of humanistic psychology by establishing the Journal and the Association for Humanistic Psychology. In the late 1960s he also supported the emerging transpersonal psychology. Maslow died of a heart attack on June 8, 1970, at the age of sixty-two.

CARL R. ROGERS

Carl Ransom Rogers was born on January 8, 1902, in Chicago, the fourth of six children. His parents came from a farm background and were well educated, upper–middle class. His father was a civil engineer and an independent contractor. His mother was a woman of strong puritanical convictions. In his recollections, Rogers reported that his parents were loving, although also "masters of the art of subtle and loving control," anti-intellectuals, and firm believers in the virtue of work. He characterized his parents' values as "austere puritanism"; the "gently suppressive atmosphere at home" was, he thought, the reason he developed an ulcer in his twenties.[6]

Rogers knew how to read before entering grammar school, which he began in the second grade. He enjoyed school activities and read extensively—Bible story books, the encyclopedia, and even the dictionary. Throughout adolescence he had little or no social life outside the family circle; he was withdrawn, dreamy, and absent-minded. When he was twelve years old, his family settled in the countryside in order to remove the children from the temptations and evils of city life. Rogers enjoyed farm activities, and his high school interest in scientific agriculture brought him to enroll in 1919 in the agriculture program at the

University of Wisconsin–Madison. Because of his strong religious inclination, however, he changed majors to history in order to pursue a career in Christian work and the ministry. Two months after graduating in June 1924 with a B.A. in history, he married Helen and enrolled in the then relatively liberal Union Theological Seminary in New York City, where he was introduced to clinical work. He soon found counseling more congenial than religious work and began attending courses at Teachers College, Columbia University, where he gained clinical experience with children. In his second year at the seminary, he enrolled full-time in Teachers College, where he specialized in clinical and educational psychology, leaving behind the pursuit of a religious career. His doctoral dissertation developed a test for measuring personality adjustment in children.

After his graduation in 1928, Rogers joined the Rochester Society for the Prevention of Cruelty to Children in New York State as a child psychologist. He spent the next twelve years carrying out a wide range of psychological services involving the diagnosis and treatment of delinquent children. In Rochester, Rogers came under the influence of Otto Rank's "relationship therapy." At this time, he was reluctant to participate in academic psychology because of what he perceived to be its sterility and "rat orientation," but he became increasingly involved in the social work profession, where he quickly moved up to local and national offices. In an attempt to integrate the theory and practice of child guidance with his own experience, he wrote *The Clinical Treatment of the Problem Child* (1939). This work brought him immediate national fame and led to a full professorship at Ohio State University the following year.

In the second year at Ohio, Rogers published *Counseling and Psychotherapy* (1942). This volume was, in great part, a crystallization of his own clinical work and Otto Rank's relationship therapy. The book focused on the theory and technique of nondirective therapy, the basic tenet of which was that healthy psychological growth occurs when the therapist creates a permissive climate that enables the client to freely express his or her feelings. The therapist must be nonjudgmental of his client's feelings and make the client feel free from all coercion or pressure. The theoretical assumption was that such a counseling relationship could induce the client to self-acceptance and understanding—which, in turn, was the first step toward a healthier personality reorientation.

During the Ohio years, Rogers established the first practicum or supervised therapy within a program of academic training in counseling psychology. This practicum was in part responsible for the University of Chicago's invitation to Rogers to establish a counseling center there—an invitation he gladly accepted in 1945. Along with the development of the counseling center at Chicago, Rogers immersed himself in the theoretical formulation of the helping relationship. *The Client-Centered Therapy* (1951) was a product of this interest.

In this work Rogers argued that a constructive change in personality and behavior is possible if certain basic conditions are experienced by the client in the counseling relationship. These "necessary and sufficient conditions of therapeutic personality change'' are: (1) the realness and congruence of the therapist who provides; (2) unconditional positive regard; and (3) the empathic understanding of the client's situation. No special intellectual or professional knowledge is essential in this process, since the focus is deliberately on the feeling aspects of the immediate situation rather than upon the intellectual aspects. In *Client-Centered Therapy*, Rogers abandoned the term ''nondirective'' for the term ''client-centered,'' thus alluding to his theoretical shift. He thought that the individual has a drive toward growth, health, and adjustment. In this context, therapy was viewed as a matter of freeing the person for normal growth or self-actualization.

In 1957, Rogers accepted an appointment at the University of Wisconsin–Madison in psychiatry and psychology and set himself to study psychotic individuals. But he encountered departments of psychology and psychiatry that were heavily experimental, ''rat-oriented,'' distrustful of clinical psychology, and skeptical of his views. Deeply disappointed with what he considered to be the antiquated and primitive structure of graduate education in psychology at Wisconsin, he resigned from the psychology department. Retaining, however, the appointment in psychiatry, he continued to explore the therapeutic potential of the client-centered approach upon schizophrenic patients. With the problems in the organization of the research staff and the antagonism of the psychology faculty, Rogers characterized the Wisconsin years as the most painful and anguished of his professional life. *The Therapeutic Relationship and Its Impact* presented the conclusions of Rogers and his associates on psychotherapy with schizophrenics.[7]

Rogers presented additional theoretical developments in client-centered therapy in *On Becoming a Person* (1961). In this work, he argued that the human organism has an ''actualizing tendency'' to develop all its capacities in order to maintain and enhance its existence. Applying this insight to psychotherapy, Rogers argued that the task of the therapist is to release this organismic capacity in order to induce growth and psychological well-being. In this context he thought that individuals have the capacity to penetrate their own complexities if they are only given a suitable psychological climate. The client is ultimately the expert in dealing with his or her own feelings and life situation. The function of the therapist is merely a facilitative one.

Disappointed with the antagonism and skepticism toward his views at Madison, Rogers resigned and moved to the Western Behavioral Sciences Institute (WBSI) in California, a nonprofit organization devoted to humanistic research in interpersonal relationships. At the WBSI, among a congenial interdisciplinary group and free from bureaucratic entanglement, Rogers turned to research on the experience of normal individuals within what he called an encounter group. The result was *Encounter Groups*, published in 1970.

During the WBSI period, Rogers was also involved in educational projects. Disappointed with the educational system at Madison, he linked his experience with encounter groups to education. In *Freedom to Learn* (1969), Rogers tried to show how educators could facilitate learning even within an antiquated and fossilized system by being personal and innovative. In two other publications of this period, *Becoming Partners* (1972) and *Carl Rogers on Personal Power* (1977), Rogers explored intimate relationships and political reality in the context of his overall thinking.

After leaving WBSI, Rogers worked at the Center for the Studies of the Person (CSP), which was near his home in La Jolla, California. He considered the CSP to be a "pilot study" for the organization of the future. It was a loosely organized group of forty-five people offering programs for the training of encounter group facilitators.

In the late 1970s Rogers developed an interest in psychic and paranormal phenomena, such as altered states of mind and phenomena not perceptible by the five senses. He read the psychic, Carlos Castaneda. Soon after the death of his wife, Helen, Rogers held a spiritualist seance with a medium through whom he believed he had talked to the surviving soul of Helen. He came to believe that the human soul is of a spiritual essence that lasts over time and occasionally incarnates in a human body.[8]

Despite advanced age, Rogers remained active until his death in February 1987. During his last years, he explored the application of encounter group techniques to the solution of international conflicts, primarily in central America, and in cultural exchange with the Soviet Union.

ROLLO R. MAY

Rollo Reece May was born in Ada, Ohio, on the early morning of April 21, 1909, and grew up in Marine City, Michigan. May characterized his parental upbringing as austere and strict, based on Victorian discipline and Methodist beliefs. His father and the general midwestern mentality permeated his childhood with anti-intellectualism and fear of "thinking too much," a "disease" he later came to hate and refer to as inhuman and destructive.[9]

May's first experience with higher education at Michigan State University ended abruptly because of his editorship of a radical student magazine. He transferred to Oberlin College in Ohio, graduating in 1930 with an A.B. degree in English. Throughout his college days, he was fascinated with ancient Greek art and philosophy. Many years later, he described this as the beginning of a "love affair with the indomitable spirit of the Ancient Greek," much more spiritual and real than the anti-intellectualism of his midwestern upbringing.

Unable to resist his passionate curiosity about Greece, soon after graduation he secured a teaching position at the American College in Salonika for three years (1930–1933). Greece represented for him not only an intellectual emancipation but also a new spiritual freedom and interest in artistic creativity. Salonika became his home base for summer excursions into the backwoods of Poland, Rumania, Turkey, and Greece, where he painted and studied the natives and their art. He also attended brief seminars in Vienna with Alfred Alder, with whom he had intimate discussions.

Upon his return to the United States in 1933, Rollo May was a counselor at Michigan State University (1934–1939) and soon afterwards enrolled at the Union Theological Seminary. He abhorred many aspects of organized religion, but he felt that he could understand the authentically human dimension of life only by studying theology. In 1935 he was described as an "idealistic youth headed for the ministry." Upon completion of the Bachelor of Divinity (cum laude) degree in 1938, May married Florence De Frees and entered the ministry, serving at a Congregational parish in Verona, New Jersey. Soon, however, he became disillusioned with his vocation and enrolled in the graduate school of Columbia University, where he received in 1949 the first Ph.D. degree in counseling psychology awarded by that institution.[10]

In 1942 May interrupted his studies at Columbia because he had contracted tuberculosis. His confrontation with death during the eighteen months of convalescence at Saranac Sanatorium in upstate New York was one of the most significant events in his intellectual and personal development and one he often mentioned in his writings. "It was a valuable experience to face death," said May many years later, "for in the experience, I learned to face life."[11]

After his recovery, May took up the position of counselor at the College of the City of New York (1943–1944) and completed his dissertation, *The Meaning of Anxiety* (1950), under the supervision of Paul Tillich. His complex and touching lifelong friendship with Tillich was of major significance in May's personal and intellectual growth; it was vividly narrated in *Reminiscence of a Friendship* (1973), which he wrote after Tillich's death. May first became acquainted with Tillich at Union Theological Seminary soon after Tillich's arrival in the United States as a German exile.

The lectures by Tillich that May attended at the seminary called forth convictions, May recalled, that he had vaguely intuited but had never dared to articulate. Their friendship expanded and, in the late 1930s when Tillich gave Sunday sermons in Union's chapel, they had an "inspired discussion" afterwards. As a dissertation mentor, Tillich was, in May's words, most "arduous and concerned." It was as a result of their mutual questioning and the development of May's concept of normal anxiety in the dissertation that Tillich wrote *Courage To Be*. According to May, Tillich was a friend, mentor, spiritual father, and teacher "who gave me more than all teachers I ever had combined."[12]

In 1948 May joined the faculty of the William Alanson White Institute of Psychiatry, Psychoanalysis, and Psychology in New York City. In 1952, he became a fellow at the institute, in 1958 its president, and in 1959, supervisory and training analyst.

Rollo May was a strenuous critic of Western civilization. Most of his writings clarified the dilemmas of the human predicament in an age of anxiety. He persistently alerted his generation to the dangerous shaping of human nature upon the image of the machine, resulting in an increasing feeling of hopelessness and loss of a sense of significance. More specifically, he energetically fought the attempt of the great majority of behavioristic psychologists of his generation to make people objects of control and scientific manipulation. He openly criticized their attempt to imitate the methods of the physical sciences, pointing out that although these methods were impressive in gaining mastery over nature, they were trivial and unreliable in the understanding of people. Against this tendency he persistently asserted the value of subjective aspects of human experience such as the place of wish, will, decision making, and the significance of the humanistic disciplines in the study of these issues. It was not surprising when Arthur Compton called Nobel Prize winners, historians, philosophers, and scientists for a conference on science and human responsibility in 1954, Rollo May was the only invited psychologist. This was because, according to Compton, they could not find any other psychologist concerned and committed to the issues of the conference.[13]

Everywhere in his writings May legitimated social rebellion, advocating the necessity to defy law and order when called upon it by our subjective values. "Every human being," he said in an interview, "must have a point at which he stands against the culture." When writing on the humanity of the rebel, he went so far as to define human nature as "the capacity to rebel," thus adopting the statement by Albert Camus that "I rebel—therefore we exist."[14]

In the early and mid–1950s May was at the center of a war in the New York State legislature against the American Medical Association attempt to make psychotherapy a medical specialty by limiting it to practitioners affiliated with the AMA. Faced with the extinction of his professional life, he fought the battle at the New York legislature that led to the winning of the war nation-wide against the monopolistic threat of the AMA. In the following decade (late 1960s and 1970s) he fought at home against the war in Vietnam. In this fight he was particularly critical of the deceptive notion of freedom and power in American culture. He argued that it is impossible to escape the need and use of power and repress these under the pretense of innocence. In this context he also wrote on the nuclear arms race, race relations, and violence. In the late 1970s and 1980s, acknowledging that he had become more of an essentialist, he ranged against those who went to extremes of subjectivity and denial of any objectivity. He was as critical of the denial of the evil aspects of human nature—or daimonic, as he preferred to call it—and naive optimism of the Human Potential Movement and encounter groups as he was of the radicalism of the women's liberation movement.[15]

Rollo May's most influential writings were *The Meaning of Anxiety* (1950); *Man's Search for Himself* (1953); *Existence* (1958), for which he served as an editor and contributor; *Psychology and the Human Dilemma* (1967); *Love and Will* (1969); and *Power and Innocence* (1972).

In the dissertation *The Meaning of Anxiety*, May argued that the process of valuing and anxiety are intimately related. Anxiety is a human reaction to the threat to something we care about, value, or identify with our existence. The death threat is, for example, the most powerful producer of anxiety. We overcome anxiety only to the extent that our values are stronger than the threat. Moreover, if anxiety is a threat to what we value, then no one is completely free from anxiety. May distinguished in this context between neurotic and normal anxiety. While normal anxiety plays a significant role in the clarification of our values, neurotic anxiety blocks self-awareness. When people lose touch with themselves, they no longer know who they are and what they ought to be. The insecurity associated with anxiety forces them to search for an inner center of values so they may overcome the threat of anxiety. This "normal" type of anxiety is proportional to the threat, does not involve unconscious motivation, and—when met constructively—is a life stimulant that is an integral part of growth and is vital for creative expression. Neurotic anxiety, on the other hand, results from unmet normal anxiety. The goal of any psychotherapy, argued May, is not to free patients from anxiety but rather to help them accept, bear, and live constructively with neurotic anxiety.

In *Man's Search for Himself* (1953), May wrote on the loss and search for meaning in an age of anxiety, alienation, and apathy. According to May, the modern predicament results from the absence of a framework that orchestrates these difficulties into a meaningful human structure. The resolution, argued May, was in the rediscovery of selfhood and self-realization.

In the two chapters that May wrote for *Existence* (1958), he attempted to unite psychology and ontology by dissolving the misleading Western distinction between the objective and subjective worlds. He explained that human meanings have no ontological existence separate from individuals. There is no subjective human world juxtaposed with objective realities, but rather a subject that projects and creates meanings. May also discussed the implications of this existential view for psychotherapy.

In *Psychology and the Human Dilemma* (1967), May explained the predicament of living in an age of anxiety; he interpreted the thorny dilemma involved in the individual's experience of self as subject and object; and he elaborated on the danger of self-identification with a world of objective realities. The self, he argued, requires a pole of centeredness preserved only by self-direction and affirmation. Anxiety in this context is a way of awakening the self to the need of discovering an inner pole of centeredness.

In *Love and Will* (1969), he focused on the meaning of love and its relation to will, wish, choice, and decision. He argued that the will is the ability of the self to give meaning to things, and thus it is related to choice and decision making. Illness, on the other hand, is the inability to will. *Love and Will* was on the best seller's list for more than a year; it brought May the Ralph Waldo Emerson Award for Humane Scholarship in 1970.

In *Power and Innocence* (1972), May interpreted the human predicament in an age of anxiety as related to the nature of power. He argued that the feeling of powerlessness drives people to apathy, which, along with repressed needs for a sense of significance, leads to uncontrolled aggression and violence. Those who have power, on the other hand, do not want to recognize that fact.

In addition to extensive publishing, part-time teaching, and training and supervision of analysts, May maintained a private practice of psychotherapy throughout most of his adult life. May was not a scholar in a strict academic sense. Once he empathically complained that "it was a waste of time to write only for a limited number of one's colleagues and a denial of the wisdom our discipline of psychology should exemplify." Instead, he wrote for what he considered a large audience of intelligent, open-minded, questioning, motivated lay people, endeavoring to interpret what it means to be authentic and human in an age of alienation and anxiety. He once said that he was honored to be considered by some a philosopher rather than a psychotherapist.[16]

JAMES F. T. BUGENTAL

James Frederick Thomas Bugental was born on the late Christmas evening of 1915 in Fort Wayne, Indiana. He spent his early childhood in Ohio, Illinois, and Michigan. His father, Richard Francis, who thought of himself as a street-smart and tough man, was anxious to be valued and become an important person; but, like many others of his generation, he was doomed to spend the prime years of his life in the Great Depression. His mother, Hazel Jeanette, was an aspiring pianist who gave up a career in music in order to marry. During the Depression she supported the family by teaching music. Bugental described her as an admirer of "cultured people."[17]

The religious education of young Bugental was mixed and confusing, for he attended whichever Protestant denomination and even unorthodox "new thought" churches were in the vicinity of the Bugentals' many relocations. At a tender age he was an avid reader. While attending grammar school he read all its library holdings. At the age of twelve, he and his family relocated to California, where he finished high school and junior college, doing well in subjects he enjoyed but doing poorly in those he did not. Upon graduation he held several unsatisfactory jobs, got married, and was admitted to West Texas Teachers College, where he earned a B.S. degree in 1940. His exceptional record and faculty support won him a fellowship at the George Peabody College in Nashville, Tennessee.

Graduating with an M.A. degree in sociology in 1941, he began his studies for the Ph.D. and concurrently accepted a position with the Tennessee State Civil Service preparing examinations. In a year he became the head of that organization and abandoned his graduate studies as the members of the Peabody psychology department scattered in war-related assignments. In the following year he accepted a position with the federal civil service system in Atlanta, Georgia. In 1943 he was invited to became an assistant professor of psychology as well as acting director of the Veterans Guidance Center at the Georgia School of Technology. Having been deferred from military service up to 1945 because he worked in "essential" positions, he was in that year drafted into the army and, after basic training, assigned to the Lawson Army General Hospital in Atlanta as a psychologist.

In 1945, the reading of Rogers's *Counseling and Psychotherapy* (1942) opened up a whole new realm for Bugental. Soon after he was discharged from the army (1946) under the GI bill, he enrolled in the doctoral program in psychology at the Ohio State University. Here he found, as he wrote many years later, a new confidence in his intellectual abilities. He studied with Victor Raimy and George Kelly, worked in several departmental positions, and received the Ph.D. degree for his dissertation, *An Investigation of the Relationship of the Conceptual Matrix to the Self-Concept* (1948).

During his post-dissertation years, Bugental was a teacher and researcher at UCLA, where he concentrated on the field of psychological interviewing. Soon, however, he moved into clinical practice in Los Angeles with individuals and groups. Between 1953 and 1969 he was a founding partner in a psychological service group, Psychological Services Associates, which rendered clinical and industrial services.

The 1960s and 1970s were extremely active decades for Bugental: He underwent a divorce; remarried; became involved in local, state, and APA professional and academic activities; and published extensively on the humanistic orientation in psychology. Between 1960 and 1961 he was president of the California State Psychological Association, and in 1962–1963, the first president of the AHP. His "Humanistic Psychology: A New Breakthrough" (1963) was particularly influential in helping the recently established Association for Humanistic Psychology to delineate its goals and policies. He edited one of the first books in humanistic psychology, *Challenges of Humanistic Psychology* (1967), and served at different times as consultant at the Stanford Research Institute and as a clinical instructor at the Stanford Medical School, the U.S. International University, and the Saybrook Institute.

In *The Search for Authenticity: An Existential-Analytic Approach to Psychology* (1965), Bugental developed what he named an "existential orientation to the psychology of personality." The emphasis of this orientation was the need to relate authentically to the existential givens of our being-in-the-world, and the anxieties associated with it. From this perspective, one is said to be authentic when one possesses "organismic awareness," an awareness that Bugental viewed as a central fact of human existence. The avoidance, however, of confrontation with the existential givens and the authentic self generates anxiety, distress, and lack of meaning. The task of psychotherapy is to reduce these distortions and to restore greater authenticity.

In *The Search for Existential Identity* (1976), Bugental vividly narrated six case studies (or dialogues, as he preferred to call them) illustrating the existential orientation developed in *Authenticity*. He further extended this orientation for student therapists in *Psychotherapy and Process: The Fundamentals of an Ex-*

istential-Humanistic Approach (1978). In *The Art of the Psychotherapist* (1987), as the title implies, he viewed his profession as an artistic and creative activity.

Like Rollo May, Bugental emphatically asserted that he was not a scholar of what he named the "abstruse literature" of European existentialism, but rather a "clinical observer" or psychotherapist working from an existential perspective. He constantly asked himself in his writing what it means to be a therapist. His less "imperfect" definition of psychotherapy was that it is a "window on the human soul"; its goal was to "help people who are distressed about their lives, try to make these lives more satisfying." His participation in many lives as a therapist, so he stated, was a powerful and evolving force in his basic character and understanding of human nature.

NOTES

1. For Allport's autobiographical references, see A1949b; A1967a; A1967f; A1968a:vii. For secondary biographical references, see Richard I. Evans, *Gordon Allport: The Man and His Ideas*, New York: Dutton, 1970; Joseph P. Ghougassian, *Gordon Allport: Ontopsychology of the Person*, New York: Philosophical Lib., 1972; *American Psy.*, 1964, 19:942–45; J. W. Mann, "Gordon Allport, 1897–1967," *Psychologia Africana*, 1968, 12:65–74; Thomas F. Pettigrew, "Gordon Willard Allport: 1897–1967," *J. Pers. and Soc. Psy.*, 1969, 12:1–5; Koji Sato, "Prof. Gordon Willard Allport (1897– 1967)," *Psychologia*, 1968, 11:125–26.

2. A1967a:10.

3. A1967a:8.

4. *American Psy.*, 1964, 19:942.

5. For significant autobiographical references for Maslow, see M1954a:ix; M1957c:22; M1961c; M1962d:9; M1962i; M1967e:11; M1967g:41; M1968f; M1969f:3; M1971a:xi-xxi; M1971b; M1972a; M1973a; M1979a. For secondary sources, see Edward Hoffman, *The Right To Be Human: A Biography of Abraham Maslow*, Los Angeles: Jeremy Tarcher, 1988; Frank G. Goble, *The Third Force: The Psychology of Abraham Maslow*, New York: Grossman, 1970; Carroll Saussy, *A Study of the Adequacy of Abraham Maslow's Concept of the Self to His Theory of Self-Actualization*, unpublished doctoral dissertation, The Graduate Theological Union, 1977; Richard Grossman, "Some Reflections on Abraham Maslow," *J. Hum. Psy.*, 1985, 25(4):31–34; *Psy. Today*, Aug. 1970, p. 16; Misako Miyamoto, "Professor Abraham H. Maslow (1908–1970)," *Psychologia*, 1970, 13:120; Richard J. Lowry, *A. H. Maslow: An Intellectual Portrait*, Monterey, Calif.: Brooks/Cole, 1973; Thomas Robert, "Beyond Self-Actualization," *Revision*, Winter 1978, pp. 42–46; Colin Wilson, *New Pathways in Psychology: Maslow and the Post-Freudian Revolution*, London: Gollancz, 1972.

6. R1967a:344. For Rogers's significant autobiographical material, see R1961a; R1964a:36; R1967a; R1967b; R1968b:21–30; R1970a; R1970b; R1971c; R1973b; R1973e; R1973h; R1974e; R1977k; R1978b; R1978d; R1979a; R1980f; R1983f. For significant secondary biographical sources, see *Perspective (AHP)*, May and March 1987; André de Peretti. *Pensée et Verité de Carl Rogers*, Toulouse: Privat, 1974; Constantine A. Dallis, *The Development of Rogerian Thought and Its Implications for Counselor Education*, unpublished doctoral dissertation, University of Wisconsin–Madison, 1965; Richard I. Evans, *Carl Rogers: The Man and His Ideas*, New York: Dutton, 1975;

Richard Farson, "Carl Rogers, Quiet Revolutionary," *Education*, 1975, 95(2): 197–203; Howard Kirschenbaum, *On Becoming Carl Rogers*, New York: Delacorte Press, 1979; Helen E. Rogers, "A Wife's-Eye View of Carl Rogers," *Voices*, 1965, 1(1):93–98; J. T. Wood, "Carl Rogers, Gardener," *Human Behavior*, Nov./Dec. 1972.

7. R1967a:371.

8. R1980e:91–92.

9. For significant autobiographical references for May, see MY1973a:13; MY1939a:92, 102, 125, 129, 166; MY1940a:26, 77; MY1943b:4; MY1950a:92, 247; MY1951A:297, 304; MY1953a:163, 196; MY1954b:585; MY1955c:45; MY1955d:43; MY1959e:87–88; MY1960a:25; MY1961a:i; MY1962d:vii; MY1964a:130; MY1964b:114; MY1965d:303; MY1967a:xi, MY1967b:59; MY1967g; MY1968c:65; MY1968f:220; MY1969a:25, 53, 239; MY1972a:13, 15, 61, 76, 157, 167, 173; MY1973a:1–24, 57, 74, 88–89, 94–96; MY1976e:33; MY1977b; MY1981a:166, 208–210; MY1982a:20. For significant secondary biographical sources on May, see Clement Reeves, *The Psychology of Rollo May*, San Francisco: Jossey-Bass, 1977; Murray Bilmes, "Rollo May," in Ronald S. Valle and Mark King, eds., *Existential-Phenomenological Alternatives for Psychology*, New York: Oxford University Press, 1978, pp. 290–94; J. G. Harris, "The Devil and Rollo May," *Psy. Today*, 1969, 3:13–16; "Rollo May: Man and Philosopher," special issue of *Perspectives (Humanistic Psychology Institute)*, 1981, 2(1); H. Spiegelberg, *Phenomenology in Psychology and Psychiatry: A Historical Introduction*, Evanston, Ill.: Northwestern University Press, 1972, pp. 158–64; W. S. Sahakian, ed., *Psychotherapy and Counseling: Studies in Technique*, Chicago: Rand McNally, 1969, pp. 249–50; *Time Magazine*, June 22, 1970, p. 66, and Nov. 13, 1972, pp. 53–54; Carl A. Whitaker, "A Commentary on Rollo May's 'Contribution of Existential Psychotherapy'," in Alvin R. Mahrer and L. Pearson, eds., *Creative Development in Psychotherapy*, Cleveland, Ohio: Case Western Reserve University, 1971, pp. 180–85; *Who's Who in America with World Notables*, Chicago: Marquis, 1971, vol. 36, p. 1481.

10. Carl A. Whitaker, "Commentary," p. 180.

11. *Time Magazine*, June 22, 1970, p. 66.

12. MY1973a:23–24.

13. MY1967g:29; MY1967a:x–xi, 202.

14. MY1967g:26; MY1972a:220, 227; MY1961e:32–33; MY1963f:214; MY1975a; MY1981a:72.

15. MY1962d:10; MY1972a:34, 35, 69, 55, 239, 255; MY1973c; MY1977b:301; MY1981a:196.

16. MY1977b:296.

17. Autobiographical material on Bugental is scarce. I wish here to thank Dr. Bugental for filling that gap by providing me with his vita, bibliography, and personal reminiscences in an interview that took place in San Francisco on March 8, 1985 and in letters. For significant autobiographical references, see B1948b:343; B1948c:237–38; B1962f:273; B1963b:361; B1968b:13; B1970a:286, 291, 293; B1976a:x, xvii, 11, 15, 278–96; B1976b:49; B1978b:45, 145–50. See also Spiegelberg, *Phenomenology in Psychology and Psychiatry*, pp. 158–64.

4

Humanistic Psychology and Behaviorism

The humanistic psychology advocated by Allport, Maslow, Rogers, May, Bugental, and the first members of the AHP was an outcry against what they thought was, using Maslow's terminology, the "mechanomorphic" image of human nature and the academic sterility of behaviorism.[1] Since the writings of the humanistic psychologists often contrasted behavioristic and humanistic views of human nature by means of negation, behaviorism substantially contributed to the emergence and conceptualization of humanistic psychology. Conversely, the persistent and somewhat provocative critique of behaviorism by humanistic psychologists contributed to the decline of behaviorism in the 1960s.[2]

Both Allport and Maslow had been nurtured in the best behavioristic traditions—Allport at Harvard, where psychologists received J. B. Watson's behavioristic proposal of 1913 enthusiastically, and Maslow in the early and mid-1930s in the primate laboratory of Harry Harlow in Madison, Wisconsin. Great familiarity with behaviorism was often evident in the behavioristic critique of not only Maslow and Allport but most humanistic psychologists, including Rogers, May, and Bugental. Allport's criticism of behaviorism intensified from the late 1940s until the early 1960s; Maslow's critique developed during the 1940s in the context of his theory of human motivation; throughout the 1950s and 1960s Rogers debated with Skinner; and May and Bugental were still challenging behaviorism in the 1960s and early 1970s. In their critiques of behaviorism, humanistic psychologists addressed the concept of behavior, the psychological and ethical implications of the control and prediction of behavior, the definition of scientific method in the psychological sciences, and the image of human nature implicit in behaviorism.

CONTRASTING CONCEPTS OF BEHAVIOR

Most of Allport's training in psychology at Harvard occurred under behaviorists. In the years 1923–1924, however, Allport spent a postdoctoral fellowship in Germany, where he encountered Gestalt psychology, Max Wertheimer, Wolfgang Kohler, William Stern, and Eduard Spranger. Upon his return to the United States, he found himself out of touch with positivism in general and behaviorism in particular. "Germany," wrote Allport many years later, "had converted me from my undergraduate semifaith in behaviorism."[3]

The common theme throughout Allport's critique of behaviorism during the 1950s and 1960s focused on what May called the "behavioristic symbol of S–R." Allport introduced an "o" in this formula to stand for organism: S–O–R. In the last interview before his death in 1967, Allport argued for a small "s" and a small "r," but a very large "O," because "it seems to me that all the interesting things in personality lie in the inferences we must make about what's going on in these intervening variables in terms of motivation, interests, attitudes, values, and so on." According to Allport, the organism made all the difference in the relation between stimulus and response. Most of his critique of behaviorists, whom he once called "person destroying psychologists," centered on this theme.[4]

Allport summarized his critique of behaviorism in two APA presidential addresses in 1939 and in 1946. At the 1939 APA annual meeting, Allport reported on the changing trends in the history of psychological research in America during the last fifty years. In the first six months of 1939, he told the audience, psychological literature mentioning operationism had doubled in relation to the previous year. There was, argued Allport, a strikingly accelerated trend in the use of statistical methods, the study of animal subjects in the laboratory under experimental conditions, and physiological research. This new trend went hand-in-hand with what Allport thought was an austere empiricism. He thus proposed in the address to review this trend in historical and philosophical perspective in order to anticipate its long-range effect on psychological science; the result was a severe criticism of behaviorism. Seven years later, in the first presidential address to the recently established Division of Personality and Social Psychology, Allport elaborated on the idea proposed in his 1939 address that individual prediction is more precise when the "frame of reference" of the individual is known. He particularly emphasized the principle of "expectancy" because, he thought, the stimulus-bond was the most purposive principle derived from the mechanistic philosophy of conditioned reflex experimentation.[5]

Like Allport, Maslow had a romance with and tragic divorce from behaviorism. Maslow first encountered behaviorism as a philosophy student during his undergraduate days at Cornell. His dislike of the speculative character of philosophical discourse attracted him to the empirical and physiological nineteenth-century psychology advocated in America by Edward Bradford Tichener. It was, however, when reading Watson in his early twenties that he realized the potential of behaviorism. The discovery of Watson's behavioristic program, he wrote many years later, produced such "an explosion of excitement" that he went "dancing down Fifth Avenue with exuberance." All you needed, he thought, was to work hard and everything could be changed and reconditioned. The techniques of conditioning seemed to promise a solution to all psychological and social problems, while its easy-to-understand positivistic, objective philosophy protected him against repeating the philosophical mistakes of the past. With such ideas in mind, Maslow joined the graduate program of the Department of Psychology at the University of Wisconsin–Madison, where his entire training and education were behavioristic.[6]

Maslow's M.A. thesis of 1931, an experimental study of the effect of varying simple external conditions on learning, initiated him into the science of prediction and control of behavior. His doctoral dissertation, written under the supervision of Harry Harlow and dealing with the role of dominance among primates, was also behavioristic in concept. A year after graduation, however, Maslow departed Wisconsin and left behind the behavioristic approach of his teachers. In New York City, while teaching first at Teachers College of Columbia University and then at Brooklyn College, Maslow read Freud, the Gestalt psychologists, and the embryologist Ludwig von Bertalanffy; at the same time, he became disillusioned with English philosophy, particularly as represented by Bertrand Russell. Also in New York City, he met Alfred Adler, Max Wertheimer, Kurt Goldstein, and Ruth Benedict; under their influence he replaced Harlow's primates with New York college women in his experimental studies. Along with his research on dominance, Maslow developed the theory of motivation that was to make him famous.[7]

Maslow's critique of behaviorism may be said to fall within three phases. During the first phase, which began with his arrival in New York City and lasted until the early 1940s, Maslow regarded human behavior as not merely the result of a linear connection between a single and isolated stimulus and a single response, but also as determined by all the feelings, attitudes, and wishes that constitute a complete personality. These personality determinants Maslow believed to result in great part from the introspection or interiorization of social convictions and ethical norms of the group. During the second phase, which covered the period of the 1940s when he wrote the key essays on human motivation compiled in *Motivation and Personality* (1954), Maslow made these ideas an integral part of his theory of human motivation. He repeatedly argued that the study of isolated single behaviors and the idea that such behaviors are self-contained is a simplistic and misleading approach to the understanding of personality. After the critique of behaviorism implicit in the theory of motivation formulated in the 1940s, Maslow continued writing on method and theory in psychology, but thereafter his criticism addressed positivistic psychology in general. In *The Psychology of Science* (1966), he criticized behaviorism in a short chapter on the prediction and control of human behavior.[8]

Rogers's lifelong critique of behaviorism was highlighted by his public debate with B. F. Skinner in the 1950s and 1960s on freedom and the control of human behavior. In the 1940s and early 1950s, Rogers had published enough critical remarks about behaviorism to attract the attention of Skinner himself, who in reply invited Rogers to a friendly public debate at the APA meeting of 1956. The purpose of the debate was to clarify the divergent trends they represented regarding the use of scientific knowledge in molding or controlling human behavior. Skinner's position, with which Rogers totally disagreed, was that psychologists should use their power to assume control of human affairs. The debate stirred the emotions of the large audience it attracted. Rogers expressed dissatisfaction, mainly because the argumentation was of the either-or type.[9]

Rogers again encountered Skinner when Skinner presented a paper four years later to the American Academy of Arts and Sciences on the subject of the individual and the design of cultures. During the next two years, Rogers continued writing critiques of Skinner and behaviorism that helped to create a well-publicized schism in the psychological community during the 1950s.[10]

Since both Skinner and Rogers felt they were touching an important nerve in American culture, another debate was scheduled for the summer of 1962 in Duluth, Minnesota. The resulting nine-hour confrontation attracted an audience of 900 people. Rogers recognized later that this debate was the most thorough exploration yet of the conflict between humanistic psychology and behaviorism concerning education and the control of human behavior. Later, he often complained that the tape of the dialogue was intended to have been made public but that Skinner was reluctant to give his permission. Feeling the "profession was cheated," Rogers called Skinner's attitude "needlessly fearful." Many years afterward, Skinner replied that he had not given permission for the release of the tapes because he did not want them to circulate without editing his portion; he also complained about the poor quality of the recording. The tapes were eventually released to the public in 1976, but by then the confrontation and the issues involved had been largely forgotten.[11]

The last public encounter between Rogers and Skinner took place in a symposium on phenomenology and behaviorism in 1963 at Rice University that attracted quite a bit of attention both within and outside psychological circles. Rogers's lecture was philosophical in tone and not specifically addressed to Skinner and behaviorism. He discussed at some length the experimental, phenomenological, and humanistic views of human nature and scientific method, trying to accommodate subjective and objective philosophies of science. Much later, Rogers thought that this presentation was a new direction in his thinking and work.[12]

Rogers's last critique of Skinner took place in 1964. Rogers was elected the "humanist of the year" by the American Humanistic Association that year, and his APA address, "Freedom and Commitment," criticized Skinner's philosophy of social control as described in *Walden Two*. Rogers contrasted the humanistic meaning of freedom with Skinner's views. It has been suggested that Skinner's *Beyond Freedom and Destiny* (1971) was an answer to Rogers's critique.[13]

Rollo May's lifelong battle with behaviorism was summarized in the early 1980s, when May wrote that behaviorism was misleading in three main respects: behaviorism assumed that the self does not exist, that all behavior is conditioned, and that freedom is an illusion. May's critique of behaviorism falls within two periods: before the 1960s, when he wrote brief and general criticisms of behaviorism; and after the 1960s, when his critique concentrated mostly on freedom, power, and the control of behavior. In the early writings, May suggested that what he considered twentieth-century American psychology's exaggerated concern with behavior was an attempt to imitate outmoded mechanistic models and techniques from physics and biology. In the 1960s, mainly in *Psychology and the Human Dilemma* (1967), and throughout the 1970s, May explored the problem of freedom and control of behavior as part of what he thought were the dilemmas of an age anxious about freedom and power.[14]

Bugental's critique of behaviorism was confined largely to the 1960s and early 1970s, a decade that was part of what Bugental termed the "behavioristic interregnum." Not incidentally, the 1960s were also Bugental's most active years in the professional development of humanistic psychology.[15]

Earlier, Bugental had regarded behavior as determined by and pertinent to one's phenomenal field, the phenomenal field being the "universe including himself as experienced by the individual at the moment"—indeed, a broad phenomenological definition. He therefore thought that Watson's proposal that only behavior be studied in psychology represented "tunnel vision." In the early 1960s Bugental went even farther, arguing that behaviorism carried the name of "psychology" by mere historical accident. Its scientific attitude was simplistic and obscure, a "parochial interruption" or "brief hiatus" where the study of superficial external behavior replaced the richness of subjective life, thus bringing narrowness and conformity into psychology.[16]

In the early 1970s, Bugental's critique of behaviorism centered on the problem of control, both individual and social. Bugental was concerned about Skinner's utopian world of *Walden Two*. He blamed the world macroproblems on the behavioristic concept of imposed control, and he suggested the implementation of self-directed control as the only alternative for survival and the creation of a true synergic society. The objectivism and scientism of behaviorism had become, thought Bugental, a pathological defense mechanism. Behaviorists, he suggested, were psychologists who were unable to confront their own subjectivity and who were therefore willing to rely on objective criteria and measurements. In *The Search for Existential Identity* (1976), Bugental illustrated this point in his report on a psychologist of behavioristic persuasion who had come to him for therapy.[17]

All five humanistic psychologists shared the idea that behavior was not to be studied in isolation from its containing organism. All five proposed alternatives to the behavioristic view of human nature. In different ways these alternatives shared a proactive, intentional, and optimistic image of human nature that they termed humanistic. They also criticized the methodological foundations of behaviorism.

CRITIQUE ON METHOD

Allport, Maslow, Rogers, May, and Bugental were critical of behaviorism's attempt to imitate the exact sciences. They thought that behaviorism's excessive concern with method had been largely imported from physics. Behaviorism also inherited from the biological sciences the evolutionary point of view and the animal model. ''The freshening winds of biology,'' wrote Allport in 1938, ''have threatened to push every vestige of humanism out, leaving psychology with a plague of rats.'' Behaviorism's interest in animal research arose, argued Allport, precisely because this data had ''delightful suitability for the exercise of objective and approved methods.'' Rollo May alone completely denied the value of scientific method in the psychological sciences; Allport, Maslow, Rogers, and Bugental thought that behavioral psychology should be complemented by artistic and humanistic perspectives.[18]

Behaviorism was a method-centered science, a ''methodolotry'' in Bugental's words. In a similar manner Allport described behaviorism in the 1939 APA address as a prejudiced empiricism derived from a metaphysical presupposition of extreme nominalism and fidelity to method. Humanistic psychologists agreed that the ability to employ precise techniques and methods gave behaviorists a kind of scientific legitimization. But for this very reason, in Maslow's estimation, behaviorists were mere ''technicians'' and ''apparatus men,'' not psychologists.

All five humanistic psychologists recognized that some behavior may be explained physiologically as a matter of conditioning. But all five also argued that behaviorism's stress on quantification unfairly excluded all problems that did not fit the technique; this in turn, they argued, left psychology with preselected, simple, invalid, and trivial questions. What was not organic or physiological about human nature—that is, what could not be quantified, such as values, consciousness, freedom, and responsibility—the five accused behaviorism of pushing aside and, in extreme cases, of denying completely. Behaviorism was on surer ground in the realm of the either-or of ''psychonomy'' than in the human realm of uncertainties. In short, what behaviorists actually did, argued Maslow, was to compile huge amounts of information on human behavior as if it were an object or a thing. Although it was rigorous methodologically, this approach blocked the development of new techniques, ideas, and questions; in short, it limited the jurisdiction of psychology by making it abstract, formal, and depersonalized. ''My plea,'' said Allport at the 1939 APA convention, ''is that we avoid authoritarianism, that we keep psychology from becoming a cult from which original and daring inquiry is ruled out by the application of one-sided tests of method.''[19]

CRITIQUE ON BEHAVIORAL CONTROL

Behaviorists, such as B. F. Skinner in *Walden Two*, argued that active control of the individual and society has always been exercised for selfish purposes.

They argued that the time had come for scientists to seize political institutions and rule by objective and scientific means. If constructive forces do not control behavior, they warned, less constructive forces will.[20]

In his debate with Rogers, Skinner defended a strict social and environmental determinism. The individual according to Skinner was totally a product of environmental conditioning. One had little or no will—or capacity for self-understanding, self-direction, or control over one's own destiny—and thus had to rely on experts for measurement and evaluation. In this context, Skinner advocated a rational and objective redesign of the environment based upon behavioral engineering. In *Beyond Freedom and Dignity* (1971), for example, he argued that human nature is totally controlled by environmental forces. Freedom is an illusion, and we should not worry about powerlessness and helplessness. Going one step farther than Skinner, some behaviorists suggested that psychoactive drugs could maintain psychological moods, attitudes, and behaviors. Human motivation could thus become a matter of scientific control and prediction.

Allport, Maslow, Rogers, May, and Bugental were unanimously critical of faith in the scientific manipulation of individuals and society. All five shared the belief that human motivation is purposive or choice-oriented and that one can choose and be held responsible for one's destiny.

Rollo May elaborated during the 1960s on the problem of freedom and control of behavior in an age of anxiety. According to May, Skinner failed to recognize the distinction between rats and humans; rats may have no choice, but this did not necessarily imply that humans also have no choice. Freedom and choice, May argued, require the unique human capacity to understand when one is becoming a victim of external conditioning; then one may pause, rebel, or allow the conditioning to continue. Freedom, thought May, also implies responsibility for and commitment to one's attitudes, acts, and future. Unfortunately, such responsibility sometimes leads to anxiety. Anxiety in its turn, according to May, sometimes forces us to abdicate freedom and responsibility to the control of the state and science, thus producing a lack of commitment. Psychologists and their patients, he thought, turn to behavioral therapy precisely to escape this anxiety and feeling of helplessness. The behavioristic utopia, according to May, thus had its strongest appeal to those who hoped for a "scientific substitute" for helplessness.[21]

Skinner had proposed the development of a technology of behavior and the design of better environments; May asked whose values would dictate the environment to be redesigned. Control implies control by someone; who was going to be the controller? No group of scientists, May thought, could be so arrogant as to claim such competence for themselves. But even if a utopia such as *Walden Two* envisioned were possible, humans would revolt against the system. It would make no difference that the system was rational and technicians benevolent.[22]

May was equally critical of behavioristic therapy. He thought that behavior, drug, and other adjustment therapies did not deserve the name of therapy; they were mere mechanical modes of controlling and relieving symptoms. May was particularly worried about the development of psychoactive drugs to control emotional disturbances such as anxiety and depression. Such drugs blocked the pain momentarily, but they had no curative effect on the underlying emotional causes of disturbance. Symptoms are nature's way of telling the self that there is an underlying problem requiring attention; treating the symptoms rather than the cause is like unplugging the smoke alarm in order not to be aware that a fire is underway. Rogers had an almost identical critique of behavior and drug therapies.[23]

Maslow's critique of the concept of control and prediction of behavior was argued within terms of the needs hierarchy theory of motivation that he developed in the 1940s. This theory distinguished between expressive and coping behavior, and Maslow blamed behaviorists for concentrating almost exclusively on coping behavior, which he argued was the least significant part of personality. Expressive behavior—artistic creation, play, wonder, and love—is part of the person and a reflection of personality even if it is nonfunctional and persists without reward. It is an epiphenomenon of inner character structure, the study of which should be the goal of any psychology. On the other hand, coping behavior is functional, instrumental, adaptive, and the product of an interaction of the character structure with the world. Since coping behavior is learned or acquired in order to deal with specific environmental situations, it dies out if not rewarded or continuously bombarded with stimulus. Maslow concluded that one should be cautious in extrapolating from coping behaviors to general conclusions about human nature. The behaviorist, according to Maslow, sees only the animal-like aspects of human nature precisely because he focuses upon coping behavior. Allport made a similar analysis, critique, and distinction between expressive and coping behavior in 1961.[24]

In *The Psychology of Science* (1966), Maslow again attacked the concept of behavioral control. In this work he compared external scientific control of the behavioristic type with the internal self-knowledge posited by humanistic scientists in their ability to predict behavior. He argued that people resent and rebel against external scientific control, but they accept the increase of self-knowledge that allows them to control their own behavior. Thus, self-knowledge of the humanistic type has much more predictive power. Rogers wrote an almost identical argument in "The role of self-understanding in the prediction of behavior."[25]

Allport made a similar argument in his APA address of 1939. He agreed with the behaviorists that only the "unexplained power of predicting, understanding and controlling the course of nature for mankind's own benefit" would make psychology a science. But, like Rogers and Maslow, he thought that self-knowledge allows more predictability than external scientific control.[26]

In his argument Allport made a distinction between actuarial and individual predictions. He argued that a statement like "72 percent of group A will behave in such a way given a certain stimulus" is an abstract generalization or actuarial statement that tells nothing about each individual member of group A. Actuarial statements predict very little about individuals, although they are quite accurate within the confines of laboratory experimentation. Knowledge of the individual's personality, on the other hand, is much more efficient in providing individual predictions. Better predictions, for example, are possible in clinical psychology when there is knowledge of "single trends," "traits," or "imperatives" pertaining to the individual. Moreover, Allport argued, the human behavioral response to a stimulus has significance only in the context of the convictions or values—indeed, the frame of reference—of the individual. Psychology, suggested Allport, should thus take the world of subjective experience as the significant determinant of human behavior. But, unfortunately, the individual is automatically excluded, he complained, when an extreme behaviorism is adopted.[27]

In the case of Rogers, like his colleagues he also criticized Skinner's belief that behavior was the result of environmental reinforcement, planned or unplanned. Rogers and Skinner had agreed to an advance exchange of manuscripts before the APA debate of 1956. Skinner used the word "choice" several times in his first draft; when Rogers returned the manuscript to Skinner, he commented that Skinner's use of the word "choice" contradicted a belief in strict environmental determinism. In reply, Skinner carefully eliminated, replaced, or put the word in quotes. In the final presentation of the papers, Rogers noted the alteration and stated that "Skinner had dropped all notions that the individual makes any value choices for himself."[28]

Four years later, Rogers attended Skinner's lecture on the subject of the individual and the design of cultures; Rogers asked Skinner if he thought it was an illusion that he had chosen to come to the lecture, that he had a purpose for the meeting, and that he existed as a person. Rogers remarked that "he [Skinner] actually made certain marks on paper and emitted certain sounds here simply because his genetic makeup and his past environment had operantly conditioned his behavior in such a way that it was rewarding to make these sounds and that he as a person doesn't enter into this." Skinner answered that he did not want to deal with the question of whether he had any choice in the matter, since this was a philosophical, not a scientific, problem. But Skinner did accept Rogers's characterization of his presence. As opposed to Skinner's environmental determinism, Rogers proposed that people have the capacity to make significant subjective appraisals, choices, and decisions.[29]

Rogers was particularly critical of the behavioristic contention that people should rely on experts for measurement, evaluation, and conduct since they do not have the capacity for self-understanding and self-direction. Science, in this sense, thought Rogers, transforms people into objects that can be measured and regulated, thereby weakening, degrading, and even eliminating one's opportunity for becoming through the process of making responsible self-decisions. Rogers thought that this idea was very threatening, because the expert brings the management and manipulation of the many by the self-selected few. We will be in great danger if tools of behavioral control fall into the hands of a totalitarian regime. Rogers argued that any discussion of behavioral control must first deal with the questions of who will control, what type of control there will be, and toward what end, purpose, or value the control occurs. These questions raise the issues of purpose and values that are extrinsic to science itself. According to Rogers, even perfect random experimentation is a value choice. In other words, Rogers argued that there is purpose and choice in human action, exactly what Skinner had emphatically denied.[30]

In Bugental's critique of behaviorism, he argued that complete behavioral control was an impossibility because the techniques of behaviorism did not allow the collection, measurement, and systematization of all factors involved in human behavior. Behaviorism, he thought, chiefly served those who wanted to predict and control the behavior of other people for selfish purposes. Like Allport and Maslow, Bugental proposed a humanistic goal for psychology, one that would enable people to increase their ability to control and predict their own experiences and life, including resistance to unwanted control.[31]

Early in the 1970s, Bugental linked the world's macroproblems (such as the threats of nuclear war, pollution, and depletion of natural resources) to the behavioristic objectification of human beings, and he suggested the implementation of self-directed control as the only alternative for survival and the creation of a true synergic society. He believed that civilization was at a crucial juncture; we could destroy our world or set back the course of evolution by centuries. We should no longer view ourselves as S-R machines caught in the interplay of powerful world influences and let small groups decide our destiny. He suggested that implementation of control of the self-directed type would encourage people to take greater and more effective responsibility for rescuing their environment and civilization from disaster.[32]

Bugental distinguished between two kinds of control, imposed or extrinsic control and self-directed or intrinsic control, thus juxtaposing behavioristic and humanistic views of control and their implicit image of human nature. He blamed the world macroproblems on control of the imposed type and saw implementation of the self-directed type as the only alternative for survival and the creation of a true synergic society. In control of the imposed kind, the wishes of a person or group are enforced and carried into effect by another person or group with the former believing and making believe that they know better what is right and good. The controllees thus need to restrain their own wills and wishes. Persistent external control in the long run influences inner experience, and the individual may behave according to the controllers' wish while believing to be self-directed. On the other hand, control of the self-directed kind is exercised by the self in order to realize inner potential. It requires facilitation and opportunity based on the belief that people can be trusted in deciding their destinies. Here, control is integral to action and choice. Bugental suggested that if control of the self-directed kind were implemented, people would take greater and more effective responsibility for rescuing the world from disaster. A period of transition and growth, however, would be required for people to accept responsibility for their own lives and the survival of the planet.[33]

CRITIQUE ON THE IMAGE OF HUMAN NATURE

The founders of humanistic psychology characterized the behaviorist's image of human nature in nearly identical ways. For the behaviorists, maintained the five humanistic psychologists, a person was like an inanimate object: purely reactive, a passive helpless thing that is not responsible for its own behavior, an empty organism that can do "nothing but" respond to a stimulus. A person was in this sense a mere collection of independent habits without organization or self-identity. In 1955, Allport argued in *Becoming* that behaviorism inherited this philosophical misconception from John Locke. For Locke, the mind began as a tabula rasa, and external impressions were more fundamental than internal processes. According to Allport, behaviorists likewise assumed that motivation requires a stimulus extrinsic to the organism; what happens to the organism between stimulus and response is of no concern. Moreover, continued Allport, behaviorism inherited from Locke a belief that small and molecular (simple) ideas are more essential then large and molar (complex) ideas; behaviorism translated this belief into the doctrine that the primary concern of psychology must be the atomistic study of behavior rather than the study of personality as a whole.[34]

Maslow argued much like Allport. Even if the behaviorists could add up a collection of single behaviors, Maslow thought that the behaviorists' picture of human nature would still be incomplete; the human organism, he contested, is more than just the additive sum of each isolated and reduced part. The parts affect the whole and vice versa in a continual process of mutual transformation. Rogers, May, and Bugental also regarded the person as a unit, self, gestalt, whole, or process. In different ways, all five thought that a behavioral act has many different components that cannot be studied in isolation from the self-containing organism. They all regarded the self as a complex, internal patterning agent that organizes the stimulus and emits a response that is related to the stimulus through the organism. In Allport's terminology, the organism was the intervening variable that stood between S and R and made the crucial difference. They also agreed that human motivation is purposive, or choice-oriented, proactive rather than reactive, self-motivated rather than restricted to "anticipatory goal reaction." Every one of us, they all agreed, has a peculiar set of subjective values that provides guidance and direction to life. An understanding of such inner attitudes and motives is an absolute prerequisite to the understanding of human behavior and human nature.[35]

CONCLUSION

A few years before his death, Allport mentioned the "mighty importance" of Skinner and other behaviorists, who, he said, had energized the field of psychology. All five humanistic psychologists thought that by borrowing from the study of animal drives and behavior, behaviorism described some limited truths about human nature. What behaviorists had forgotten, they said, were the more important aspects of human nature; above all, behaviorists had ignored the concrete human experience of the self. The study of any behavior, they argued, cannot be singled out and understood apart from the subjective meaning it has in the context of the organism. Although it was legitimate to study behavior, it was not legitimate to forget human rationality and emotion merely because these had no animal counterpart.

Rogers argued that behaviorism and humanistic psychology offered an extra-scientific "philosophical choice." Maslow described the two approaches to psychology as having a "different temperament." According to Maslow, some people would like and some people would not like positivistic rigor; both types had the right to pursue their own interest. Rogers argued that behaviorism and humanistic psychology contrasted most fundamentally in views of human nature as either reactive or proactive (Allport's terminology). Once we have made our "philosophical choice" on this issue, Rogers thought, the paths of study would continue to diverge.[36]

NOTES

1. R1965g; see, for example, Bugental, AHP's first president, comments in B1967b; B1965f:10; B1966a:223; B1967a:viii, 2; B1967b; and report on an interview with the author on March 8, 1985. Allport often juxtaposed the behavioristic reactive and humanistic proactive views of human nature. Maslow did the same with the mechanomorphic and humanistic views.

2. See Rogers's statement on the decline and deradicalization of behaviorism in R1973a:83–84; R1965g:1–5; Richard I. Evans, *Carl Rogers: The Man and His Ideas*, New York: Dutton, 1975, pp. 115, 130–35.

3. Edwin B. Holt, Herbert S. Langfeld, and Hugo Munsterberg were among his behavioristically inclined teachers. See Richard I. Evans, *Gordon Allport: The Man and His Ideas*, New York: Dutton, 1970, pp. 13, 17–19; A1967a:6–12; A1967e:30–32.

4. A1953d:352–53; A1960d:303; A1961a:345; A1961h:2–4; A1968a:45, 68–70; Evans, *Allport*, pp. 13–15.

5. A1940a; A1940b; A1947e.

6. M1971b:19–20; M1966b:7; M1968f:37, 55.

7. M1936a–d; M1968f:37, 55.

8. For the first phase, see M1937c:407; M1937d:421; M1939a:30–31, 38.

9. R1948b:13, 18; R1955a; R1955c:298; R1956c:318–21; R1961a:363–64.

10. R1959a:197; R1959f:241; R1961a:ix, 363–64; R1961a:ch.20; R1961a:ch.21; R1962a:17; R1963c:271; R1974e:132.

11. Gerald Gladstein, ed., *A Dialogue on Education and the Control of Human Behavior* (A six-cassette recording of a dialogue between C. R. Rogers and B. F. Skinner), New York: Jeffrey Norton, 1976; B. F. Skinner, "Comment on Rogers," *American Psy.*, August 1974, p. 640; R1965j:182; R1967b:62; R1970b:522; R1974e:130; Rogers's letter to Louis Hoechstetter included in his *The Analytical Study of the Views of Carl Rogers and B. F. Skinner on the Study of Man*, unpublished doctoral dissertation, University of Pittsburgh, 1971, p. 311.

12. T. W. Wann, *Behaviorism and Phenomenology*, Chicago: University of Chicago Press, 1964.

13. R1964a; Evans, *Rogers*, p. 114. See also Patrick K. Dooley, "Kuhn and Psychology: The Rogers-Skinner, Day-Giorgi Debates," *J. for the Theory of Soc. Beh.*, 1982, 12:275–89.

14. See, for example, MY1955g; MY1981a:137.

15. B1966a:224; B1967b:7. He edited *Challenges of Humanistic Psychology* (B1967a), wrote key essays in the development of his thought (B1963c, B1966a, B1964h, B1967b), and served as AHP's first president.

16. B1948c:126; B1954b:55; B1962c:42–44; B1967a:346.

17. B1971b:34, 95; B1976a:191, 197, 233, 193–94; B1976b:55–59.

18. A1938c:199. MY1958b:13–14; MY1960a:13.

19. A1940a:73. M1943d; M1946b; M1961e. B1963c; B1966a; B1964h; B1967b. R1955c; R1961a:ch.20; R1961a:ch.21; R1963g; R1965j. MY1940a:32; MY1943a:144, 147; MY1943b:15; MY1953a:56; MY1955g; MY1956b:352–53; MY1956c:170; MY1957b:174; MY1958b:13–14; MY1959a:130–33. A1938c; A1940a; A1940b; A1943g:115; A1947e.

20. Evans, *Rogers*, p. 114.

21. MY1960c:12–13;   MY1962c;   MY1963b:205;   MY1963e;   MY1963d; MY1967a:130–33; MY1968f:187; MY1972a:22–23, 106–107; MY1981a:194–203.

22. MY1962c; MY1963d:199; MY1963f:205; MY1981a:194–203.

23. MY1962d:16–17;   MY1967g:26;   MY1969a:263;   MY1955g:184–85; MY1963d:202; MY1956c:170; MY1972a:22; MY1981a:194. R1948b:13, 18; R1955a. R1955c:298; R1956c:318–21.

24. M1949b; M1943b:103; M1954d:291–92. A1961a:ch.19.

25. R1948e; see also R1956f:lxiii; M1966b:40–44.

26. A1940a; A1921a:38; A1940b; A1946a:135; A1950a:vi.

27. A1940a.

28. R1973a:83–84; R1956f; see also R1970b:521–23; R1973b:46; R1974f:198–99; R1977a:19.

29. R1962a:17; R1963c:271; R1974e:132.

30. R1956f; R1955a; R1964a; R1948b:13, 18; R1955c:298; R1956c:318–21.

31. B1963c; B1964h; B1966a; B1967b.

32. B1971d; B1971b; B1974b; B1971b:34, 95.

33. B1971d; B1971b; B1974b.

34. A1955a:7–12.

35. A1937a:248–58; A1937b:87; A1947e; A1940a; A1940b; A1961a:27–28, 314–19; A1961h:2–4; A1962c:68–70. M1943a: see mainly page 72, note 2; M1943b; M1943d:55; M1951a:350–51; M1966b:55; M1968b:2; M1968c:64. R1939b:4; R1946d:422; R1947c:367; R1948e; R1951a:ch.11; R1965f; R1961a:chs.20, 21; R1963a:3; R1963g; R1964a; R1970b:521–23. MY1940a:32; MY12943a:144, 147; MY1943b:15; MY1953a:56; MY1955g; MY1956b:352–53; MY1956c:170; MY1957b:174; MY1958b:13–14; MY1959a:130–33. B1963c; B1966a; B1963b:97; B1964h; B1965f:11; B1967b; B1976b.

36. A1940o:293;   A1964b:19–23;   A1967a:23;   A1967f:1–2;   A1968a:12,   45. MY1940a:32; MY1943a:147; MY1943b:15; MY1957b:174; MY1963b:75; MY1972a:76. R1973a:83–84. Evans, *Rogers*, pp. 115, 130–35. B1964h:25; B1966a:235; B1967b:7. M1971b:20, 49.

5

Humanistic Psychology and Psychoanalysis

When humanistic psychologists wrote of themselves as a third force, they were thinking of behaviorism as the first or dominant force in psychology; the second force was psychoanalysis. Allport, Maslow, Rogers, May, and Bugental often set their views in contrast to Freudian psychoanalytical views, arguing that humanistic psychology was a protest or outcry, not only against behaviorism but also against the formalism, determinism, and dogma of classical psychoanalysis. However, the founders of humanistic psychology also paid a tribute of reverence to Freud. Quite often they even referred to humanistic psychology as complementing rather than replacing Freud's observations by providing a broader phenomenological and existential conception of human nature. A distinction, however, must be made within the psychoanalytical movement between Freud or classical psychoanalysis and the neo-Freudians. All five were also more indebted to the neo-Freudians than they usually cared to admit.[1]

This chapter traces the impact of the neo-Freudians on the humanistic psychologists' intellectual development and concentrates on their criticism of what they understood to be classical Freudian psychoanalysis. As with behaviorism, it was the particular view of human nature implicit in psychoanalysis—the concept of the person as a helpless being caught in an insoluble conflict between biology and society—that permeated most of their critique.

HOMAGE TO FREUD

Rollo May described Sigmund Freud as a genius and one of the most influential and original thinkers of all time, comparable to figures such as Socrates, Newton, and Einstein. Freud, along with Kierkegaard, Nietzsche, and Schopenhauer, recognized the significance of the irrational, dynamic, unconscious, instinctual, and sexual side of human nature. He was, according to May, the first to expose the futility of the Victorian/Puritan notion of willpower and to study the other side of human nature within a scientific framework. Freud's chief contribution, wrote May, "was not in his technique (where I do disagree) but rather in his insight into the unconscious. He answered the chief problem of the 19th and 20th century—how to live in an age of repression."[2]

Gordon Allport similarly credited Freud with preserving the concept of the ego from total extinction in an age of positivism. Allport regarded classical psychoanalysis as one of several useful methods of studying personality and acknowledged that he himself borrowed from the Freudians. Like May, Allport also pointed out that Freud's main contribution was to the understanding of hidden human qualities; in the case of the neurotic personality, he noted that Freud provided the best available theoretical framework. In 1955 he stated that it was because of Freud that psychologists had begun to understand mechanisms such as denial, repression, displacement, and transference.[3]

Both Maslow and Bugental distinguished between facts and theory in Freudian thought; they praised the facts or clinical experience, but they despised Freud's metaphysics or what Bugental called Freud's "metapsychology." Maslow argued in the late 1960s that Freud the fact finder but not Freud the metaphysician was still required reading for a humanistic psychologist. Early in his own career Maslow praised Freud for introducing the concept of "dynamism" or the recognition of the essential role of motivation, especially unconscious motivation, in the study of personality. Bugental also often praised Freud's discovery of resistance and its significance in the practice of therapy.[4]

When Carl Rogers was asked in 1975 to comment on Freud's views, he answered that they all contained a germ of truth. Rogers often praised Freud as a very flexible researcher who changed, altered, and revised his terminology according to his own clinical experience. It was in the hands of his followers, thought Rogers, that Freud's psychoanalysis deteriorated into a narrow and dogmatic orthodoxy comparable to religious fundamentalism.[5]

Of the five thinkers, only Allport met Freud face to face. This meeting occurred in 1920 when Allport, then twenty-three years old, was visiting his brother in Vienna. When he was introduced to Allport, Freud replied with a "psychoanalytical silence." Not being prepared for this reception, Allport reported an event—the case of a dominant mother whose child displayed a dirt phobia—he had just witnessed on the tram car. Assuming that the report was Allport's own projection, Freud asked if that little boy was Allport himself. In recounting the encounter many years later, Allport suggested that Freud, accustomed to neurotic personalities and defenses, had read too much into his "dirty little boy" report, misunderstanding his real motivation. Allport often described his short meeting with Freud as a "traumatic developmental episode."[6]

Apparently only Maslow, May, and Bugental were psychoanalyzed. Maslow was psychoanalyzed at least three times in his life, in the late 1940s and early 1950s by Emil Oberholzer and Felix Deutsch respectively, and in the 1960s by

Harry Rand. He described his analysis as "the best of all learning experiences," and he said it had taught him about psychoanalysis "from the inside, by experiencing it." Bugental underwent analysis during his first years of practice as a therapist; however, his was a negative outcome. May was most likely analyzed by Erich Fromm, who was his supervisor in the practicum of psychoanalysis. He might, however, have been referring to other psychoanalytical experiences when he said in an interview that these experiences were "tremendously valuable, I wouldn't trade them for the world."[7]

INFLUENCE OF THE NEO-FREUDIANS

Among psychoanalysts, it was the neo-Freudians who had the deepest intellectual impact on Maslow, Rogers, and May. Allport himself had a substantial influence on neo-Freudians of ego-psychology leaning such as Hanz Hartmann, Erich Fromm, David Rappaport, and Karen Horney. It has been suggested that it was Allport's supportive attitude and later endorsement that eased the neo-Freudians' acceptance by the field of academic psychology. Allport often referred to the ego-psychologists' views on motivation as being much better balanced than those of classical psychoanalysis, and he praised the ego-psychologists for modifying psychoanalysis in the direction of his own "functional autonomy." Like Allport, the ego-psychologists no longer sought motives exclusively in the unconscious, but they consider the ego to be much more active than do classical psychoanalysts.[8]

Maslow often acknowledged his intellectual indebtedness to the writings and friendship of Alfred Adler, Erich Fromm, and Karen Horney. David Levy, Abram Kardiner, Sandor Rado, and Franz Alexander also encouraged and stimulated his early intellectual development. Most of these neo-Freudian contacts took place during Maslow's postdoctoral years in New York City in the 1930s and 1940s at a time when the city was flooded with learned émigrés from Europe.[9]

In New York City, Maslow met Heinz L. Ansbacher, who introduced him to Alfred Adler's informal seminars being held at the hotel where Adler lived. After Adler read Maslow's dissertation on the social behavior of primates, Adler encouraged Maslow to present a summary of his conclusions in the *Journal of Individual Psychology*. Maslow's essay invited comparison between the behavior of humans and apes, and Adler's encouragement thus had an important role in causing Maslow to replace primates with college women as experimental subjects in his studies of dominance and sexual behavior. Maslow and Adler remained friends, occasionally dining together until Adler's death in 1937. Heinz Ansbacher believes that as the humanistic psychology that Maslow advocated matured, it came to resemble the individual psychology of Adler ever more closely.[10]

Friendship in New York City with Fromm and Horney was also to prove important to Maslow's intellectual development. They were to become—along with Adler, Kurt Goldstein, and Rogers—Maslow's most quoted authors. In the late 1930s and early 1940s, Maslow often discussed his ideas on motivation with

Fromm and Horney, and he subsequently acknowledged that he had learned psychoanalysis from them and that his psychology was to a certain extent an effort to integrate the partial truths he found in their theories. Also, he often juxtaposed their ideas to those of Freud and defended them from scholarly criticism.[11]

The most influential figure to emerge from the psychoanalytical movement who had a deep intellectual impact on the formative years of Carl Rogers's client-centered therapy was Otto Rank. During the 1930s Rogers was in Rochester, New York, first as an employee and later as director of the Child Study Department of the Society for the Prevention of Cruelty to Children. Some of the social workers at Rochester had taken courses at the Pennsylvania School of Social Work, which followed the orientation of Otto Rank; their enthusiasm about Rank's new "relationship therapy" led Rogers to invite Rank to Rochester for a weekend.

Rogers was deeply impressed with Rank's description of therapy, particularly with his emphasis on the importance of listening to the feelings behind the client's words and of "reflecting" them back to the client. Moreover, Rank's claim that the person has potential to grow and that therapy should rely on human qualities rather than on intellectual skills proved to be, wrote Rogers, an effective way of working with people in distress. Rogers's first publications, including *The Clinical Treatment of the Problem Child*, were increasingly critical of classical Freudian psychoanalysis and were sympathetic to the "relationship" or "passive therapy" advanced by Otto Rank and Jessie Taft. However, in this book Rogers advocated a broad, eclectic approach to child therapy.[12]

Rollo May was the humanistic psychologist most involved with the psychoanalytical movement. May read a number of books by Freud while attending the Union Theological Seminary in his late twenties and was deeply impressed. But already in his first publications we find May praising the "disciples" of Freud, namely Carl Jung, Fritz Kunkel, Otto Rank, and in particular Alfred Adler. Adler's work, according to May, complemented the initial work of the master. As in the case of Maslow, Alfred Adler's friendship and writings had a significant impact on May's early intellectual development. After graduation, May taught at the American College in Salonika, Greece, and spent the summers studying with Adler in Vienna, an experience he described as intimate and one that led him indirectly to psychology.[13]

In the 1940s, May expressed increased sympathy for the theories of Freud's disciples. Adopting Rank's views, May criticized the determinism and mechanistic interpretation of personality at the core of psychoanalytical theory. Like Rank, May also pointed to the relevance of freedom, responsibility, and creative will in psychotherapy. From Jung, May borrowed the concepts of uniqueness and polarities or the "play of opposites" in personality; from Adler came the belief that human motivation was teleological rather than causological, as Freud had implied. In his dissertation on the meaning of anxiety, May referred to Adler, Jung, and Rank, and also to Karen Horney, Erich Fromm (who was

May's supervisor in more than 300 hours of practicum in psychoanalysis), Abram Kardiner, and Harry Stack Sullivan.[14]

During the 1950s May developed an interesting historical interpretation of the psychoanalytical movement. In this account, Freud was the first to expose the futility of Victorian/Puritan views by pointing to the unconscious and irrational sides of human nature; Freud was the first to include these aspects within a scientific framework. For this fact, he was—along with Kierkegaard and Nietzsche—one of the greatest thinkers of recent history. In the 1920s, according to May's historical account, most psychoanalysts were obsessively concerned with the patient's past; but Rank emphasized psychological "present time," arguing that "experiencing" is more important than talking about experience. In keeping with the competitive atmosphere at the time, Karen Horney and Erich Fromm during the 1930s frequently considered psychological problems to result from a repressed hostility between groups and individuals. They argued that orthodox psychoanalysis missed the crucial significance of the social and inter-personal aspects of human nature. The 1950s, May believed, was a decade of loneliness and social unease, and thus Sullivan's interpersonal psychology was of crucial significance. May argued that Sullivan's "theory may well be the most consistent basis we yet have for a unified science of man."[15]

BIOGRAPHICAL SKETCH

Allport argued that Freud had a too-ready tendency to imagine pathological personality problems and to plunge too quickly and too deeply into the uncon-scious. Allport thought that his own "traumatic" encounter with Freud illustrated Freud's tendency quite well. Allport did not deny the existence of repressed traces, neurotic dispositions, and repetition compulsion; but he argued that these apply only to neurotic personality and not to normal personality development. In non-neurotic personalities, according to Allport, human motivation is con-scious and future-oriented, rather than unconscious and past-oriented. In a healthy person, the unconscious and conscious agree; repressed traces may exist, but understanding those traces requires phenomenological insight rather than analysis of the unconscious. Allport thought that Freud's broad statements about human nature were, therefore, mistaken. Allport's more detailed critique of Freud cen-tered around two basic arguments: In non-neurotic personality development, the ego (and, along with it, human motivation) is purposive and future-oriented rather than reactive and past-oriented; and unconscious infantile motives and instinctual drives of the id do not explain motivation in the nonpathological personality. Allport's criticisms of Freud were thus consistent with Allport's own "functional autonomy" theory of human motivation.[16]

When Maslow arrived in Madison, Wisconsin, for graduate school, he ex-pressed some interest in psychoanalysis. Later, the behavioristic orientation of the faculty seemed to have eclipsed this interest. Maslow wrote in the 1940s that his attitude toward Freud was one of reverence with reservations. Maslow accused Freud and other classical psychoanalysts of studying only half of personality and of being the "worst offenders" among all psychologists in their depiction of human nature. Maslow praised Freud for having introduced the concept of "dynamism" or the recognition of the essential role of motivation, especially unconscious motivation, to the study of personality. But, according to Maslow, Freud was mistaken in considering all behavior to be determined by unconscious motives. Like Allport, Maslow also distinguished between neurotic motivation and healthy motivation, the latter being much less directed by unconscious forces. This distinction suggested Maslow's study of self-actualization in healthy people.[17]

In the 1950s and 1960s Maslow criticized Freud for always considering the unconscious and regression to be unhealthy processes needing to be controlled and examined. Maslow argued that they could also be the sources of creativity, art, love, humor, gaiety, and the like; they could be healthy aspects of personality that should be accepted and nurtured. Toward the end of the 1960s Maslow blamed Freud for studying only the basic needs humans share with animals and neglecting the "higher human qualities" unique to mankind.[18]

Rogers first encountered psychoanalysis in the mid–1920s at the Institute for Child Guidance in New York City, where he fulfilled the internship requirement for his doctorate degree from Teachers College, Columbia University. Rogers remembered that "Freud was a dirty word" and that the approach was rigorous and scientific at Teachers College; but he recalled that at the Institute for Child Guidance he "soaked up the dynamic Freudian view of the staff." Rogers's first clinical treatment of a child in the institute was based almost exclusively on psychoanalytical theories. During the 1930s, while in Rochester, Rogers gradually came under the spell of Otto Rank. In the following decade of the 1940s, Rogers formulated his critique of classical Freudian psychoanalysis in terms of the "assimilated intellectual interpretation" implicit in psychoanalytical therapeutic procedures.[19]

Rogers's first clear formulation of client-centered therapy, described in 1942 in *Counseling and Psychotherapy*, included a comprehensive critique of Freud. Rogers argued that client-centered therapy allowed greater independence and self-interpretation on the part of the individual than did classical psychoanalysis. In the late 1940s, Rogers further elaborated this critique in terms of interrelated therapeutic concepts: directive versus nondirective therapy, resistance to therapy, and transference to the therapist. After the late 1950s Rogers continually criticized Freudian views of human nature, which he believed contrasted with his own views.[20]

Rollo May's first serious challenge to psychoanalysis as a form of psychotherapy began in the 1950s under the banner of existentialism. His dissertation on the meaning of anxiety (1950), written under the influence of Kierkegaard and Paul Tillich, discussed and praised Freud's historical influence. In his postdissertation years, however, May increasingly criticized the practice of psychoanalysis from the standpoint of phenomenological and existential psychologists.

May did not consider the existential movement in psychology and psychiatry to be another reform within the history of psychoanalysis, but a challenge to it.[21]

May challenged psychoanalysis on three main grounds. First, a psychoanalytical science of human nature could never become an objective science; second, the determinism implicit in orthodox psychoanalytical practices contributed to the passivity of the ego; and third, the splitting tendency of Freud's rational and technical reasoning was undesirable in the study of human nature.[22]

May knew that merely challenging psychoanalysis was not enough; a large body of psychological phenomena needed to be explained. From the early 1960s on, May concentrated on developing alternative theoretical explanations for the practice of psychoanalysis. He discussed the centrality of will, decision, and intentionality in human motivation; reinterpreted the Oedipus myth in the light of these ideas; worked on the relevance of symbols and myths to the understanding of man's unconscious life; and formulated a phenomenological interpretation of dreams, the unconscious, and psychotherapy.[23]

Bugental's criticism of psychoanalysis in the mid–1960s and mid–1970s stemmed from his own existential-analytic psychotherapy. Bugental opposed what he thought was the psychic determinism of psychoanalysis. He also criticized such Freudian concepts as the libido; the tripartite division of personality into id, ego, and superego; and the ideal of the therapist as a "blank screen." Bugental accepted the Freudian theory of the unconscious and often praised Freud's pioneer discovery of resistance and its significance for the clinical practice of therapy, but he also criticized Freud's understanding of human nature and reinterpreted Freudian ideas within the context of his own existential framework.[24]

MOTIVATION AND THERAPY

The founders of humanistic psychology similarly accused Freud of emphasizing too much the role of the unconscious in human motivation. They considered Freud's analysis of personality to imply the existence of basic irrational, fixed motives or biological drives in the id. Most of their criticism of Freud addressed this issue in one way or another. Allport, Maslow, and, to some extent, May dealt specifically with the problem of conscious versus unconscious motivation; Rogers and Bugental addressed psychoanalytical therapeutic procedures.

Allport and Maslow distinguished between neurotic and non-neurotic motivation. Both thought that Freud's mechanisms explained the neurotic personality quite well; but they argued that it was a mistake to extend the conclusions of such studies to generalizations about all humankind. When developing his needs hierarchy theory of human motivation in 1940, Maslow argued that the behavior of healthy individuals is much less unconscious than that of neurotics. Healthy behavior, he wrote, was not always directly related to an underlying and ultimately unconscious aim.[25]

As Maslow explored self-actualization and peak-experiences, he also argued that Freud was mistaken in describing the unconscious as irrational, dark, and obscure. Id impulses, he suggested, need not be signs of sickness, regression, and enslavement. The unconscious could also be good, beautiful, and desirable. In cases of artistic creation, inspiration, humor, love, and the like, unconscious impulses were, indeed, revelations of the inmost core of human nature. Growth toward self-actualization, he argued, relies on this essential unconscious core of the person, which needed to be accepted, respected, and loved. One should use the unconscious rather than fear it; accept it rather than control it. In self-actualizing individuals, Maslow argued, the Freudian id, ego, and superego, the dichotomies of conscious and unconscious, and all internal conflicts are much less sharp than in unhealthy personalities. In peak-experiences, for example, these oppositions tend to dissolve. Healthy people have a sense of themselves as conscious, active agencies rather than as helpless victims of unconscious forces. Their behavior is understandable without reference to their unconscious life.[26]

Allport challenged Freud's concept of instinctual and biological id drives in terms of the "functional autonomy" or "progressive internal organization" of an individual's motives. In spite of a continuity in personality development, he thought that motives in adult life supplant and are radically different from the motives of infancy. The tensions involved in any acquired system of motivation are not of the same kind as the antecedent tensions from which that acquired system developed. Motivation, concluded Allport, is determined by contemporary conscious "structural dispositions" such as interests, ambitions, values, goals, plans, intentions, ideals, and hopes; these dispositions involve long-range terms and are persistent, dynamic, directive, and aimed toward the future. He called the process by which motivation evolves the "course of becoming."[27]

Allport often criticized classical psychoanalysts for accepting Freud's view of the ego. The ego as described by Freud, Allport argued, was a helpless, rational, and passive percipient agent; it was devoid of dynamic power and vulnerable to the conflicting pressures of the instinctual forces or drives of the id; it was also vulnerable to the superego and the pressures of the external environment. All the ego could do was attempt to reconcile or steer these warring forces; anxiety occurred when this attempt failed. Rejecting the reactive view of the ego, Allport proposed a purposive or proactive view in which the ego was recognized as a "fighter for ends," an executive and planner. For Allport, the ego had a dynamism of its own; it was active, autonomous, and not dependent upon the primitive instinctual desires and drives of the id. Allport described a "conflict free ego" that allowed humans to live according to conscious motives, interests, values, plans, and intentions.[28]

Like Allport, Rollo May also argued for the functional autonomy of motives— but focusing on the psychoanalytical significance of wish, will, and intentionality, he introduced to the discussion an existential component. May argued in 1966 that psychoanalysis was in a state of crisis because psychoanalysts had failed to find a balance between wish and will. According to May's view, psychoanalytical therapy systematically destroyed the patient's will and created indecision, thus worsening the very problem psychoanalysts hoped to cure. May argued that biological drives and wishes were linked to willpower by intentionality. Wish gives content and richness to will, whereas will gives self-direction, freedom, and maturity to wish; wish and will are both means of achieving intentions. Once blended with will, wish becomes more than a blind drive of response to primitive biological needs. It carries meaning, selects and molds one's actions. It allows one to fantasize and to hope, thus shaping one's future.[29]

Using existential terminology, May asserted that intentionality requires the committing of attention to something. Every will and every wish involves movement toward something to which we are committed as part of our very being in the world. One is able to pay attention to something only when one is able to experience that thing. In a therapy session, for example, the patient is able to remember repressed past experiences only when the patient is ready to cope with those experiences. Attention as such, May explained, is one's belief that one can achieve something one commits oneself to do. Attention is an "I can" that implies an "I will." The Cartesian *cogito, ergo sum* thus became, for May, an "I think–I can–I will–I am," where the crucial experience of individual self-identity derived from "I can–I will." According to May, the goal of psychotherapy is, first, to bring wish into consciousness where it becomes will (I-am-the-one-who-has-these-wishes); and, second, to make the patient accept responsibility for his choices and learn that intentions can shape his peculiar being-in-the-world.[30]

Rogers and Bugental criticized classical psychoanalysis on therapeutic grounds. As early as the 1940s, Rogers focused his critique on psychoanalytical procedures that required "assimilated intellectual interpretation." He argued that classical psychoanalytical therapy was overintellectualized in that it aimed to change patient attitudes through the patient's assimilation of the intellectual interpretation of his own behavior. But an intellectualized interpretation of behavior, argued Rogers, cannot itself alter behavior, no matter how accurate that interpretation may be. Self-understanding is achieved inwardly; it is emotional, not rational, and it cannot be imposed. Rogers believed that "resistance" to the therapist was not an inevitable consequence of the therapy, but that it took place when the therapist confronted the client too rapidly with a highly intellectualized explanation.[31]

Client-centered therapy, Rogers stated, aimed at greater independence and self-interpretation on the part of the individual than did classical psychoanalysis. It aimed at helping the client solve his own problems efficiently and without need of a therapist. There was more emphasis in client-centered therapy upon the emotional and immediate situation than upon personality reorganization through an intellectualization of the client's past experiences.[32]

As Rogers's thoughts on therapy matured, he criticized classical psychoanalysis in terms of his distinction between directive versus nondirective therapy.

Rogers argued that traditional psychoanalysts believed they must control the therapeutic relationship because they had no confidence in the client's own capacity to achieve self-understanding. The philosophy of client-centered therapy stood at the opposite end. He was thus critical of psychoanalysts' tendency to manipulate the therapeutic process by the use of "directives." Rogers argued that therapists should trust the capacity of the client for self-understanding in the therapeutic setting if only given a supporting relationship.[33]

Rogers also criticized the Freudian concept of "transference." Therapeutic improvement is more rapid and efficient, he argued, if the client's emotional transference of attitudes to the therapist is openly expressed and accepted by the therapist with "unconditional positive regard." In so doing the client will eventually understand that transference has taken place, thereby dissolving that transference. Under no circumstances should the existence of transference be discussed with the client before he himself consciously experiences the transference attitudes; otherwise the client will resist the transference explanation.[34]

Bugental likewise criticized Freud's views on psychotherapy. He accepted and valued Freud's concept of resistance, but he sought to give it a broader, more existential setting. The resistance to the therapist and the therapeutic process he saw as less significant than the fact that the same resistance is the force that brings about the client's life difficulties. The ways in which a client resists therapy are isomorphic with the ways in which that person holds off the reality of his or her being-in-the-world. Thus, psychotherapy must be sought to aid the client in redirecting the resistive energies toward greater authenticity in being. Psychotherapy of the existential-analytical type that Bugental advocated meant, in a simplified form, "training in authenticity." It sought to uncover the patient's symptoms in order to expose his underlying existential anxiety, thus producing a greater degree of subjective awareness that could lead to recovery.[35]

CONCLUSION

In considering the intellectual influence of psychoanalysis on the founders of humanistic psychology, a distinction must be made between Freud—or classical psychoanalytical thought—and the neo-Freudians. Although all five humanistic psychologists examined in this book paid homage to Freud, they also often criticized Freud's psychoanalytical interpretation of human nature. Their relationship with the neo-Freudians was less ambivalent, however. Adler, Fromm, and Horney had a great deal of influence on May and Maslow. Rank influenced Rogers and May; and Jung and Sullivan influenced May. Conversely, Allport had a substantial impact on the ego-psychologists themselves.

In their earlier writings, Allport, Maslow, and May criticized psychoanalytical explanations of motivation. On the other hand, Rogers, Bugental, and (to a lesser extent) May criticized the psychoanalytical understanding and practice of psychotherapy. Allport and Maslow made a distinction between motivation in neurotics and healthy people, arguing that motivation among the latter is much less unconscious and instinctual than among the former. Allport utilized his theory of the "functional autonomy" of motives to criticize Freud, and Maslow used his theory of human motivation. In the existential context of the concept of intentionality, May argued that motivation was teleological in character and that psychology could never become the naturalistic science envisioned by Freud. Rogers criticized the "assimilated intellectual interpretation" of psychoanalysis. Finally, Bugental provided an existential reinterpretation of the Freudian concept of resistance.

In their mature writings, all five humanistic psychologists broadened their attacks on Freud by criticizing what they understood to be the psychoanalytical views of human nature. They all argued that Freud's assessment of human nature was overly pessimistic, too fatalistic, too deterministic; Freud, they said, focused too exclusively on the dark side of human nature, not taking into account an individual's sense of personhood, freedom, and dignity. They believed that Freud accepted the need for control, both in society and personality, mainly because he considered the individual to be innately destructive, irrational, and unsocial. They understood Freud to mean that destruction, incest, murder, and other crimes would follow if one's inner nature was allowed a free expression.

Freud erred, said the humanistic psychologists, by believing that a person's entire life is merely a reaction to early childhood fixations, castration threats, and Oedipal fantasies. It was as if an individual was forever a prisoner, condemned never to escape the primitive passions that originated in these fixations. They argued that Freud considered personality to be the "willy-nilly" product of powerful and unrestrained biological drives. According to Freud, they said, a person can direct but can never transform the id's basic structure. Thus, Freudian personality dynamics could do no more than restrain the forces of the id, seeking either their sublimation or equilibrium.

The five humanistic psychologists offered a proactive and teleological alternative to Freud. They believed the human organism possessed a capacity for self-direction and could take responsibility for shaping its way of being-in-the-world. With the exception of Rollo May (who believed that human nature was the product of a tension between polarities), they had an essentially optimistic view of human nature. They argued that freedom from internal and external controls would allow for the emergence, in Maslow's and Rogers's terminology, of a fully functioning and self-actualizing person.

NOTES

1. On the humanistic psychologists' protest against psychoanalysis see, for example, A1933b:264; A1955a:37; A1967a:7–8; A1967f:1. Richard I. Evans, *Gordon Allport: The Man and His Ideas*, New York: Dutton, 1970, pp. 3–12. M1939a:4–5; M1956d:21; M1959c:141; M1962b:60; M1964b:6, 8; M1968b:2–3; M1968c:65; M1970a:xi. R1937b:56, 323; R1951a:4; R1954a:32; R1963g:72; R1974c:23. MY1939a:45–49;

MY1958b:6–7; MY1959e:87; MY1961c:641; MY1964b:111–15; MY1966a:55–60; MY1981a:22–23. B1964h:22, 25; B1965f:10, 16; B1966a:223–24.

2. MY1939a:7, 19, 44–77, 228; MY1940a:21, 42; MY1943a:146; MY1950a:132; MY1953a:13–14, 266; MY1958b:7, 33; MY1961a:11; MY1961e:31; MY1963b:16–17; MY1964b:112–15; MY1967g:25. See also May's letter to the author dated May 23, 1989.

3. A1933b:264; A1955a:37; A1961a:145; A1967f:2. Evans, *Allport*, pp. 3–12.

4. M1943a:66–67; M1943b:103; M1951b:638–39; M1956d:21. A1970a:xiii. B1964h:22, 25; B1965f:10, 16, 58, 63, 88; B1966a:223–24.

5. R1959h:191; R1961a:ix. Richard I. Evans, *Carl Rogers: The Man and His Ideas*, New York: Dutton, 1975, pp. 6–8, 88–89.

6. A1967a:7–8. Evans, *Allport*, pp. 3–6. As to Allport's "traumatic" encounter with Freud, recently two psychoanalytical writers have argued that Allport's exaggerated response stemmed (1) from an unwillingness to recognize his own motives for seeking out Freud, such as his own "clean little boy phobia," and (2) from his misconception of Freud and psychoanalysis in general. M. D. Faber, "Allport's Visit with Freud," *Psychoanalytic Rev.*, 1970, 57:60–64; Allan C. Elms, "Allport, Freud, and the Clean Little Boy," *Psychoanalytical Rev.*, 1972–1973, 59:627–32.

7. M1954a:x; M1962b:xi; M1966b:xix. B1976a:281. MY1967g:72.

8. A1937a:viii; A1953b:95, 107; A1955a:46; A1961a:103, 216–17; A1967a:7–8; A1967f:4.

9. Maslow wrote about New York City in this period as being the center of the psychological universe of that time (M1954a:ix). See also the following two notes.

10. Throughout Maslow's extensive list of writings, Adler was indeed one of the most quoted authors after Freud. He mentioned Adler by name at least seventy-seven times; see Jenny Scheele, *Register Referring to the Complete Published Works by A. H. Maslow*, Delft, The Netherlands: Delft University of Technology, 1978, p. 411. M1935b:47; M1943b:90–91; M1954a:x; M1962f:125; M1970a:xi. Author's personal correspondence with H. L. Ansbacher of October 29, 1985; Heinz L. Ansbacher, "Alfred Adler and Humanistic Psychology," *J. Hum. Psy.*, 1971, 11:53–63.

11. M1941a:xii–xiii; M1943e:401; M1954a:x; M1956d:21; M1962c:34–35; M1970a:xi; M1971b:20. Scheele, *Register*, pp. 435, 444.

12. R1937a:239, 241–42; R1937b:56–57; R1939b:338, 346; R1954a:32; R1961a:9; R1967a:356–60; R1977k:128–29.

13. MY1939a:7–10, 19, 44–77, 227fn2; MY1961e:31; MY1964b:113; MY1967g:25.

14. MY1940a:20–26, 39–43, 148–51, 187–88, 244–59; MY1943a:146–50; MY1950a:133–70, 191–239, 247.

15. MY1951a:304; MY1953a:13–14, 266; MY1953b:16–17; MY1958b:7.

16. A1935b:4–5; A1936a:10; A1937a:12–15, 181–89; A1937b; A1947e:118–19; A1950f:204; A1953b; A1955a:37, 45–46, 49, 65–68; A1957a:10; A1958a:37; A1961a:103, 149–55, 202–3, 206–9, 216–17, 229; A1961h:4; A1962c:71–73; A1965a:176–89; A1967a:7–8; A1967f:2, 4–5; A1968a:71–73. Evans, *Allport*, pp. 3–12, 79.

17. M1939a:4–5; M1943a:66–67, 77–79; M1943b:90–91, 101; M1949b:193–98; M1951b:636–39.

18. M1956c:56–57; M1959c:141–42; M1961a:182–83, 196; M1962a:196; M1962b:60, 207–8; M1964b:6–8; M1966b:19; M1968b:2–3; M1968c:64–65.

19. R1940a:163; R1961a:9. See also R1967a:356–57.

20. R1942a:25–28, 151, 195–96, 439–40; R1942e:430; R1945e:140; R1946d:418–19;

R1947b:112–13; R1953c:91; R1957b:25; R1959h:191, 248; R1960a:218; R1977a:16–18. Evans, *Rogers*, pp. 30–31, 88–89.

21. In the introductory article of *Existence* (MY1958a), May argued that the emergent existential movement in psychology and psychiatry was not another dissident neo-Freudian faction or a clarification of dubious psychoanalytical theories, but a challenge to classical Freudianism (MY1958b:6–7).

22. MY1958b:6–7, 32–36.

23. MY1969a:48–52, 81–88. On the unconscious, see MY1960c:18; MY1961c:641; MY1961b:31–40; MY1963g:41–50; MY1965g:125–27; MY1981a:84. On May's interpretation of the Oedipus complex, see MY1953a:248–53; MY1959e:98–108; MY1960c:34–35; MY1961a:11–30; MY1972a:212–13. For "dreams," see MY1967d; MY1968a:3–14. See also Medard Boss, "Dreaming and the Dreamed," *Soundings*, 1977, 60(3):246–54 for a critique of May's views on dreams, and MY1964b for a summary of the critique of Freud's views on therapy.

24. B1962g:244; B1964h:22, 25; B1965f:16, 59, 63, 71, 89, 93, 142–43, 332; B1966a:224, 228; B1978b:64–65.

25. M1939a:4–5; M1943a:66–67, 77, 79; M1943b:90–91, 101; M1949b:193–98; M1951b:636–37.

26. M1956c:56–57; M1959c:141–42; M1961a:182–83; M1962a:196; M1962b:56–57, 207–10; M1964b:6–8.

27. A1935b:4–5; A1937a:12–15, 181–89; A1937b; A1950f:204; A1953b; A1955a:65–66; A1961a:103, 149–55, 202–3, 206–9, 229; A1965a:176–89; A1967a:7–8; A1967f:4–5; A1968a:71–73. Evans, *Allport*, pp. 3–12, 79.

28. A1936a:10; A1947e:118–19; A1955a:37, 45–46, 49, 65–68; A1957a:10; A1958a:37; A1961a:216–17; A1961h:4; A1967f:2.

29. May's discussion of the concepts of will, wish, and intentionality is of major significance in his thought and challenge to classical Freudian psychoanalysis. May developed these concepts throughout most of his writings, but mainly during the 1960s. Reeves's treatment of this theme is particularly relevant (Clement Reeves, *The Psychology of Rollo May*, San Francisco: Jossey-Bass, 1977, ch. 4, pp. 147–221). See also May's comment on Reeves's statements on pp. 264–309. The key essays of May on will, wish, and intentionality are MY1961b:31–40; MY1963b:77–81; MY1969a:chs. 7, 8, 9, 10. May's presidential address to the William Alanson White Psychoanalytic Society in 1966 is particularly significant (MY1966a).

30. MY1958b; MY1958c.

31. R1940a:163; R1942a:151; R1942e:430.

32. R1942a:25–28, 195–96, 439–40.

33. R1946d:418–19; R1947b:112–13.

34. R1945e:141; R1951a:197–218; R1953c:81–82. Evans, *Rogers*, pp. 30–31.

35. B1965f:59, 63, 89, 93, 332; B1976a:291.

6

Humanistic Psychology, Existentialism, and Phenomenology

This chapter discusses the significance of the phenomenological and existential tradition of Continental philosophy in the emergence and conceptualization of humanistic psychology. All five humanistic psychologists agreed that this tradition of thought not only had an important impact on the shaping of humanistic psychology as a source of inspiration but was also a mainstream within humanistic psychology.

BIOGRAPHICAL SKETCH

We find a substantial discussion of existentialism in Allport's writings only from the late 1950s on. He often used the generic and misleading term "existentialism," but he rarely mentioned by name specific existential thinkers—with the exception of short references to Viktor Frankl and Paul Tillich. Some are of the opinion that Allport paved the way in America for the introduction of existentialism; for example, it is pointed out that he introduced the logotherapy of Frankl into America.[1]

Although Allport was careful in evaluating the potential benefits of existential thought to American psychology, he was certain that psychology in America needed a "blood transfusion," or a "generous injection" of existentialism, mainly because American psychology neglected the study of subjectivity—which he regarded as crucial in understanding human nature. Allport argued that the overdeterministic orientation of American psychology would be greatly enhanced by existentialism's discussion of freedom, choices, and responsibility. He also believed that existentialism's comprehensive analysis of man's relation to the inanimate world, humans, and himself (*Umwelt*, *Mitwelt*, *Eigenwelt*) would provide an important counterbalance to the common practice in American psychology of isolating profiles of human behavior and relating them to nonhuman models. The belief in objectivity widely held by American psychologists could thus be tempered by the existentialist's study of subjectivity, the mysteries, fate, and paradoxes of life.[2]

Maslow first encountered existentialism in the late 1950s when Adrian Van Kaam, Rollo May, and James Klee introduced him to the literature of existentialism. In the early 1960s he already acknowledged that existentialism was a powerful influence in humanistic psychology. With the exception of scarce references to Jean-Paul Sartre and Martin Buber, he rarely discussed in writing the work of any of the existentialists. He referred to Sartre as being "flat" wrong in his views of human nature. As to Buber, he considered the "I-thou relationship" an example of the emerging humanistic paradigm in psychology.[3]

Maslow complained that existentialism was difficult and inaccessible to him. When he studied this literature, however, he questioned, "What's in it for me as a psychologist?" Like Allport, he thought that existentialism would enrich American psychology, although he saw many of the existentialists' insights as stressing conformation of trends in humanistic psychology. Maslow identified himself in particular with the existentialists' emphasis on the concept of identity and the focus on subjective experiential knowledge. Praising the existentialists for studying the unique characteristics of human nature, he was impressed by their discussion of existential dilemmas, vision of the human predicament as simultaneously comprising aspirations and limitations, worm and hero, and the mystery and tragic aspects of life.[4]

Whereas during the 1940s Rogers was under the spell of Otto Rank and Jessie Taft, in the late 1950s he turned to Kierkegaard's and Buber's writings. During the early 1950s Rogers became increasingly divided between the tenets of logical positivism and subjectivism. At the insistence of some theology students at Chicago, he read the basic writings of Buber and Kierkegaard. Then, during two consecutive winters in Mexico and Granada, he immersed himself in the writings of Kierkegaard. This reading helped him to formulate controversial personal opinions on education and to write a paper on "Persons or science" that was significant to his intellectual development.[5]

Reading Kierkegaard, wrote Rogers, had a "loosening up" effect, encouraging him to trust and to express his own experience. He thought that Kierkegaard's insights and convictions expressed views he himself had held but was unable to formulate. One of these insights was found in the passage from *The Sickness unto Death*, in which Kierkegaard argued that the aim of life is "to be that self which one truly is." Rogers interpreted the passage to mean that the most common despair is created not by being responsible for becoming what one truly wants to be, but rather by desiring to be something else. In other words, Rogers understood the passage to mean that one ought to allow one's innermost nature to surface. This idea was, indeed, a cornerstone of Rogers's thought on the self and on therapy.[6]

The theology students in Chicago also introduced Rogers to the thinking of the Hasidic philosopher, Martin Buber. Between 1953 and 1960, Rogers wrote extensively on the significance of the therapist as a person in the successful outcome of psychotherapy. He thought that in addition to "unconditional positive regard" and the immediacy and realness of the therapist, a deep sense of communication and unity between therapist and client was crucial. In this sense, therapy meant for Rogers a genuine person-to-person experience. This was exactly what Buber had described in the "I-thou relationship." Buber thought that the deep mutual experience of speaking truly to another without playing a "role"—that is, the meeting between two persons at a deep and significant level—had a healing effect. Buber named this process "healing through meeting." It was a process Rogers argued to have experienced in the most effective moments of the therapeutic relationship.[7]

To write about Rollo May and existentialism is to write about the introduction of existential psychiatry and psychology in this country. The chief milestone was the book *Existence: A New Dimension in Psychiatry and Psychology*, edited in 1958 by Rollo May, Ernest Angel, and Henri F. Ellenberger. *Existence* presented the American public for the first time with the translation of the writings of leading European phenomenological and existential psychologists such as Ludwig Binswanger, Eugene Minkowski, Erwin Strauss, Viktor Emil von Gebsattel, and Roland Kuhn. May wrote two introductory chapters that were no less influential than the rest of the volume. May's chapters were epoch-making. They were republished many times and became classic writings in the field. Thereafter, May was commonly viewed as the spokesman for the existential approach to psychology. Many years later, Bugental confessed that the reading of May's essays in *Existence* had had a kind of conversion effect on him. Alvin Mahrer, president of the humanistic psychology division of the APA in the 1980s, wrote that *Existence* had been his Bible in the 1960s.[8]

Following the publication of *Existence*, May was active in the growing existential movement in American psychology. In 1958 and 1959, he organized two symposia on existential psychology, one at the recently formed American Academy of Psychotherapists and the other at the APA meeting in Cincinnati. The Cincinnati symposium attracted a great deal of interest. May, Maslow, and Rogers presented papers. Allport wrote the "comment on earlier chapters" for the book—*Existential Psychology*, edited by Rollo May—that published the papers. In 1959 May also started a mimeographed journal, *Existential Inquiries*, which was later transferred to the University of Duquesne under the editorship of Adrian Van Kaam. In the early 1960s, and with the collaboration of May, the recently formed Association of Existential Psychology and Psychiatry began publishing the journal *Review of Existential Psychology and Psychiatry*.[9]

Among the so-called existentialists, it was Tillich—May's dissertation adviser and lifelong friend—who had the greatest impact on May's thinking. May regularly attended Tillich's courses at the Union Theological Seminary, where Tillich introduced him to Kierkegaard, Martin Heidegger, and other European existentialists and phenomenologists. May read Kierkegaard's *The Concept of*

Dread while recuperating in a tuberculosis sanatorium and before he began writing his dissertation, *The Meaning of Anxiety*.[10]

In the dissertation, May advocated that the experience of anxiety is related to the development of the self, thus linking two of the main themes in the literature of existentialism; this idea also ran through most of May's writings. Viewing anxiety initially from the perspective of the individual, he moved on to a discussion of anxiety in relation to the human predicament, love, power, and aggression. He described modern people living in an age of anxiety and loneliness caused by the dichotomy between reason and emotion, isolation from community, and tragic loss of a center of values and a sense of self. But May also argued that it is exactly this predicament that sets us in search for ourselves. He thought that personal integration in a disintegrated world was possible only if we find a center of strength within ourselves.[11]

Bugental used the word "existentialism" quite freely, and often as a form of psychotherapy. For example, he named his approach to psychotherapy "existential-analytic" and "existential-humanistic." He rarely discussed in writing the European existentialists and phenomenologists. His knowledge of this tradition came from the reading of Kierkegaard, Sartre, Binswanger, Medard Boss, and May's two essays in *Existence*. When confronted with the similarities between his concepts of existential anxiety and authenticity and the philosophy of Jean-Paul Sartre, he answered that he had tried to read *Being and Nothingness* but did not go beyond the first pages of the work. He indicated that he had deeply enjoyed, however, reading the other works of Sartre such as his plays.

May was the most influential thinker on Bugental's thought. May's essays in *Existence* expressed what Bugental thought psychology was all about. "In *Existence* May spoke my language," he said. Bugental often quoted May on the concepts of intentionality, centeredness, and the I-am experience.[12]

The Cincinnati symposium on existential psychology organized by May at the 1959 APA meeting and the publication of the papers that followed constituted a particularly significant event, since it cemented the final identification of Rogers, Maslow, May, and Allport with an American brand of existential psychology. It was only in the mid–1960s that this homegrown existentialism was labeled humanistic psychology. "The earlier 'shock troop' work of the existential psychologists," wrote May a decade later, "opened the way and provided some of the impetus for these developments." Thus, in the mid–1960s, Allport stated that American psychologists sympathetic to existentialism belonged to the third force of humanistic psychology. In 1965 he rhetorically asked, "What form does existential therapy take in the US?" and answered by pointing to Rogers's work on client-centered therapy as a "home-grown existentialism." Along the same lines, when asked to define existential psychotherapy, May was said to answer, "examine the work of Carl Rogers and his associates and you will get a pretty good idea of what existential psychotherapy is."[13]

It is historically inaccurate to say that humanistic psychology is an import of European existentialism. The idea of "parallelism" is much more accurate than the "root" analogy. When our five thinkers discovered existentialism in the late 1950s, they had already formulated most of their original ideas. In the 1970s and 1980s, May, Rogers, Maslow, Allport, and Bugental often protested that they had not merely imported existentialism into America in the 1950s. They proudly argued that they had defended existentialist beliefs long before they had heard about European existential psychiatry and psychology. Or, in the words of May, "I valued these developments long before I heard about contemporary existential psychiatry in Europe." "Every European stress has its American equivalent," Maslow wrote. It is true, however, as in the case of Rogers, that the reading of Kierkegaard and Buber had a loosening-up effect. Rogers wrote that he had been pleased "to find [about 1951] that there are friends here that I never knew I had," and was surprised that the "central aspects of my therapeutic work could justifiably be labeled existential and phenomenological."[14]

HUMANISTIC PSYCHOLOGY AND EXISTENTIALISM

Allport shared with the existentialists the views of the person as a being in the process of becoming, and of the uniqueness of personality. He shared with them also the belief that in mature nonpathological personalities, motives undergo transformations. In this process, which Allport labeled the "functional autonomy of motives," the personality structure and motives change in the course of life, thus placing us in a permanent process of becoming. Most of the European existentialists would have agreed with Allport that human life is not limited to a strict list of McDougallian instincts, psychoanalytical drives, or stimulus-response conditioning, but is instead a result of continuous personal choices and decisions. Allport also shared with the existentialists the belief in human dignity and freedom that was so crucial to the European writers. Allport, however, went too far—at least from a Sartrean existentialism point of view—when, in reply to the criticism that functional autonomy lacks unity and congruence, he reinforced the concept of the ego as the unifying and patterning element.[15]

Rogers, like Kierkegaard, thought that the goal of life was to move away from "oughts" and facades. But while the main aim of Kierkegaard was to purify Christianity, Rogers addressed issues of psychotherapy instead. In therapy, argued Rogers, when the individual becomes what he is inwardly, he is able to hear the inner messages and meanings of the self. When this happens, a deep desire to be fully oneself in all one's complexity and richness follows, withholding and fearing nothing that is part of the inner self. Self-experience becomes a friendly resource and not a frightening enemy. Psychotherapy was, for Rogers, an avenue to what Kierkegaard thought was the most important thing in one's life—to become truly what one is inwardly.

Rogers persistently argued that the client-centered approach to therapy deeply respected the integrity of the individual and the right to choose one's own direction, both in psychotherapy and in life. If the conditions that promote growth in psychotherapy are present (such as unconditional positive regard, empathic understanding, and self-understanding), the choices of the individual will be true to his or her nature. Psychotherapy makes it possible for the person to consider choices with greater objectivity and to select those that promote a healthy biological and psychic growth. The task of the therapist is merely to form an alliance with the natural forces of the person.[16]

Maslow agreed with Rogers's favorite quote from Kierkegaard that the aim of life is "to be that self which one truly is." Like them, Maslow also thought that if people are free to grow and to actualize inner potential, they make the right choices. Self-actualizers, argued Maslow, always choose what is good for them, primarily because the inner core of their real self is good, trustworthy, and ethical.[17]

After Sartre, whose views on human nature Maslow thought were "flat" wrong, Martin Buber was the existentialist most often mentioned by Maslow. Like Rogers, Maslow thought that Buber's description of the I-thou relationship constituted a new paradigm in psychotherapy. Following Buber, Maslow argued that the I-thou knowledge that emerges in the experience of deep communication between two people is more valid than the "objective" I-it type of knowledge. The latter, he argued, belongs to the medical paradigm, where the physician treats the patient as an object. The I-thou paradigm, on the other hand, is based on the intimacy of the encounter between two equal individuals and is much more therapeutic.[18]

Rollo May accepted the claim of many existentialists that understanding of human nature should rely on the immediate experience of the individual. Like the existentialists, he argued that one ought to understand the individual with the fewest possible preconceptions, so that one will encounter the people as they truly are rather than filtered through one's own theories. Like most of the existentialists, May studied the central role of freedom, choice, decision, and responsibility in human existence. Also like them, he argued that these themes should be at the center of psychology.

May's most original contribution on this issue was on the problem of identity, or what he named the "I am" experience. According to May, one experiences identity not when one thinks (as René Descartes had argued), but rather when one asserts oneself. One needs to experience oneself as a being in one's own right in order to feel identity. The main disease of our age—the alienation of people from themselves—stemmed, according to May, precisely from the failure to become a self; a failure to express an "I-ness" affirming oneself against the world. Often May referred to this as the problem of "achieving selfhood." Selfhood for May was not, however, the same as the ego in psychoanalytic ego-psychology. It was a center of subjective experience, or of "centeredness."[19]

In this sense, argued May, Descartes was wrong in assuming that the identity of the "I" is found in thinking. It is, rather, a product of self-affirmation. It is the affirmation of the self ("I-can" rather than "I-think") that builds identity and individualizes oneself. Every time one affirms "I can–I will," one experiences identity. Throughout the 1960s, May rewrote the Cartesian formula in different ways, but the idea remained the same. We find it as "I think–I can–I will–I am," "I am, therefore, I think, I feel, I do" (or "I act"), and "I conceive–I can–I will–I am."[20]

Bugental, like the existentialists and Sartre in particular, thought that we find ourselves existing in a world we do not comprehend and being restricted by many contingencies. We are permanently confronted with choices and are forced to take responsibility for the conduct of our life. However, when we neither assume responsibility for our actions nor have a meaningful stance for our existence, explained Bugental, the "existential anxiety of emptiness and meaninglessness" (terminology he borrowed from Tillich) assails us. But when we learn to live with and incorporate our existential anxiety into our own being, then we become "authentic."

On the other hand, the failure to attain "genuineness and awareness of being" leads us to seek "real" meanings in the world of objectivities. There is an attempt to deny the despair, limitedness, guilt, and freedom that are inseparable from our existence by erecting defenses made of objectivizations such as deities, virtues, natural laws, magic, and science. This attempt, which results in "unauthentic being," was, according to Bugental, the source of neurosis. Being authentic, on the other hand, comprises awareness of possibilities and the experience of choice. In other words, we create ourselves by committing ourselves to a pole of "centeredness" (terminology Bugental borrowed from May) within our existence. Authenticity was, indeed, a main theme in Sartre's analysis of the human condition.[21]

The task of the psychotherapy Bugental named "existential-analytic" and "existential-humanistic" was to help the patient move through his or her unauthentic way of being by releasing the distortions created by the evasion of commitment or centeredness. In doing so, psychotherapy also facilitates the liberation and realization of human potential. Bugental named this constructive facet of psychology "ontogogic."[22]

CRITIQUE OF EXISTENTIALISM

Although Allport, Maslow, Rogers, May, and Bugental had much in common with the existentialists, they were at times critical of some trends in existentialism. The most persistent critique—and one they addressed specifically to Sartre— was of Sartre's statement that "freedom is existence, and in it existence precedes essence." Sartre had argued that there are no essences in human nature. There is no inner structure of reality that defines human nature. Human existence is a "nothingness," a "non-substantial absolute" or "being-for-itself," which exists merely by virtue of its relation to "being-in-itself." In this sense, argued Sartre, human existence was defined primarily by its freedom and was the result of our "project" in life.[23]

The humanistic psychologists agreed with Sartre that "man is his own project." It is commitment and determination, one's will and responsibility that make oneself. All five humanistic psychologists wrote extensively on these themes. But they equally thought that Sartre had gone too far in assuming that we are a "nothingness" and that the process of becoming has no biological basis.

Throughout the 1960s Maslow specifically addressed this issue, often writing that his research was a "flat rejection" of this type of Sartrean "arbitrary existentialism." He agreed with Sartre that one is ultimately responsible for one's decisions and life project, but he also thought that there is a biological or "instinctoid" basis of human nature. According to Maslow, there is potential in human nature pressing toward actualization, potential that desires by nature to be actualized in the same way an acorn desires by nature to become an oak tree. These potentialities, however, are dormant, and they require a culture in order to awaken. "Culture permits or fosters or encourages or helps," wrote Maslow, "what exists in embryo to become real and actual."[24]

Unlike Sartre, Maslow argued that one's life project is not created at random by psychological and life paradoxes, but primarily by trends, bents, and tendencies intrinsic to human nature. "To discover" one's nature was for Maslow a much better term than "to create." He thus thought that humanistic psychology was closer to psychodynamics than to Sartre's existentialism. The "uncovering" therapies of the former were meant to help the person discover one's true identity rather than to create a self in the existentialist sense. Allport's concept of the ego is a good illustration of Maslow's statement.

Rogers also emphasized the biological basis of the process of becoming. In the late 1970s, Rogers explained this belief as the "actualizing tendency of organic life" and "the organismic tendency towards fulfillment." Like Maslow and Allport, Rogers also spoke of the process of therapy as a process of "discovering" a settled, inner biological self. According to Rogers, humans—like animals—are organisms that develop or grow according to the dictates of innate qualities. What is different in the human species, he argued, is that at a certain point in the biological development, consciousness or awareness arises and changes everything.[25]

In his critique of Sartre, May pointed out that one's power to create oneself is already a nature or essence of human nature. Moreover, in the introduction to an English translation of Sartre's work, May argued that there is no freedom without some structure in which one acts; that is, freedom implies some kind of structure in which one acts. He was also critical of what he considered undesirable anti-scientific and anti-genetic dimensions in existentialism.[26]

In conclusion, the five humanistic thinkers argued that there is a biological core or essence in human nature that precedes existence, exactly what Sartre had most denied. All five, perhaps with the exception of May, also found existentialism to be overly pessimistic. They thought that their humanistic brand of existentialism provided more hope and optimism in confronting the mystery, anguish, and despair of life. Rogers once referred to the existentialists as "despairing existentialists." In his opinion (and in the opinion of Maslow, Allport, and Bugental), humanistic psychology was more positive in its view of human nature and closer to Kierkegaard and Buber than to the radical French existentialism. Rogers attributed this phenomenon to the fact that, as a nation, Americans had been more fortunate than the French because they had not suffered two world wars in their homeland.[27]

HUMANISTIC PSYCHOLOGY AND PHENOMENOLOGY

Often, the founders of humanistic psychology equated phenomenology with a method of studying subjective reports of immediate experience and of introspective nature. They rarely referred to the classical phenomenological studies of Franz Brentano, Edmund Husserl, and Martin Heidegger on the intent and constitution of consciousness. Their little knowledge of that tradition in Continental philosophy was from secondary sources.

In Allport's eclectic approach, phenomenology was one of several avenues to the study of human nature. In the early 1960s, however, he was of the opinion that phenomenology was the most appropriate tool for the study of the unique structure of personality. Several years before his death, he said that phenomenology had been neglected in American psychology, and for that reason he was not ashamed of being too phenomenological in his approach. According to Allport, phenomenological studies were the foundations of good mental science because they addressed the complexities of phenomenal consciousness. He cited Francis Galton's account of the imagery of his correspondents as a typical case of an early phenomenological document. In *The Nature of Prejudice*, another good example, the phenomenological study of prejudice was for Allport the study of the actual act of prejudice as encountered in the world. However, the study of the act of prejudice as such, he argued, reveals a blend of historical, social-cultural, situational, and psychodynamic factors.[28]

Throughout the 1960s Maslow often juxtaposed the phenomenological world of the self to the physical world of the scientist, arguing that external validation of the positivistic and atomistic type was no more real than the subjective phenomenological world of the experiential self. He believed that phenomenological studies were more truthful to the individual because they focused on how it feels from the internal point of view of the self.[29]

Maslow praised in particular the attack of the existentialists on abstract systems of philosophy that have nothing to do with actual concrete human experience. There was no place to turn, Maslow agreed with the existentialists, but to the inner self as the source of all validation. In this sense, existentialism, he thought, would supply psychology with the underlying experiential and phenomenological basis it so desperately needed.[30]

According to Rogers, the client-centered therapy was phenomenological at its very foundations. Rogers's first clear statement of the phenomenological character of the ideas he advanced in personality dynamics and behavior relied basically upon the concept of the self as an explanatory construct, which he advocated as early as 1951 in *Client-Centered Therapy*. In this work, the self functioned as a gestalt or "internal frame of reference," both in the organization of one's continuing and changing world of experience as well as in the perception of reality. In this sense, there was no perception without a meaning because the organism immediately attaches meaning—patterned upon its gestalt—to whatever it perceives. Objective reality, even if there was one, was always "reality-as-perceived" by the phenomenal field of the self. This phenomenal self, he argued, had to be accepted with unconditional positive regard if therapy was to be successful. Throughout the 1950s, when Rogers first formulated these thoughts, he advocated a technique developed by his associates for the "objective analysis of phenomenological data," which he named the Q-technique. The Q-technique aimed to treat objectively the complex data drawn from the internal frame of reference of the individual.[31]

Not by coincidence, Bugental's early thinking followed Rogers's thoughts on phenomenology. In his doctoral dissertation, Bugental expanded on the self-concept theory of personality of Victor Raimy, a close associate of Rogers when he was at Ohio State University in Columbus (1940–1945). Like that of Rogers, Bugental's approach was partly phenomenological, partly quantitative. Focusing on the way people see themselves in their own frame of reference, he studied the significant aspects of the interaction between the individual and the environment—or, in other words, between what one does and does not regard as part of the self. Like Rogers, Bugental explicitly stated that this approach to the psychology of personality was phenomenological, but also like Rogers, he took a quantitative approach to processing and synthesizing the phenomenological data. This procedure would raise the eyebrows of any European phenomenologist, who would certainly question Rogers's and Bugental's definition of phenomenology. Most of Bugental's references to phenomenology were drawn from American thinkers such as Donald Snygg, Roy McLeod, and George Kelly.[32]

Allport had a similar approach to a quantitative phenomenology. Like Rogers and Bugental, he defended methods, which he first named "idiographic" and later "morphogenic," that would allow "scientific" access to the uniqueness of individuality.[33] Along similar lines, May regarded phenomenology as a method opposed to the causal approach of the physical sciences based on observation and description. In the late 1960s, however, he brought most of his thoughts on phenomenology under the banner of intentionality, which was, indeed, a central theme in European phenomenology. He wrote on the historical development of the concept of intentionality with brief references to Brentano and Husserl, but his knowledge of these thinkers came to him via Tillich and a certain Professor Cairns, who showed him that his concept of "centeredness" was similar to Husserl's "integration" in the *Ideas*. His most original contribution to phenomenology, however, dealt with the interpretation of dreams, the unconscious, myths and symbols, and the achievement of selfhood, or the "I-ness" experience already discussed.[34]

Like Rollo May, Bugental also argued that intentionality is an essential element of human existence; indeed, he believed that identity and authentic existence are the product of the purposeful intent-orientation of the self. Intentionality was for Bugental a process by which one is fully responsible for one's conduct. Intentionality involves full participation of our wishing, wanting, and will; requires action; and results in actualization. This process consists of awareness, choice, and intentions simultaneously—"being-aware-and-choosing" as opposed to an "I" identified with a "me" that is the result of external objectivizations.[35]

Allport, too, rarely referred to the classical phenomenological studies of Brentano, Husserl, Heidegger, and Max Scheler—although, like May and Bugental, he wrote on intentionality and the constitution of consciousness. Allport defined intention as "what the individual is trying to do" and as a "direction of his endeavor" based on attitudes that rely on a subjective set of values. Most of Allport's discussion of intentionality and attitude is found within his discussion of functional autonomy in human motivation.[36]

CONCLUSION

In the late 1950s, when American psychologists noticed European existentialism and phenomenology, the humanistic psychologists had already developed the core of their psychological thinking. The similarities of thought between the Americans and Europeans was thus more a case of philosophical parallelism rather than the import, translation, or Americanization of the European tradition—although the latter certainly had a loosening-up effect on the founders of humanistic psychology.

Allport, Maslow, Rogers, May, and Bugental were surprised to discover in the 1950s that humanistic philosophy was present in various forms in the Continental phenomenological and existential tradition. In different ways, both the Americans and Europeans pointed to the restrictivenss of a positivistic approach to the study of human nature, which they thought should focus on the uniqueness of subjective existence. Since the acknowledgment of this philosophical parallelism, there has been a fruitful cross-fertilization of ideas between American humanistic thought and European existentialism and phenomenology, for the most part in the field of psychology.

The founders of humanistic psychology shared with the existentialists the general ideas often used to characterize this idiosyncratic and ill-defined group of thinkers in Continental philosophy. Like the existentialists, the humanistic psychologists were perplexed by the uniqueness of people. They all agreed that people have no fixed and determined nature, but are a process of becoming. They all focused their studies of human nature on the authentic or inner self, not on objectivities, oughts, or facades. In different ways, they all understood the crucial significance of intentionality in the study of personality and behavior. Their favorite themes of study were anxiety, choice, freedom, responsibility, meaning, and intention.

With the exception of May, none of the five, however, had a deep knowledge of existentialism. Allport and Maslow had only a general interest in existentialism and wrote nothing really specific about it. In the case of Rogers, it was Kierkegaard and Buber who had the most significant impact on his thinking. Sartre and Tillich had an indirect influence on Bugental. Of the five, May was the most well versed on existential psychiatry and psychology; it was the reading of Kierkegaard and friendship with Tillich that helped shape his psychological thinking. Concerning phenomenology—especially the classical works in the field by Brentano, Husserl, and Heidegger—their knowledge was even more limited. The little they knew was from secondary sources. For them, phenomenology was a method for the study of subjective reports.

Allport, Maslow, Rogers, and Bugental—and to a much lesser extent, May— were also critical of what they understood to be the pessimistic features of existentialism. Existentialists were too pessimistic and abstract for their pragmatic and optimistic American tastes. With the exception of May, the humanistic psychologists believed that human nature is inherently good. For them this was not an abstract metaphysical concept, however, but a characteristic grounded on our very biological being. Thus, they spoke of authentic "growth" and "self-actualization," hoping that their studies would help bring out the best in us. This attitude was radically opposed to the conclusions of some of the existentialists that lead to despairing nihilism (Nietzsche), nothingness, denial, paradoxes (Sartre), and absurdisms (Camus). They were as severely critical of this attitude toward human nature as they were of behaviorism's S-R philosophy and Freud's psychic determinism. In this sense, the founders of humanistic psychology were certainly closer to the Kierkegaardian, Buberian, and Tillichian theological brand of existentialism.

NOTES

1. Richard I. Evans, *Gordon Allport: The Man and His Ideas*, New York: Dutton, 1970, pp. 57, 133; see also the preface by Allport to Viktor E. Frankl, *From Death-Camp to Existentialism*, Boston: Beacon Press, 1959; A1959b:ix-xii; A1960d:305; A1961a:217, 282, 555–56, 560; A1964e:134; A1965a:174.

2. A1955a:79, 83; A1955c:195; A1957a:19; A1961a:x, 555–64; A1964b:17–18; A1965a:175.

3. M1959e:20–21; M1962b:ix, xi.

4. Maslow explicitly stated his views on existentialism in a paper he presented at the Symposium on Existential Psychology at the 1959 convention of the APA. Rogers and May also presented papers at this symposium. The enthusiastic interest it attracted led Random House to invite Rollo May to edit the papers published under the title *Existential Psychology* in 1961. Maslow's paper, "Existential Psychology—What's in It for Us?" was also published in the first pages of *Existentialist Inquiries* (M1960b) under the title "Remarks on Existentialism and Psychology." It was reprinted twice, translated into Japanese, and revised for *Toward a Psychology of Being* (M1962b). In the *Eupsychian Management* (1965g:127–32), he wrote five additional pages to be added to the original

essay. These notes were also reprinted in the *Journal of Humanistic Psychology* (M1964d). See also M1960b:59; M1962b:174.

5. R1961a:273; R1955c:199–200; R1960a:208; R1952c:342. Richard I. Evans, *Carl Rogers: The Man and His Ideas*, New York: Dutton, 1975, p. 69.

6. Soren Kierkegaard, *Fear and Trembling and the Sickness unto Death*, trans. Walter Lowrie, Garden City, New York: Doubleday, 1954, p. 29; R1956g:198; R1957d:172; R1960d; R1961a:166, 199, 200; R1961f:5–6.

7. In 1957 Maurice Friedman, a Buber scholar, was instrumental in arranging a public dialogue between Rogers and Buber at the University of Michigan. This dialogue is particularly useful in delineating the points of agreement and disagreement between Buber and Rogers (R1960a). R1950d:26; R1952c:342; R1955c:290; R1961b:175; R1965e:26; R1973e:12. Evans, *Rogers*, pp. 25, 69.

8. MY1958a. For references to May as a "spokesman," see, for example, MY1967g:25. Interview with Bugental in San Francisco on March 8, 1985. Mahrer's letter to the author, October 25, 1985.

9. In 1964 it was renamed *Journal of Existentialism* and it continued in 1966 as *Existential Psychiatry*. MY1960b. R1961b:164.

10. MY1950a.

11. May's most influential works that discuss these and other themes are *Man's Search for Himself* (MY1953a), *Psychology and the Human Dilemma* (MY1967a), *Love and Will* (MY1969a), *Power and Innocence* (MY1972a).

12. B1965f:10. Interview with Bugental in San Francisco, March 8, 1985.

13. A1955a:81; A1957a:11; A1962c:73; A1964e:135; A1965a:174; A1967f:1. Evans, *Allport*, pp. 55–58. R1974i:11–12; R1959i:196. MY1968f:191.

14. MY1959e:87. M1960b:59. R1960c:96; R1961a:200; R1967a:378; R1974j:256. Evans, *Rogers*, p. 70. MY1963b:75.

15. A1961a:217; A1964f:167; A1967a:15; A1967f:3–4. M. Brewster Smith, "Allport, Murray, and Lewin on Personality Theory," *J. Hist. Beh. Sci.*, 1971, 7:353–62. Evans, *Allport*, p. 119.

16. See, for example, the early writings: R1942a:208–10; R1943a:285; R1943b:113 and the later R1979a.

17. M1962b:168; M1968h:186.

18. M1965g:128–29; M1966b:52, 102–7.

19. Reference to this issue in May's writings would have to include most of his bibliography. In MY1969a:ch.9, however, one finds a concise discussion of the main issues involved at the climax of May's thought. I have chosen to refer to the following items because they were useful in the preparation of this chapter or in illustrating one point or another: MY1951a:306–22; MY1953a:ch.3; MY1961a:2; MY1961e:31–40; MY1962c:14–19; MY1962d:19; MY1963b:74–81; MY1966a:68.

20. MY1958c:46; MY1961a:4; MY1966a:68; MY1969a:243.

21. B1965f:102; B1967c:286; B1967e:629; B1976a:54, 99–100; B1978a:184.

22. Ibid.

23. For Sartre's discussion of this issue, see Jean-Paul Sartre, *Being and Nothingness*, trans. Hazel E. Barnes, New York: Washington Square Press, 1956, p. 725.

24. M1959a:131. See also: M1959a:130–31; M1962a:190–91; M1962b:167, 174–75; M1964b:xvi; M1964e:128; M1968h:186; M1970a:xvii–xviii; M1971a:315–16, 349; M1971b:22–23.

25. R1971c:87–90; R1973b:45–46; R1979a.

26. MY1953a:165–67;   MY1953c;   MY1961e:34–36;   MY1962e:147–57; MY1967a:135–37; MY1968f:212–17; MY1969a:157.

27. For the problem of existentialism versus essentialism, see Paul Tillich, "Existentialism and Psychotherapy," in Hendrick M. Ruitenbeek, ed., *Psychoanalysis and Existential Philosophy*, New York: Dutton, 1962, pp. 3–16. R1959g:100fnl; R1959h:251; R1965j:183; R1966c:5–6. Evans, *Rogers*, pp. 70–71. M1968h:186. A1957a:11; A1955a:81; A1964e:135; A1962c:73; A1965a:174; A1967f:1. Evans, *Allport*, pp. 55–58.

28. A1954a:207; A1955a:17–18; A1961h:6–7, 11. Evans, *Allport*, p. 44.

29. M1959d:99; M1964b:26, 41; M1965d:136; M1966b:76.

30. M1960b:52–60. See also M1959e:20–21.

31. R1947c:367; R1951a:ch.11; R1951d:344; R1954e:9, 429–30; R1963g:77; R1974j:255. Evans, *Rogers*, p. 9.

32. B1948c; B1951c:12; B1962b:427–30.

33. See, for example, A1962b; A1967f.

34. MY1950a:137; MY1951a:305; MY1963b:76; MY1964b:111–27; MY1969a:1200, 226. For May's "original contribution," see this work's ch. 5, note number 23; MY1961c:641; MY1968a:vi.

35. B1969a; B1967f:30–39; B1968c:384; B1976a:291; B1977a:138–39.

36. A1943a:305; A1945a:144; A1947e:191–93; A1955a:14; A1961a:223–25.

7

Other Sources of Influence in Humanistic Psychology

The revolt against behaviorism and classical psychoanalysis, encounters with the neo-Freudians, and phenomenological and existential psychologies were not the only sources of inspiration in the making of humanistic psychology. Kurt Goldstein, the personality theorists, and Gestalt psychology also contributed to the conceptualization of humanistic psychology.

KURT GOLDSTEIN

Kurt Goldstein substantially influenced Rogers, May, and especially Maslow. Maslow met Goldstein in the late 1930s in New York City, an event that he recognized many years later as fortunate. In gratitude Maslow dedicated *Toward a Psychology of Being* (1962) to Goldstein. Goldstein showed him that some aspects of Gestalt psychology could be integrated with the psychodynamic psychologies. Maslow's holistic-dynamic approach stemmed from Goldstein's organismic psychology in the sense that it was holistic, functional, dynamic, and purposive, rather than atomistic, taxonomic, static, and mechanical.[1]

Maslow was well known in psychological circles for his studies on self-actualization. It was, however, Goldstein who coined the term "self-actualization." He employed the concept in his studies of brain-injured war veterans to explain the reorganization of a person's capacities after injury. According to Goldstein, a damaged organism in the struggle for survival reorganizes itself into a new unit that incorporates the damages. In this sense, the organism is active, generating and recreating itself as it strives toward self-actualization. Maslow acknowledged to have adopted the concept of self-actualization from Goldstein, although he used it in a broader sense.

Maslow compared Goldstein's studies of brain-injured subjects and Skinner's behavioristic psychology, examining in particular the reduction to the concrete and the inability to abstract. Unable to integrate separate phenomena, the brain-injured of Goldstein's studies do not think in terms of general categories. When they see a color, for example, they see it in isolation and are unable to compare it to any other color or category. This phenomenon represents "selective attention" or "obsessional neurosis" at its best, wrote Maslow; he compared it to Skinner's stress on predictability, control, lawfulness, and structure. In both cases, the subjects maintain equilibrium by avoiding what is strange and unfamiliar, neatly arranging and ordering their restricted world so they can count on it and guarantee that changes will not occur. In order to avoid problems they are unable to handle, they narrow their worlds.[2]

Like Maslow, Rogers acknowledged that his thought on the process of therapy had been influenced by Goldstein. In different contexts, Rogers wrote that Goldstein enriched his thinking, mentioning specifically the "actualizing tendency" or "growth hypothesis." Rogers believed that the motivational constructs of effective therapy and the actualizing or growth tendency of the patient resembled Goldstein's organismic psychology.[3]

Goldstein also had a significant impact on the development of May's thought, particularly while May was writing his dissertation on the meaning of anxiety. During that period May had many stimulating hours of discussion with Goldstein. In the dissertation, May wrote on Goldstein's views on fear, anxiety, self-actualization, and the organism. Like Maslow and Rogers, May also often referred to the brain-injured patients. In the epoch-making essays of *Existence*, May interpreted Goldstein's thought in an existential context.[4]

As to Allport and Bugental, they often referred to Goldstein's concepts of self-actualization and organismic psychology, identifying him with the emerging humanistic paradigm in psychology. Bugental referred to Goldstein as a "pioneer" of humanistic psychology because of his insistence on the uniqueness of the individual during what he thought were the "lonely years of the behavioristic interregnum."[5]

PERSONALITY PSYCHOLOGY

Historically, humanistic psychology was closer to personality theory than to any other current in psychology. Allport's name, for example, is almost synonymous with personality psychology. He was at the forefront of the field of personality for most of his life. Allport's dissertation was the first in this country on the component traits of personality; his course on the psychology of personality, first offered at Harvard in 1924, was a pioneer enterprise; and his book *Personality: A Psychological Interpretation* (1937) was the first American textbook on personality theory.

When Allport went to Germany for a postdoctoral fellowship he was already active in the field of personality. However, his encounter there with William Stern and Eduard Spranger was, as he wrote many years later, part of his "formal training." *A Study of Values*, which he developed upon his return to America, expanded on Spranger's concept of six fundamental types of human values. Allport considered Stern to be a true personality psychologist. He credited Stern with teaching him that when one studies the person one ought to focus upon the organization, not the mere profiling, of traits. Among the personality theorists, it was Stern who had the greatest influence on Allport's intellectual development.[6]

Like Allport, Maslow might also be grouped with the personality theorists. Maslow often complained about the lack of emphasis on the study of personality in mainstream psychology. The concept of self implied in his notion of organismic growth tendency justifies including him among the personality theorists.[7]

Among the personality psychologists, it was Gardner Murphy who had the closest professional contacts with Maslow. Murphy recommended Maslow's dissertation to the *Journal of Genetic Psychology* for publication, and Maslow's *Principles of Abnormal Psychology* and *Motivation and Personality* were published in a series edited by Murphy.[8]

Rogers's emphasis on the study of the self as a process of becoming also places him among the personality theorists. His article "A theory of personality and behavior" included in *Client-Centered Therapy* (1951) was the earliest expression of his interest in the study of personality. Explaining that the best way to understand the self was to study the "internal frame of reference" of the individual, he concluded that his theory of personality relied heavily upon the concept of the self as an explanatory construct. In several encyclopedia essays on the client-centered therapy written in the 1970s, Rogers duly emphasized his interest on the self and personality theory.[9]

The personality theorist Rogers referred to most often in his writings was George Kelly. Kelly had been a colleague of Rogers at the Ohio State University. In 1956, Rogers reviewed for *Contemporary Psychology* Kelly's *Psychology of Personal Constructs*, praising it lavishly as a "highly rewarding reading." The most original and valuable section of the book, wrote Rogers, was the theory of personality and behavior known as the psychology of constructs, a theory Rogers occasionally employed to clarify issues in client-centered therapy.[10]

Bugental's emphasis on the study of the self as a process of becoming also places him among the personality theorists. As in the case of Rogers, the personality theorist who had the most significant impact on Bugental was George Kelly. Bugental acknowledged his intellectual indebtedness to Kelly, who had been one of his dissertation advisers. According to Bugental, Kelly "set a standard of freedom of thought which constantly encouraged this exploratory project." About twenty years later, Bugental was particularly nostalgic for the teacher of his Ohio days. He wrote that he was proud to have had Kelly as a teacher, and he repeatedly quoted Kelly's remark that "the key to man's destiny is his ability to reconstruct what he cannot deny."[11]

GESTALT PSYCHOLOGY

Allport first heard of Gestalt psychology while he was in Germany during his postdoctoral fellowship. His encounter with Max Wertheimer, Wolfgang Kohler,

Kurt Lewin, and Eduard Spranger during that time had a powerful intellectual impact on his thinking. They legitimated what he had intuited but had been unable to express. When Allport attended the Leipzig Congress of Psychology in 1923, the report he sent home contained a short history of Gestalt psychology. The following year he wrote an article, "The standpoint of Gestalt psychology." In *Personality* (1937), he referred to Kohler and Lewin as rebels in psychology because of their emphasis upon the patterns and totality of mental life. At the end of the manuscript he included a chapter on the unity of personality, discussing at great length the work of Kurt Lewin. As an eclectic and as an admirer of Gestalt psychology, Allport included in all of his major works a discussion of Gestalt psychology. Later in life, Allport viewed the Gestalt movement within the Leibnitzian tradition, which he opposed to Humean empiricism.

Allport's most often praised Gestalt psychologist was Kurt Lewin. He referred to Lewin in a memorial tribute shortly after Lewin's death as a genius and as one of the most original thinkers in twentieth-century psychology. In a different context, Allport once said that Lewin supported whatever line of development his thinking took, calling Lewin a first cousin of his thinking.[12]

Maslow learned Gestalt psychology from Max Wertheimer and Kurt Koffka at the New School for Social Research in New York City in the late 1930s. Maslow was particularly impressed by Max Wertheimer. He described Wertheimer as a loving person, who—acting like a parent—allowed Maslow to attend his classes and always answered his questions. In the prefaces to all of his major publications, Maslow expressed his indebtedness to Gestalt psychology and to Max Wertheimer in particular.

Maslow emphatically complained that the lessons of Gestalt psychology had not been integrated into mainstream psychology. For the Gestalt psychologists, a person was an irreducible unit in which every aspect of personality is part of an interrelated pattern based on varying relationships within the individual and between the individual and the environment. Maslow's discussion of the "syndrome"—a complex of symptoms occurring together in an organism—in his holistic-dynamic theory is a good example, as Maslow himself pointed out, of his borrowing from Gestalt psychology. But Maslow was not a mere follower of Gestalt psychology. He emphasized that his health-and-growth psychology was an integration of Gestalt theory with dynamic and functionalist psychologies. In "A theory of human motivation" (1943), for example, Maslow himself argued that his theory of motivation fused the functionalist tradition with the holism of Gestalt and the dynamism of psychoanalysis.[13]

There were as well points of contact between Gestalt psychology and the thought of Rogers—"parallels rather than roots," in Rogers's words—who referred, in particular, to the Gestalt psychology advocated by Kurt Lewin. As early as 1947, when Rogers formulated the theoretical implications of client-centered therapy to the understanding of personality, he realized that, like Lewin, he also employed a field theory. Both assumed that the experience of the present field determines behavior; thus they studied the person at the present moment, not in the sense of historical development or genetic determination. In "Some observations on the organization of personality," a 1947 paper Rogers considered to be a new direction in his thinking and work, he pointed to this relationship by rephrasing Lewin's comment that behavior is primarily a reaction to "reality-as-perceived." Alterations in the perception of the self alter behavior as well.[14]

In the case of Rollo May, we find few references to personality and Gestalt psychologies, perhaps because he was largely under the influence of existential psychology and the neo-Freudians. Nevertheless, Gestalt and personality theorists had a significant influence on him during graduate school. While he was at Columbia University, May wrote an essay referring to Lewin's theories as the most novel and stimulating work in the new dynamic movement.[15]

EASTERN THOUGHT

Too often, the impact of Eastern thought on humanistic psychology is over-estimated. Among the founders of humanistic psychology Maslow was the one who most often referred to Eastern thought—Taoism in particular. In the late 1950s Rollo May made some short comparisons between Eastern thinking and existential psychology, but only in the 1980s did he express some enthusiasm for Eastern wisdom. Rogers, on the other hand, found close resemblances between Zen Buddhism and person-centered philosophy only in the early 1970s. As to Bugental and Allport, we find very few references to Eastern thought in their writings, although in the late 1960s Bugental, like Maslow, included the followers of Zen Buddhism as a subgroup within humanistic psychology.

Maslow first heard of Taoism in Wertheimer's seminars at the New School for Social Research. As early as 1949, Maslow employed the term "Taoism" to describe the purposeful spontaneity in the expressive component of behavior. Later, he referred to Taoism as synonymous with passivity or resignation in the understanding of nature and the self, arguing that Western psychologists should learn from the "taoistic fashion," "taoistic let-be," "taoistic listening" when studying human nature. Scientists should be receptive and let things happen without interference in order to attain inside experiential knowledge. He also explored the similarities between the concepts of satori, nirvana, peak-experiences, and self-actualization. In *The Psychology of Science* (1966), Maslow dedicated a chapter to "taoistic science." He described this approach as complementary to Western science and argued that the classification and conceptualization methods of Western science remove our perception of reality to an abstract and rational realm invented by the mind. This negative aspect of Western science should be balanced against taoistic non-intruding, receptivity, and passive contemplation of experience. In a later work he referred to "taoistic objectivity" as opposed to "classical objectivity."[16]

In the two epoch-making articles of *Existence*, May wrote on the similarities between Zen Buddhism and existentialism. He argued that both deal with ontology, or the study of being. He praised Eastern thought for not having suffered the radical split between subject and object so characteristic of Western thought. Three years later, however, in discussing the negative trends of existential psychiatry, he pointed out that the identification of existential psychology with Zen Buddhism oversimplifies both. He was also critical of the simplistic use of the Eastern concept of transcendence as a means to bypass and evade anxiety, tragedy, guilt, and the reality of evil. In *Freedom and Destiny* (1981), however, May wrote on Eastern thought much more enthusiastically. He praised acupuncture, Eastern medicine, and the concept of freedom in its social, cultural, and philosophical contexts.[17]

When Rogers discovered Zen Buddhism in the early 1970s, he realized that there was also a distinct oriental flavor to the person-centered philosophy. He found particularly congenial Zen's stress on personal experience as a way of learning, as well as its emphasis on avoiding to manipulate people, but rather allowing them to become. On one occasion he used Zen stories to initiate an encounter group with counselors in training and was enthusiastic about the outcome.[18]

As to Allport, we find only one significant reference to Eastern thought. In *Patterns and Growth* (1961), he included in the concluding chapter (along with a discussion of several schools of thought in Western psychology) the Hindu formulation of human nature.[19]

We find no in-depth discussion of Eastern philosophy in Bugental's writings, except for references to its wisdom as evidence for or validation of humanistic psychology. In the late 1960s Bugental included "interpreters of Zen Buddhism" as a subgroup within humanistic psychology. On one occasion he also compared Zen's equation between light and the fullest realization of one's being with his own concepts of the I-process and transcendence.[20]

The intellectual impact Maslow, May, and Rogers had on Bugental, the youngest, requires a short digression at this point. Bugental first came under the spell of Rogers through Victor Raimy, a former student of Rogers at Ohio State University who had written a dissertation expanding upon Rogerian thought. Rogers himself often referred in writing to the research of Raimy, whom he called a close associate. In the "phenomenal self" Raimy aimed to illustrate Rogers's point that successful therapy changes the perception of the self and reality, which in turn changes behavior. Several years after Rogers left Ohio for Chicago, Bugental submitted his dissertation expanding on Raimy's ideas. It aimed to quantify the phenomenological data that validated Raimy's phenomenal self. In later writings, however, Bugental referred only infrequently to Rogers.[21]

It was May's writings and friendship that most influenced Bugental's thought on existential therapy. He submitted manuscripts of at least two of his major publications to May for criticism and comments. Bugental's writings include several lengthy discussions of May's thought on intentionality, choice, will, and responsibility. As Bugental himself pointed out, there were resemblances between his I-process and May's concept of centeredness—although, unlike May, he preferred to regard intentionality as a process rather than as a structure.[22]

Bugental was also thankful for Maslow's intellectual stimulation, encouragement, and friendship. He often employed Maslowean terminology; his concept of the "emergent man" is a slight variation of Maslow's self-actualization.[23]

CONCLUSION

The primary intellectual sources of the humanistic psychologies of Allport, Rogers, May, and Bugental were their revolt against behaviorism and classical psychoanalysis, their encounters with the neo-Freudians, and their discovery of Continental existentialism and phenomenology. There were, however, additional sources of inspiration. Kurt Goldstein's organismic psychology was crucial in the development of Maslow's health-and-growth psychology and Rogers's theoretical framework of the client-centered therapy. The boundaries between the thinking of Allport, Maslow, and Rogers and that of the personality psychologists are so blurred that the humanistic psychologists were and still are often identified as personality theorists. Gestalt psychology also had a substantial influence on Maslow, Allport, and Rogers; Max Wertheimer influenced Maslow and Allport, and Kurt Lewin influenced Allport and Rogers. Concerning Eastern thought, we found little or no significant impact on the founders of humanistic psychology, although in the 1970s they did explore the similarities between humanistic psychology and Eastern philosophical wisdom.

NOTES

1. For Kurt Goldstein, see, for example, Joseph I. Meiers, *Kurt Goldstein Bibliography 1903–1958*, Washington, D.C.: American Documentation Institute, 1958, Doc. 5816; "Papers in Honor of Kurt Goldstein," *J. Indiv. Psy.*, 1959, 15:1–19; Marianne L. Simmel, ed., *The Reach of Mind: Essays in Memory of Kurt Goldstein*, New York: Springer, 1968; Herbert Spiegelberg, *Phenomenology in Psychology and Psychiatry*, Evanston, Ill.: Northwestern University Press, 1972, pp. 301–18.

2. Maslow's significant references to Goldstein are: M1941a:xiii; M1951b:645; M1954a:ix, 27, 36, 80, 89, 91, 95, 109, 116, 124, 161, 166, 192, 206, 262, 286, 287, 291, 296, 342, 383; M1955a:2,5,13; M1959e:19; M1961f:7; M1962b:ii, v, ix, xi, 118; M1962h:247; M1965b:v; M1966b:23,42,69; M1968f:55; M1969d:132; M1971a:119,252.

3. R1951a:481,489; R1959a:193; R1963a:3; R1979a:100.

4. MY1950a:xi,62–70, 96–100, 108, 115, 120, 122, 161, 167, 213, 221, 225, 286, 376, 383, 384, 390; MY1953a:224–25; MY1958a:50–52,60,72.

5. A1961h:8. Richard I. Evans, *Gordon Allport: The Man and His Ideas*, New York: Dutton, 1970, p. 54; A1955a:16, 50, 80; A1960a:166, 107, 303; A1960d:302,305; A1961a:212, 215, 269, 348, 558, 569; A1968a:73. B1966a:224.

6. See, for example, A1930c; A1931a; A1937c; A1938b; A1943g; A1967a:10–11; A1967f; A1968a:271–97. Evans, *Allport*, p. 18.

7. See, for example, M1948c:116; M1951b; M1955a.

8. M1936a:261; M1941a; M1954a.

9. R1947c; R1951a:481–533; R1956g; R1961e; R1973h; R1974j.

10. R1956d; R1961e:35; R1963e:11.

11. B1948c:188; B1952a:435; B1962g:245; B1965f:xvi,403; B1969a:96; B1970a:286; B1971a:37; B1976a:320; B1982b:47; B1984a:549.

12. A1923b; A1929a; A1930c:695; A1930d; A1937a:15–17, 343–65; A1947a:100; A1948a:vii–xiv; A1955a:12–19; A1967a:10; A1968a:360–70. Evans, *Allport*, p. 18.

13. M1941a:xii, xiii; M1943b:80,97; M1943d:31–37; M1956d:32; M1961d:215; M1961f:7;   M1962i:23;   M1963c:117–19;   M1965b:v;   M1967g:42;   M1968f:55; M1971a:42,118; M1971b:21.

14. R1947c:366; R1951a:57, 481–533; R1967a:366, 383; R1974j:256. Richard I. Evans, *Carl Rogers: The Man and His Ideas*, New York: Dutton, 1975, p. 28.

15. MY1943a:144–45.

16. M1966b:96. M1949b:182; M1950a:207; M1954d:291; M1955a:25; M1956d:30; M1956c:55; M1959c:136; M1959d:78; M1959f:119; M1961a:184; M1962d:12,14,16; M1962h:6,7,105,154; M1962i:23; M1963c:115,124; M1963f:251–255; M1964b:x, xiii, 33, 80, 100; M1966b:95–101,124,103; M1968h:189, 191; M1971a:16–18.

17. MY1958a:18–19; MY1961e:34; MY1981a:77–82, 164, 180, 208–11.

18. R1963e:9; R1959d:25: R1965a:4; R1974j:256; R1973e:12.

19. A1961a:564–65; A1961h:9.

20. B1964h:21; B1965f:10,205,279,399; B1968b:17; B1973a:157.

21. B1954b:556; B1954c:72; B1962c:44; B1962e:88; B1963b:107; B1965d:181; B1965f:xvi, 71, 89; B1978b:65.

22. B1962e:102; B1965f:27, 56, 217, 275, 335; B1966a:231; B1967b:346; B1967f:32; B1968b:16; B1969a; B1971b:66; B1977a:139–40; B1978b:83; B1984a:546.

23. B1962g:247; B1963d:78; B1964e:274; B1965f:xvi, 50, 73, 213, 251, 263, 316, 367, 395; B1967b:345; B1967d:7; B1972b:18–19; B1976a:10.

8

Human Nature in Humanistic Psychology

The founders of humanistic psychology believed that any psychology deserving the name entails a view of human nature. A view of human nature, they argued, determines the focus of psychological research, the gathering and interpretation of evidence, and above all, the construction of psychological theories. Gordon W. Allport, for example, acknowledged that the "type of psychology one chooses to follow reflects inevitably one's philosophical presuppositions about human nature." Abraham Maslow similarly wrote in 1956:

> Everyone, even the year-old child, has a conception of human nature, for it is impossible to live without a theory of how people will behave. Every psychologist, however positivistic and anti-theoretical he may claim to be, nevertheless has a full-blown philosophy of human nature hidden away within him. It is as if he guided himself by a half-known map, which he disavows and denies, and which is therefore immune to intrusion and correction by newly acquired knowledge. This unconscious map or theory guides his reactions far more than does his laboriously acquired experimental knowledge.[1]

All five humanistic psychologists devoted great effort to the delineation of their views of human nature. These views were not ambiguously or vaguely implied between the lines of their texts, but were explicitly stated at the core of their writings. Their assessment of human nature created the frame of reference within which humanistic psychologists discussed general topics such as ethics, education, and politics. In the long run, it was that image of human nature that became the common and unifying ground of the humanistic movement.

Humanistic psychologists shared a conviction that a person is a "being-in-the-process-of-becoming." People at their best, they said, are proactive, autonomous, choice-oriented, and mutable—indeed, continuously becoming. Each human being, they argued, is a unique organism with the ability to direct and change the guiding motives or "project" of life's course. In the process of becoming, one must assume the ultimate responsibility for the individualization and actualization of one's own existence. To reach the highest levels through the process of becoming, a person must be fully functioning (Rogers) or functionally autonomous (Allport); the self must be spontaneously integrated and actualizing (Maslow); there must be a sense of self-awareness, centeredness (May), and authenticity of being (Bugental). Humanistic psychologists believed that the process of becoming was never simply a matter of genetics, biology, or the contingencies of external reinforcement, and they were convinced that the rejection of becoming was a psychological illness that should be the main concern of psychotherapy.

Although they agreed that the process of becoming characterizes human nature, humanistic psychologists disagreed on the exact causes of that process. Maslow, Rogers, and, to a lesser degree, Allport believed that the process of becoming had a biological basis; but they were extremely careful not to revert to simple biological determinism. Maslow thought that human beings had an "instinctoid" inner core that contained potentialities pressing toward actualization. In a similar vein, Rogers argued that the human organism had a directional and actualizing tendency toward the fulfillment of an inner potential. May and Bugental, however, regarded all biological assumptions as overly vague. They explained the process of becoming as a product of self-awareness and affirmation in the face of anxiety when dealing with existential contingencies. Allport, Maslow, and Rogers believed that human nature was inherently good when given the proper environment and opportunity for growth and self-actualization. May was to a certain extent optimistic regarding human nature, but he also believed that evil and anxiety had a major role as motivators of choice, responsibility, meaning, and authenticity.

GORDON W. ALLPORT

"What sort then of creature is Man?" With a characteristic eclecticism, Gordon Allport replied to his own rhetorical question by writing that "Man is both reactive (positivism) and proactive (personalism); that he is moved by unconscious urges (psychoanalysis) and that he is able to transcend them (existentialism)."[2]

Allport thought that the views of human nature stated by behaviorists and psychoanalysts must be supplemented by those of the personality theorists. He believed that human personality was a product of many causes acting both separately and conjointly. "A narrow model" of personality, he wrote, "insults human nature." Allport often blamed "die-hard temperamental particularists" (probably referring to behaviorists and psychoanalysts) for caricaturing human nature by dealing with isolated profiles of the person and ignoring everything that they deliberately decided to neglect. To avoid such particularism, Allport proposed a "systematic eclecticism" that aimed at a comprehensive metatheory of human nature.[3]

However, Allport believed that even eclecticism would fall short in describing human nature. Human personality was, for Allport, the unique pattern or agglomeration of generic attitudes, formations, or traits operating within the person. The mere listing of these, however, falls short of a complete picture of personality. The whole and integrative personality, he argued, is more than just the sum of its parts. Allport's systematic eclecticism pictured human nature as the assemblage of personality profiles that, operating jointly as a coordinating principle or center of gravity, binds together the individual profiles and, in so doing, becomes an internal patterning agent. Allport referred to this agent as the organism, person, self, or ego. It is the "intervening variable" or "o" (meaning "organism") that stands between stimulus and response in the S–R formula. Since it is responsible for our subjective values, attitudes, motives, ambitions, goals, intentions, and self-awareness, it guides or directs the process of becoming a person.[4]

Essential to Allport's view of human nature was his concept of "trait," which he defined as an "integrated system of action tendency" that constitutes a unit of the total personality structure. According to Allport, there are both common and individual traits. The common traits are social in nature; they are affiliative or symbiotic in the sense that culture and upbringing molds the development of each person.[5] Individual traits, on the other hand, encompass the dispositions, conflicts, urges, fears, and beliefs that guide, direct, and make up each person's unique personality. Whereas the social mode shapes the person into a mirror image of his or her environment, the personal mode allows creativity, purpose, and the uniqueness of personality.[6]

Allport called the patterning element that ensures the congruity and unity of the various traits and motives within personality the ego. The ego for Allport is autonomous, purposive, proactive, choice-oriented; it is a self-motivated executive and fighter for ends that plans the future. Since it is neither dominated by the superego nor in constant conflict with the instinctual forces of the id, it is a relatively independent entity.[7]

In a nonpathological personality the structural dispositions of the self undergo a continuous metamorphic process of transformation and alteration in the motives of action. Past-oriented, unchanging, unconscious, and instinctual motivation is a sign of neurosis. The ego, nevertheless, ensures that dominant character traits persist throughout life; what changes is the internal organization of motivation. Adult motives, noted Allport, are radically different from the motives of childhood. A newer system of motivation made up of adult motives is not the same as the older system—childhood motives—out of which it emerged. In spite of continuity in personality development, motives in adult life supplant and are different from the motives of infancy. In other words, the tensions involved in any acquired system of motivation are not of the same kind as the antecedent tensions from which that acquired system developed. There is a progressive internal organization of the person's motives. Human motivation is thus determined by contemporary conscious and changing structural dispositions, such as ambitions, values, plans, and hopes. These dispositions involve long-range terms and are persistent, dynamic, directive, and future-oriented. This is the reason, argued Allport, why healthy personality and motivation are a never-ending process of becoming. In Allport's terms this was the principle of the functional autonomy of motives. Spelled out in the context of a theory of personality and social psychology, Allport's principle of the functional autonomy of motives shares the autonomy, proactivity, formative tendency, and actualization features of the growth hypothesis view of human nature advocated by Maslow and Rogers.[8]

ABRAHAM H. MASLOW

Human nature, according to Abraham Maslow, depends upon both biology and culture. It seemed obvious to him that there could be no such thing as human nature without the existence of the human body. But it seemed equally clear to him that a simple biological determinism could not explain human nature.

Central to Maslow's view of human nature was the concept of an "instinctoid" inner core within the human organism. Innate human capacities, talents, and idiosyncrasies, he thought, have a biological basis in that inner core. However, the biological inner core exists merely as potential "raw material" waiting to be subjectively developed or actualized by the individual. The inner core was nothing like an all-powerful animal instinct but rather was an instinct-remnant, very subtle and easily suppressed and repressed or developed and actualized. There were, according to Maslow, both cultural and psychological dimensions to the process of actualization. The species-specific potentialities of the human body were, on one hand, shaped by family, education, environment, and culture; and on the other hand, they were determined by people themselves; by their choices, will, and decisions; by all the things that Sartre had called the "project."[9]

Because Maslow believed that human biological potential is malleable, he emphasized the importance of a proper cultural environment. A synergetic society, he argued, must create conditions that encourage the free expression of instinctoid human nature; more important, it must allow the human organism to actualize itself positively by means of subjective choice. Subjective choice did not mean for Maslow what it meant for post–World War II Sartrean existentialism. Choices for Maslow were determined by the species-specific biological core residing within the individual. The individual needed to recognize the impulses of the body, love and respect the self as a biological organism, and then actualize its potential. In spite of the biological foundations of human nature, however, the person as a subjective entity is responsible for the manner in which he or she individuates and actualizes his or her own existence. Ultimately it is the person who is the active agent, the mover and chooser, and the master of him or herself.[10]

Signifying the importance of the individual in the unfolding of his or her inner potential, Maslow argued that the inner core develops only by a process of self-discovery and "creation." Although the organism develops from within by virtue of intrinsic growth tendencies, the manner in which this development is accomplished depends upon the person. Maslow agreed with Carl Rogers that there are "positive growth tendencies" within the human organism driving it to fuller and fuller development. He also agreed with Rogers that a primary task of psychotherapy is to create an environment conducive to self-discovery and the conscious exercise of will.[11]

Maslow was deeply interested in ethics, and he argued that it was possible to have a scientific study of human values. Values, he thought, were deeply embedded within the structure of human nature, and he believed that the possession of wrong values was a kind of mental illness. Wrong values included the suppression of one's inner biological core, the inhibition of growth, and wanting "what-is-not-good-for-us." Mental health, on the other hand, was synonymous with "good-growth-toward-self-actualization," or the development and actualization to the fullest extent of the capacities latent within the biological core. Maslow considered values leading to self-actualization to be the right values. Actualization is always possible, argued Maslow, because human nature is fundamentally trustworthy, self-governing, and self-protecting. Provided with a synergetic environment and full freedom of self-expression, human nature will unfold and grow in the right direction. Maslow believed that Carl Rogers's ideal of a "fully functioning person" suggested the ethical implications of his own concept of self-actualization.[12]

Maslow's other well-known concept was the hierarchy of needs. The inner core of human nature, argued Maslow, consists of urges and instinct-like propensities that create basic needs within the individual. These needs have to be satisfied; otherwise, frustration and sickness will result. The first and most basic needs are physiological and are related to our survival. If the physiological needs are not satisfied, all other needs are temporarily pushed aside. Once basic physiological needs are fulfilled, relatively higher and higher needs emerge—such as those for safety, love, and esteem. When safety needs are satisfied, love needs and esteem needs arise. The social needs stand at the top of Maslow's hierarchy of needs.[13]

According to Maslow, the drive to gratify needs is instinctoid; needs must be gratified or illness will ensue. Mental illness is manifested by the person who compulsively seeks gratification of a particular need and does not move on to fulfill higher needs. Maslow agreed with Allport that the satisfaction of certain needs in healthy individuals become ends in themselves, only distantly related to the original needs. Higher needs are relatively independent and are functionally autonomous from lower needs.

At the top of the hierarchy of needs, Maslow placed the need for self-actualization, or the desire to become all that one is capable of becoming. A desire for self-actualization arose with the emergence of a need to know, a need to satisfy our curiosity about nature, a need to understand the perplexities of life; it was also a response to the needs for meaningful work, responsibility, justice, creativity, and the appreciation of beauty. In *The Farther Reaches of Human Nature* (1971), Maslow also discussed a yet higher need than that of self-actualization, one that was transcendental and centered on cosmic rather than human awareness. All humans, said Maslow, possess an instinctoid need to penetrate the cosmic mysteries and to live in a realm of symbols and religion.[14]

The desire to transcend one's own nature, said Maslow, was just as much an aspect of human nature itself as were all of the lower needs. Denial of this ultimate need could be just as pathological as a denial of one's need for vitamins and proper nutrition.[15]

CARL R. ROGERS

Humanistic psychologists often described human nature in terms of growth and development. They also often argued that the process of development must be understood in both biological and nonbiological terms. Carl Rogers's views on human nature illustrated both of these propensities. According to Rogers, the unfolding of an organism's potential is a process largely determined by genetics; what separates human beings from the rest of nature, he maintained, was the development of consciousness.

Rogers placed his view of development within a broad evolutionary context that was, although distinct, reminiscent of the evolutionary systems of Jean-Baptiste Lamarck and Herbert Spencer in the nineteenth century. Rogers thought that a "formative directional tendency" permeates all beings in the universe, from crystals to stellar space and organic life. He saw this directional tendency within evolutionary terms as the development toward greater and greater complexity, interrelatedness, and order. In living organisms, the directional tendency, he said, becomes a "formative tendency." All organisms desire to maintain, enhance, and reproduce themselves; they also desire to gain independence from external control, to become self-regulated, and even to transcend their own nature. Although the actualizing tendency can be inhibited by an adverse environment, Rogers believed that it can never be destroyed as long as the organism is alive. Rogers agreed with Maslow that certain lower conditions must be fulfilled before higher needs emerge to press the organism toward further actualization. Like Allport, he also believed that actualization is relatively independent of antecedent needs.[16]

The actualizing tendency does not, however, involve the development of all the potentials within the organism. It is selective and directive only toward positive objectives; it does not, for example, actualize the capacity for nausea, self-destruction, or the ability to bear pain.[17]

Rogers believed that there is a biological base to human nature. At a certain point in evolution, however, the formative tendency of the human organism achieved consciousness of itself. According to Rogers, consciousness created a "symbolizing capacity, topping a vast pyramid of nonconscious organismic functioning." To be conscious, said Rogers, meant to be aware of one's own growth and development. Consciousness also brought along the ability to understand one's inner self. If a person makes choices that are in tone with his or her own organism, Rogers argued, these could be called good choices. However, these were not "objective" or "real" choices because they were ultimately determined by the subjective actualizing tendency, which Rogers described as a kind of "automatic pilot."[18]

Rogers considered a "fully functioning person" to be one who is in touch with his or her own inner nature; one who trusts and allows his or her own organism to function freely; and one who selects from among all the organismic potentialities what is most genuinely satisfying. "The basic nature of the human being," wrote Rogers, "when functioning freely is constructive and trustworthy." Constant change is thus also natural to human nature. A healthy individual, according to Rogers, is one who is continually in the process of becoming. On this last point Carl Rogers agreed completely with Gordon Allport and Abraham Maslow.[19]

Rogers made the actualizing tendency the central hypothesis of his person-centered approach to psychotherapy. He believed that people can learn to tap their actualizing tendency and fulfill their potential if they are surrounded by a "definable climate" of facilitative attitudes. The task of psychotherapy was thus to facilitate self-understanding in the hope that it will allow the individual to direct his or her own life in constructive and fulfilling ways according to the dictates of his or her own organism.

Rogers stated three conditions that comprise what he called the "definable climate" of a facilitative attitude. First, the client ought to perceive genuineness, realness, and congruency on the part of the therapist, so that he or she may learn firsthand how to achieve an authentic relationship. Second, the client ought to feel that the therapist positively and unconditionally accepts, cares, and values him or her as a person. Third, the therapist ought to understand and empathize with the client so that the therapist can make the client more self-aware of his or her own inner world and feelings. By these means, Rogers argued, the therapist could enable the client to tap into his or her own actualizing tendency, thus releasing constructive changes leading to mental health and personal growth.[20]

ROLLO MAY

According to Rollo May, unlike animals and vegetables, there is in human life a distinction between nature and being, between the self as an object and as a subject. As objects, humans are expected to fulfill the predetermined external realities and values of their social environment. As subjects, they are free to mold their way of being from personal feelings about the intrinsic significance of that objective world. According to May, it is impossible to evade the dilemma implicit in the objective-subjective polarity and focus exclusively on either pole. It is, however, in the dialectical relationship between the two poles that human freedom emerges. In this context, May, like the European existentialists, asserted that "Man is his freedom."[21]

Along with other humanistic psychologists such as Allport, Maslow, and Rogers, May viewed human nature as a process of becoming; unlike them, however, he did not believe that this process was a one-dimensional organismic growth analogous to the growth of a seed into a plant. May thought that this definition of becoming was based on "vague biological assumptions about growth." He argued instead that the process of becoming resulted from the attempt to balance the dialectical tension or "play of opposites" between the objective and subjective poles and the freedom implicit in that condition. "Man does not grow automatically like a tree, but fulfills his potentialities only as he, in his own consciousness, plans and chooses," wrote May.[22]

Human life and growth, according to May, result from the perpetual tension between the pole of perfection one seeks (what it ought to be) and the pole of imperfection one is. A healthy personality, claimed May, has the ability and courage to tolerate the tension produced in the dialectical play between the two poles, to sustain a state of flux, and to direct the tension into creative channels. Exclusive focus on one of the poles is a sign of psychic illness. The worst and the best, pleasure and pain, good and evil, happiness and tragedy depend and are attached one to the other. Without one pole, the other would have no meaning. It is "this polarity, this dialectical relationship, this oscillation between positive and negative," wrote May, "that gives the dynamic and the depth to human life."[23]

The force behind the dialectical play of opposites was, according to May, the biological drive, wish, urge, or impulse in humans to affirm, assert, and increase their existence. May named the conglomerate of these forces the "daimonic." The daimonic puts the dualistic tension of the play of opposites into either constructive or destructive use. If integrated in the personality, it empowers the person with creativity; if, however, not integrated or if focused exclusively on one pole, it may dominate the personality and be expressed by destructive means.[24]

Human nature, in May's view, is both good and evil. If our evil pole (anger, hostility, and lust, for example) is not denied, then the opposite pole will emerge and balance it out. In a public polemic May carried on in the late 1980s with Carl Rogers on the issue of evil. May wrote that the client-centered therapist's denial of the evil pole of human nature was a dangerous error with narcissistic overtones. The refusal to frankly recognize the inner daimonic is already a partnership with its destructive facets. The more one comes to terms with the daimonic, the more its constructive side emerges. "When we can deal with this evil, then and only then what we say about goodness will have power and cogency."[25]

Experience of identity, argued May, stems from the ability to take a stance in relation to the subject-object play of opposites and the daimonic. The human predicament of our age—the alienation of the individual from himself and his world—stems precisely from the inability to take such a stance. Identity, or the Cartesian "I," he asserted, is not a result of doubting or thinking, but rather of affirmation and willingness ("I can–I will"). It is only by turning and committing attention that we gain "centeredness," or a sense of the self as a center of subjective experience. This centeredness individualizes and provides subjective identity ("achieving selfhood") and existential meaning to life. The crucial experience of identity ("I-ness," in May's terminology) could thus be expressed in a Cartesian manner as "I think–I can–I will–I am."[26]

May thought that psychotherapy should aim at assisting the patient to will, so he might achieve "centeredness." In this process, the patient has to encounter and transmit the biological wishes and drives (the daimonic) into consciousness and incorporate them into the will. Only when patients recognize that they cannot avoid responsibility for their choices and lives do they learn to exploit intentionality in the shaping of their being-in-the-world. In other words, the patient learns to focus attention on and to accept the inner and unconscious self. In doing so, the patient acquires a pole of centeredness for subjective identity and being-in-the-world, thus deliberately becoming a product of his or her own choices.[27]

May argued that the task of psychotherapy was also to help the patient tolerate the tension in the dialectical play between opposite poles. The negative pole of the daimonic should not be avoided, but rather should be respected and allowed constructive expression into creative outputs. If one seeks perfection, then help should focus on the development and ability to bear imperfection. It is also an important goal of psychotherapy to raise consciousness of the strength given to each pole. Another important goal is to learn to live with the indefinite, the unsettled, and the paradoxical that are inescapably human and are never fully resolved.[28]

JAMES F. T. BUGENTAL

In Bugental's view, the human world is one of contingencies far beyond our control and understanding. The resulting sense of incomprehension and fear leads to feelings of hopelessness over the circumstances and destiny of our being in that world. This predicament generates what Bugental, along with other existentialists, termed "the existential anxiety of emptiness and meaninglessness." In order to cope with this existential anxiety, we seek constructs that enable us to understand the world and attach meaning to our existence. If these constructs rely on self-awareness and on realistic acceptance of the world's contingencies, then, thought Bugental, we are in harmony with inner and outer realities and, hence, we are authentic people.[29]

For authentic people, open confrontation with existential anxiety is positive ("ontogogic" in Bugental's terminology), since it forces them to accept responsibility for their process of becoming. In this process they actualize inner potential and grow with greater authenticity. In this sense, self-actualization or personal growth results from dealing authentically with the existential anxiety imposed upon us by life contingencies and not from the biological determinism of the body. Only greater knowledge and awareness of the inner self and surroundings allows the person to grow properly and authentically.[30]

Awareness of the self and the givens of life's contingencies ("organismic awareness of our human situation"), however, by itself is unauthentic and disruptive; only when combined with intentionality does it constitute a process that allows the individual to construct a unique way of being-in-the-world. One can never really be self-aware. The I-process of the self is just that, a process. It cannot be seen because it is seeing, and too much preoccupation with it occludes the process of becoming. Without intentionality, therefore, one does not truly exercise choice and becomes authentic in terms of having a sense of one's own being as subject and creator of one's existence. Although self-awareness is something we always work toward but never fully achieve, it nevertheless gives us spiritedness or vitality in the measure that we attain it.

Awareness alone is not enough for the construction of identity. Active and full participation, wishing, wanting, and willing are also necessary. Human nature, argued Bugental, is simultaneous awareness and choice; it is a flowing process of "being-aware-and-choosing." A person is involved in his or her behavior, and his or her response to stimuli is dictated by an all-embracing "self-and-world-concept" that is vital in understanding "who-I-am-and-what-my-world-is." It is, indeed, the self-and-world-concepts that provide the road map for the orientation of our being-in-the-world; they are, thus, the elements of identity building.[31]

The self-and-world-concepts, however, are not static, fixed, and immutable. The center of commitment and identity they provide is an ongoing process. "I am subjective awareness continually in process," or "I am the I-ing!" It is an I-process that is the expression of authenticity and self-actualization. In this context, Bugental's concept of the "emergent man" had much in common with Maslow's self-actualization and Rogers's organismic growth—but without the genetic tones implied in the concepts of his colleagues. The self-actualization of Bugental's emergent man is, rather, a product of authenticity and the freedom to commit oneself to a chosen center of being.[32]

Avoiding confrontation with existential anxiety and contingencies, on the other hand, reduces authenticity of being. Since humans are unable to live without meaning, they tend to seek external absolutes—such as moral principles, magical incantations, and scientific "certainties"—that dictate their conduct and give meaning to their existence. In this process, people disenfranchise themselves from responsibility for their conduct and lose touch with their inner selves, thus becoming puppets determined by everything except personal choice. That is, they become unauthentic.

Psychotherapy, in Bugental's understanding, reverses this process. It helps to reduce the distortions or unauthenticities, supports the patient's courage to confront the existential contingencies, and facilitates deeper awareness. Once the patient becomes aware of his or her subjecthood, intentionality may support more authenticity of being. Psychotherapy, argued Bugental, helps the patient to center his or her life "in subjective awareness"; it provides "training in authenticity." In this context, Bugental understood the concept of "resistance" as a "process of non-being" by which one avoids responsible and aware being. Resistance distorts awareness as a defense against the dread of an unbearable threat to one's distorted way of being.

NOTES

1. M1956d:23. A1967c:271. The following are explicit statements on the crucial role of an image of human nature in social thinking: A1962c; A1967a:14,15,23; A1967f:1. M1954f:353; M1962a:189; M1962b:220; M1968c:64; M1971b:20,40. R1946d:418–19; R1948b:17; R1950d:26; R1952c:352; R1957b. MY1956c; MY1959e:87,90–91; MY1963b:75; MY1967a:3–22; MY1978d:vii. B1951c:194–200; B1964h:23; B1965f:142, 193; B1966a:228; B1967b:7.

2. A1961h:11.

3. A1955a:vii; A1960d; A1961h:11–12; A1962b; A1964b; A1967f.

4. A1953d:352–53; A1960d:303; A1961a:345; A1961h:2–4; A1968a:45,68–70. Richard I. Evans, *Gordon Allport: The Man and His Ideas*, New York: Dutton, 1970, pp. 13–15.

5. A1955a:35; A1960a:v–vi; A1961a:347; A1965c:43; A1967f:3.

6. Ibid.

7. A1955a:37,45–46,49,65–68; A1957a:10; A1958a:37; A1961a:216–27; A1961h:4; A1967f:2. Evans, *Allport*, pp. 22–43.

8. A1937b; A1950f:204; A1953b; A1955a:65–66; A1961a:103,149–55,202–3,206–9; A1965a:176–89; A1967a:7–8; A1967f:4–5; A1968a:71–73.

9. M1954a:9,139,382; M1962b:3–4,138; M1964b:xvi; M1968h:186; M1970a:xvii; M1971b:22–24.

10. M1954a:9,124,145,153,349,382;   M1962a;   M1968c:64–65;   M1968g:36; M1968k:223; M1971a:101,148,223.

11. M1954a:116,124; M1962b:138; M1971b:22–24.

12. M1954a:116; M1957a:116; M1962b:81,130,167–85; M1968k:211; M1971a:28.

13. M1943b; M1954a:80,106,116,154,345–47,379–90; M1955a:3.

14. M1954a:183; M1961c:3; M1964b:xvi; M1968b; M1970a:xxvil; M1971a:186.

15. M1954a:146–51, 379–90; M1962b:222; M1968b:3.

16. Rogers's view of human nature permeates almost everything he wrote since *Counseling and Psychotherapy* (1942). The following sources, however, were particularly significant in writing this section of the chapter: R1954a; R1957d; R1963a; R1963b; R1963g; R1965e; R1977k; R1979a.

17. R1979a:101.

18. R1948a:29–30; R1951a:522; R1957d:186–87; R1971c:87–89; R1979a:103.

19. R1954a:122; R1956g:206; R1960a:171; R1961a:27; R1963b:17–26.

20. R1954a:33–36; R1957a; R1961a:60; R1974c:23; R1979a:98–99; R1984b:26–27.

21. MY1952a; MY1956b:356; MY1963d; MY1967a:3–20,217; MY1974e:16,61; MY1981a:xi.

22. MY1940a:58–60,114–27,249–51; MY1956b:356; MY1963f:216; MY1963g:45; MY1964b:116; MY1967a:ix,19–20,215; MY1967g:28,73; MY1969a:112, 278, 311, chs.5–6; MY1972a:54,75,110,122,217,238,254; MY1973c:48,95–96, 121, 239; MY1973e:17; MY1975a:20; MY1976d:27; MY1976e:48; MY1981a:66; MY1982a.

23. MY1982a:19.

24. MY1956b:355–57; MY1966c:21; MY1967g:29; MY1969a:123–29; MY1974e:55; MY1977b:304.

25. MY1982a:19. See also: MY1967a:ix,17,19,216; MY1972a:255–80.

26. MY1951a:306–22; MY1958b; MY1958c:46; MY1961a:2; MY1961b; MY1961e:31–40; MY1962c:14–19; MY1962d:19; MY1963b:74–81; MY1964b:117; MY1966a; MY1967a:94; MY1969a:chs.7–10.

27. MY1958b; MY1958c; MY1963b:77–81; MY1967a:108–9.

28. MY1967a:ix; MY1982a:19.

29. B1962g:245–48; B1965b; B1965f:15,22,24,74,94,102,195–99,319; B1967c:286; B1967e:629; B1967f:30–39; B1976a:54,99–100,291; B1978a:178,184; B1978b:75,77.

30. Ibid.

31. B1962b:526–27; B1965f:11–20; B1968c:384; B1969a; B1977a:138–39.

32. B1964a:46–55; B1965f:213,263–76,394,425; B1966a:231; B1967c:287,292; B1976a:14,283; B1978b:133.

9

Humanistic Ethics in Psychology

Since awakening to the void in ethics inherited from the valueless interregnum of the 1980s and the heralding of a kinder and gentler decade, the search for values has been pressing in the social sciences. Not often, however, do social scientists venture into the philosophers' domain of ethics. Some even deny the significance of ethics in the social sciences; B. F. Skinner is a prime example. The founders of humanistic psychology in the late 1950s and early 1960s—such as Gordon Allport, Abraham Maslow, Rollo May, and Carl Rogers—were exceptions. Indeed, no other group of thinkers in the history and systems of psychology has been as concerned with problems of values as has this group.[1]

The founders of humanistic psychology were certain that people need a value system—a system of understanding, or frame of orientation—that gives life meaning and purpose. Nonetheless, they pointed out, we live in an age where the ultimate diseases are amorality, rootlessness, emptiness, hopelessness, and the lack of something to believe in and be devoted to. They explained that traditional ethics failed because their validation, sought in supernatural concepts, sacred books, or a ruling class, was a priori authoritarian thinking. They blamed this uncertainty in value orientation on the anachronism between rigid ethical systems of the past and the relativistic world view of science. No longer unquestionably accepting the value systems of our upbringing, we find ourselves in the dilemma of having to choose between various—and at times even contradictory—values. Science, on the other hand, has divorced itself from ethics and has not offered an alternative. Impressive twentieth-century advances in

This chapter is adapted from an earlier work published by Roy J. DeCarvalho, "Humanistic Ethics in Psychology," *Journal of Integrative and Eclectic Psychotherapy*, vol. 10, no. 2 (1990). Adapted with permission.

science and technology have mistakenly led us to believe that the separation of ethics from science will improve the human world. The result has been that without a corresponding advancement in human ethics, the mechanization of the modern world shaped human civilization upon the image of the machine, making people its servants. The human dependency on science and technology has, as a result, outrun people's ethical sense and needs.[2]

Psychology, according to the founders of humanistic psychology, had a major role in the clarification and treatment of modern ethical dilemmas. Its goal was to study the place of the person in the modern world—to enlarge people's moral sense and guide the neutralism of science and technology with human values. Unfortunately, they argued, American psychology distanced itself from the problem of values and followed the technological or mechanical model, an attitude they severely criticized. A valueless or value-free psychology, they argued, is neither desirable nor possible. A psychology obsessed with techniques unconsciously embraces a "directionless and conscienceless scientism," which is also a value. Their humanistic psychology meant to reverse this predicament by reintroducing the human perspective and values to psychology. Although they shared common concerns and a humanistic philosophy, their thoughts were also unique. While Rollo May advocated an existentialist ethics and Maslow and Rogers a naturalistic ethics based on the growth hypothesis, Gordon Allport's views were phenomenologically based.[3]

Every major work of Rollo May was an elucidation of ethics. Values, he argued, were essential in understanding human nature because they give human beings—whom he once called the ethical animal—their "sense of being" and ontology. Values, he explained, emerge from the rational and irrational, conscious and unconscious levels of human nature. Values are not a product of theoretical speculations, but of, on one hand, subjective choice exercised in the process of commitment to self-chosen centers of valuation, and, on the other hand, the collective levels or archetypes of civilization symbolically represented in myths. Values require awareness of the body and feelings, courage to affirm convictions, responsibility, and confrontation with the anxiety associated with this process. For all these reasons, values presuppose freedom.[4]

Like May, Allport also studied the process of valuing. He thought that a person's schemata of value are essential in the organization of personality. Values, he argued, are personal subjective meanings and dispositions of addressing the future that guide human motivation. Their intentional nature is responsible for the uniqueness of personality and the functionally autonomous process of becoming a person. Allport himself occasionally referred to this understanding of personality as phenomenological.[5]

Maslow and Rogers thought that the solution to the ethical dilemmas of modern age was to find a "true" validating ethical system independent of subjective values—or, in Maslow's words, a system "based squarely upon knowledge of the nature of man." Like Maslow, Rogers also complained that the study of ethics had always been in the domain of philosophy; he insisted that it was now time for psychologists to initiate scientific studies of values. It was in this context that Maslow and Rogers persistently sought a naturalistic system of ethics.[6]

Maslow was critical of all psychological attempts to explain human nature on the basis of the knowledge of sick individuals who sought psychologists for help. Instead, he selected for study those who, in his judgment, were the "most fully human" and healthy people. He thought that their "humanness," capacities, and values could be the ultimate transcendental values of the entire species. Rogers, on the other hand, studied people who grow toward psychological maturity and health in the process of psychotherapy. Both Rogers and Maslow concluded that there are universal values that are an integral part of human nature and that are experienced when the individual is in touch with his or her own organism. Organismic awareness, in their opinion, could help the individual to find within himself or herself a system of universal ethics that would answer the most perplexing value questions of our age. Such values are synonymous with psychological or physical health and are concrete, observable facts, not mere subjective phenomena. They are as biologically based and descriptive as is the concept of physical health.[7]

All four humanistic psychologists thought that it is impossible for a psychologist to be objective and not to have a view of human nature. A well-articulated view of human nature is, in their understanding, the most important value in science, psychology in particular. Any psychology deserving the name entails a view of human nature, they argued. Every one, including the most experimentally oriented psychologist, has (whether consciously stated or not) an understanding of people. "The issue," wrote Maslow, "is thus not over whether or not to have a philosophy of psychology, but whether to have one that is conscious or unconscious."[8] The unconscious theories of human nature are particularly dangerous because they guide the collection of data and research more profoundly than laboriously acquired empirical knowledge. They argued, in other words, that there are prior personal subjective views of human nature and choices of the purpose or value of scientific work. It is important that these values be stated and clarified because they cannot be tested, evaluated, or denied by scientific means. In their case, they indeed dedicated much effort to the delineation of a view of human nature.[9]

THE GROWTH HYPOTHESIS OF HUMAN NATURE

For Maslow and Rogers, the cornerstone of their views on human nature— and, consequently, their naturalistic understanding of values—was the growth hypothesis. Maslow explained that an "instinctoid" inner core of human nature contains potentialities pressing for actualization. Similarly, Rogers stated that the human organism has an actualizing tendency toward the fulfillment of inner potential. Both were inspired by Kurt Goldstein, a German-born Jewish psychiatrist and a World War II émigré who first coined the term self-actualization to denote the reorganizational capability of the organism after injury. Maslow and Rogers acknowledged that they had adopted the concept of self-actualization from Goldstein.[10]

In his version of the growth hypothesis, Maslow argued that individuals have basic needs, emotions, and capacities that are neutral, pre-moral, positive, and good. If they guide our lives, we grow healthier and happier; but if we deny or suppress them, sickness is certain. In this view, higher and lower needs are arranged in levels of potency, where the fulfillment of less potent needs relies upon the gratification of the more potent ones. The higher aspects of human nature, in other words, rest upon the fulfillment of the lower nature.[11]

Physiological needs related to basic survival, such as food, shelter, safety, and security, belong to the lower aspects of human nature and dominate the organism at the elementary level. When satisfied, however, the next higher need emerges and organizes personality differently. Belonging, affection, love, respect, and self-esteem belong to the next level, self-actualization to another, and spiritual and transcendental needs constitute the last category. A healthy person, according to Maslow, is one who develops and actualizes his or her full potential and capacities by gratifying the ascending hierarchy of needs; Maslow called such people self-actualizers. However, when a persistent active basic need is not satisfied, the person is not free to grow and fulfill the higher needs—and he is thus said to be ill.[12]

All needs, including the higher needs, are instinctoid, or physiological and similar to the need for vitamins. Deprivation of safety, love, truth, joy, and justice, for example, generates a pathological state similar to that arising from the deprivation of vitamin C.[13]

Rogers's version of the growth hypothesis has much in common with Maslow's self-actualization. Rogers thought that infants have a clear set of values. Infants choose experiences that maintain and induce growth, actualize their organismic potential, and reject what is contrary to their well-being. Since the values that guide their actualization lie strictly within their organism, they are naturalistic and objective. But, Rogers argued, as infants grow their efficient valuing process is slowly transformed into rigid artificial and organismically inefficient value systems. Their naive conception that what feels good is good is distorted by assimilation of the evaluation of adults, who make them feel sorry, fearful, and guilty about their naive values in exchange for love. In this process, they lose the wisdom of organismic awareness and incorporate the values set by the human environment. The values carried along with the love, esteem, and approval from adults force them to distrust the experience of their own organism as a guiding value system. In other words, they relinquish their trust of organismic wisdom.[14]

When the discrepancy between organismic and assimilated artificial values is acute, the individual experiences questions of meaning that are cyclically originated by or culminated in personal crisis. This estrangement of people from themselves, according to Rogers, explains modern strain, insecurity, and the lack of and search for values. The goal of psychotherapy, he argued, is to reverse that process. By confronting the individual with the lack of touch with his or her own organism, psychotherapy puts the person back in touch with his or her organismic valuing process.[15]

The belief that individuals have the capacity for self-understanding and reorganization in satisfying ways if they are only provided the necessary and sufficient conditions for personality change was the foundation of Rogers's client-centered therapy. Given an appropriate growth-inducing environment in which one is unconditionally accepted, one learns the causes of behavior and new ways of perceiving and reacting to these causes. Once the denied attitudes and behavior become conscious and accepted, the self assimilates them and reorganizes itself, consequently altering the entire personality structure and behavior. In other words, when one explores and accepts the inner self like the infant does, one learns to be in touch with and release the organismic wisdom. If given the freedom to become what one truly is, one naturally actualizes one's true identity—which, Rogers argued, could be positive in terms of enhancing the individual's nature and existence.[16]

The goal of the client-centered therapy he advocated is to set the person free from internal and external barriers so that the basic nucleus of his or her nature would be released. In the early stages of therapy, people live largely by values introspected from others; as therapy progresses, however, they realize that they are living according to the expectations of others. When this acknowledgment becomes unbearable, their valuing process changes; the judgment and expectation of others concerning their thinking and feeling is slowly replaced by their own experience, values, and standards. In this understanding of client-centered therapy, Rogers implied that the basic nature of the person when functioning freely is constructive and trustworthy. Each one of us has the capacity for self-understanding and for initiating change in the direction of psychological growth and maturity, providing only that we are genuinely free and treated with worth and significance. In this sense, he argued, the therapist merely makes an alliance with the individual's organismic forces for growth and self-actualization.[17]

MAY AND THE PROCESS OF VALUING

Maslow's concept of self-actualization and Rogers's actualizing tendency served as a breeding ground for the development of the human potential movement and were in part the foundations of the humanistic movement in American psychology. The other pillar was the existential perspective in psychology and psychiatry, of which Rollo May was the most outspoken. Entirely within the context of the humanistic movement in psychology, Rollo May was critical of the ethics of the growth hypothesis. He argued that it was one-dimensional and was borrowed from biology. Its popularity stemmed from the appeal to an easy and useful deterministic growth toward the fulfillment of unlimited potential. He thought, for example, that it is an oversimplification to say that we grow toward moral values or truth. Ethical growth is not like the growth of plants or of the economy. We do not become better than the Greeks, for example, in the same way that our bridges are better than their bridges. In human terms, mere growth does not imply right growth. Growth can also be evil; cancer, for example, is a growth.[18]

May argued that people do not automatically grow toward the development of their potential, which, according to the growth hypothesis, is always good. If they do not develop their potential, they do not become simply neuter. Without positive values to believe in when life has no constructive meaning, people become actively evil and the unused power turns into destructiveness. Human nature is both evil and good; we ought to accept the evil aspects in order to balance it out with our goodness and thereby neutralize it, rather than projecting our evil upon others or using it destructively. According to May, the ethics of growth leaves out the daimonic element of human nature, which is also necessary for growth.[19]

The understanding of "value" as a result of personal valuing (a verb rather than a noun) is crucial in May's humanistic ethics. He thought that there were no real values, but rather valuation of what is important for oneself to which to be committed. What one truly values—family relationships, possessions, ideals, and life goals, for example—one accepts as concrete realities generated by subjective commitment and assertion of personal choice and power, not as products of meaningless theoretical discussions. The process of becoming a person, he argued, relates to the capacity to experience the self as a valuing source and to affirm personal goals and values rather than adjusting to external criteria.[20]

Abstract and detached theoretical clarifications do not create values, argued May. Only the subjective experience of values provides poles around which one knows oneself as a person. Values do not exist independent from the valuing process and commitment of the individual. They have meaning only when one's motives and ethical awareness are the starting point. For May, an ethical act was thus an expression of inward motives and attitudes—an action that is chosen and affirmed by the self and an assertion of personal power. In this sense, although no one can really teach values to anyone, one may facilitate the act of valuing, an act that requires courage and commitment to do the valuing and not to be apologetic for the self-chosen personal goals and way of life.[21]

In the process of valuing, the significance is not on values but on the process of focusing oneself on centers of valuation that vary from person to person and within the person as well. It is not the case that there is only one inner, fixed center that one permanently seeks to fulfill; rather, there is an ongoing process of centering around core values that serve as psychological poles of integration and unity. These centers change over time and circumstances; they are, in other words, functionally autonomous. Adult values are rooted, but they are not extensions of the mothers' care and love; they developed as functionally autonomous from the antecedent values that generated them. The values of neurotics, on the other hand, are not functionally autonomous because they compulsively seek to satisfy few childhood values. Permanent inflexible values crystallize into dogma. Therefore, we ought not only to be committed and act from the center that our values provide, but we should also continuously clarify, reevaluate, and accommodate them to new circumstances and people. Courage is a necessary element in this process of valuation. The capacity to stand up and take risks for one's convictions and originality demands courage, which is an essential human quality that May referred to as heroic.[22]

In describing the process of centering, May wrote that it requires self-consciousness, generates anxiety, and presupposes freedom. We will discuss this and related matters later. It suffices here to say that according to May, the process of centering on one's self-chosen centers of valuation demands awareness of one's body, feelings, and intentions; decision making; responsibility; constructive confrontation with anxiety; and unconditional freedom.[23]

May thinks that the process of valuing and anxiety are intimately related. Anxiety is a human reaction to the threat to something we care about, value, or identify with our existence. The death threat, for example, is the most powerful producer of anxiety. We overcome anxiety only to the extent that our values are stronger than the threat. Moreover, if anxiety is a threat to what we value, then no one is completely free from anxiety.[24]

May distinguished in this context between neurotic and normal anxiety. While normal anxiety has a role in the clarification of our values, neurotic anxiety blocks self-awareness. When people lose touch with themselves they no longer know who they are and what they ought to be. The insecurity associated with anxiety forces them to search for an inner center of values so they may overcome the threat of anxiety. This "normal" anxiety is proportional to the threat, does not involve unconscious motivation, and, when met constructively, is a constructive life stimulant that is an integral part of growth and is vital for creative expression. Neurotic anxiety, on the other hand, results from unmet normal anxiety.[25]

ALLPORT'S SCHEMATA OF VALUES

Allport, like Maslow, Rogers, and May, persistently asserted that a view of human nature is the most significant value, and one that is crucial in the making of any psychology. Indeed, a consciously delineated view of human nature also permeates Allport's psychological thinking. In his view, personality has an ego that—according to its intentions—is involved and participates in the organization of the organism and in matters affecting its own destiny. He named these intentions that guide personality the schemata of value. A significant task of psychology, as he understood it, is to study the universality of the individual's unique schemata of values. He held this search at a high place in the scale of what he thought to be his "scientific values."[26]

Allport defined values as "meanings perceived as related to the self." One experiences value whenever something has meaning that is warm, desirable, and central to oneself. Values are a personal "matter of importance," distinct from mere matters of fact. The schemata of value are thus the goals, sentiments, hopes, attitudes, habits, and faculties that are chief ingredients in personality structure and that give people their unique features. It disposes the development of the healthy individual by selecting his or her perception of the world, giving him or her a sense of "generic conscience." This conscience points to what is right and desirable and influences behavior and decision making, thus playing a crucial role in the process of becoming a person.[27]

Nevertheless, not all value orientation is attained; neither are people always consistent with their values. Also, value orientation does not allow for prediction of what the individual will do at any given moment. Sometimes people put up appearances, give in to environmental pressures, or follow personal idiosyncrasies. Still, the schemata of values they hold exert a dynamic pressure upon daily conduct, thus allowing for the development of a personal style of living. Allport pointed out that although it is difficult to define the individual's value system, his or her philosophy of life—whether consciously articulated or not—is the major characteristic of personality. It is a distinctive mark, or engraving, of personality that unites biology with a network of personal meanings. As a matter of fact, he argued, personality problems emerge when one's values are largely unconscious and repressed, or when one lives in a state of valuelessness. Since values are the personal dispositions of addressing the future, they constitute a structure that has a decisive influence upon the further growth of personality.[28]

One holds various values, but because they constitute clusters where the larger units serve as a cataclysm to minor and temporary intentions, there are few and ascertainable value types operating in personality. Indeed, Allport thought that personality could be best known through the study of such reducible generic evaluative tendencies (*Lebensformen*) or motives. Borrowing from the work of Eduard Spranger, he postulated that there are six value-motives (theoretical, economic, esthetic, social, political, and religious) and developed a test to measure their relative prominence within personality. These are personal profiles relevant only to the individual; they are not to be cross-compared among people. Each type is an ideal value direction, a pure portrait; it does not exist singularly in actual people, but within individuals in different combinations and intensities.[29]

Personalities dominated by the theoretical value type take a cognitive attitude toward life. Their dominant interest is the discovery of truth. They are empirical, critical, and rational. They seek to reason, order, and systematize knowledge. The economic type focuses on the useful and the practical. These individuals seek to satisfy their bodily needs, to accumulate wealth, and to prosper on a mundane level. Unapplied or theoretical knowledge is a waste in their understanding. Individuals who are, on the other hand, dominated by artistic interests, form, and harmony belong to the esthetic value type. They value grace and symmetry, are highly individualistic, and equate truth with beauty. The social type is unselfish, selfless, altruistic, kind, and sympathetic. These individuals love and prize people as ends. Those who are dominated by the theoretical, economic, and esthetic values seem to them to be cold and inhuman. The political types value power over other people. They enjoy competition, struggle, achievement, and recognition for their leadership qualities. Finally, the ideal religious types seek ultimate mystical experiences, comprehension, and unity with the cosmos. They are detached from the mundane, living in self-denial and meditation. Every individual has all six of these values in different combinations and intensities. The test Allport developed on *The Study of Values* measures how an individual organizes his or her life around these six values and what constitutes his or her hierarchy of values.[30]

In the context of this view, Allport argued that human motivation is related to the futuristic character of the intentional nature of values. Nonpathological human motivation and values are future-oriented, not past-oriented. As a matter of fact, when motives and their underlying values are unconscious, persistent, instinctual, and past-oriented, the individual is neurotic and is a creature of his or her own habits. At their best, however, people are proactive, autonomous, mutable, and choice-oriented. They are motivated by values that—although rooted in their past—are nevertheless independent from their origins and are future-oriented.[31]

Although values guide the development of personality, according to Allport, the values and related tensions involved in any acquired system of motivation are functionally autonomous from the antecedent values from which the acquired system developed. In a nonpathological personality, for example, adult motives are different from the childhood motives from which they emerged. Values and the process of becoming they guide are functionally autonomous. This is why one is forever different, always a being in the process of becoming. It is not surprising that in this context Allport empathically criticized the behavioristic understanding of motivation as past-oriented and of personality as a battery of trigger-release mechanisms functioning on the bases of "expectancy" (e.g., we behave according to what we have learned, or humans are a mere response to stimulus). This philosophy, he argued, is appropriate for the understanding of animals, not human beings and their moral dilemmas.[32]

Values, he was certain, exist a priori and cannot be derived from scientific studies. However, some ethical generalizations or universalities can be validated or confirmed by science. Allport argued that values are subjective and unique, but—like Maslow and Rogers—he also thought that there are universal features based on human nature that should be studied scientifically. Like them, he also thought that it is possible to derive values from the psychological study of human nature, that is, through a naturalistic system of ethics. There are certain values—such as personal renunciation, asceticism, authoritarian morality, utopian theories, and utilitarian ethics of the hedonistic type, for example—that fare badly when scrutinized by the social sciences.[33]

HUMANISTIC ETHICS

Values, argued Allport, Maslow, Rogers, and May, are of crucial significance in describing the process of becoming a person. Every person must have a commitment, or a set of values. Thus, they often advocated the need to implant nutritive doses of values in people, without ever dictating the content of such values. Personal values are subjective, but because valuelessness is a disease, they must develop some kind of ethics. The task of psychology, education, or psychotherapy, for example, is not to dictate but merely to facilitate people in finding values within themselves and in formulating a philosophy of life.

Of the four humanistic psychologists discussed here, Allport is the vaguest when it comes to describing concrete humanistic values. Rhetorically questioning himself on what type of ethical theories social science finds most congruent with research on human nature, Allport wrote that "desires for affiliation are the inescapable groundwork of human life." People wish by nature to preserve their self-esteem (self-love) through warm, affiliative relations. Hatred results from blocked self-esteem, denial of group affiliation, personal rejection, or indignity to one's existence. Even the most healthy individual, when denied the desire for love and affiliation, becomes anxious, and his or her fear may turn into aggression and hostility. This hostility is often displaced upon irrelevant "enemies."[34]

Allport also studied the place of religious values in personality. He found a high correlation between racial prejudice and religion. On one hand, churchgoers are more prejudiced than non-churchgoers, but on the other hand, many of the most humanitarian people are religiously motivated. In this context Allport distinguished between two types of religious values, the extrinsic and intrinsic, according to the function religion plays in the lives of people. While the extrinsic religious value relates to high levels of prejudice, the intrinsic relates to low levels of prejudice. Those who hold extrinsic religious values use religion for their own selfish purposes; they benefit from religion, and they are high in prejudice. The other group, however, serves religion; they are humanitarian, they practice what they believe, and they are low in prejudice.[35]

Unlike Allport, however, Maslow, Rogers, and May wrote extensively on humanistic values. Although May disagreed with Maslow and Rogers in his understanding of human nature, the concept of authenticity permeates their ethical systems nevertheless. All four argued that in the attempt to evade the modern predicament of valuelessness (and instead of looking inward unto themselves), modern people cling instead to authority as a source of security and persist to find and fulfill "scientific" or "objective" ethical criteria. In doing so, there is a tendency toward conformity, passivity, apathy, obedience, adjustment to the anonymous authority of public opinion, overemphasis on acceptance by peers, and the need to become a social success. They called this phenomenon the ethics of adjustment.

This tendency to melt down in the "collectivist pot of conformity" results, May explained, from the absence of a center of values in society and from the loss of self-awareness and an affective center of motivation within the individual. The only alternative, he argued, is to develop a deeper understanding of ourselves, rediscover an inner ethical center of strength and integrity, and courageously confront our historical situation and traditions. A morality of conformity and adjustment, argued May, leaves out the essence of ethics: the subjective valuing process.[36]

Versions of the growth hypothesis offered by Rogers and Maslow refer to the ability of self-actualizers to transcend the environment. Like May, in this context they also criticize the identification of psychological health with the concept of adjustment. They thought that it is misleading to define a healthy person in environment-centered terms of adjustment to a reality, society, or job, and they argued that mental health should be defined instead in terms of the individuals' autonomy and transcendence of the environment. It should be defined in terms of the ability to rely upon or function within—yet transcend—the social norms; the ability to stand against, fight, neglect, or change environmental conditions. The healthy, fully grown person is not a "willy-nilly" product of public opinion; rather, he transcends other people's opinions. According to Maslow and Rogers, healthy individuals are, in this sense, said to be authentic, original, and creative, but not well adjusted.[37]

Authenticity, not adjustment, was also the goal of psychotherapy for Rogers, Maslow, and May. Psychotherapy, argued Maslow and Rogers for instance, should help the less fortunate to reach the level of authenticity and the individuation found among self-actualizers. It meant, in Maslow's understanding, not to create but to reveal and facilitate integration with the biological core, or inborn preferences, talents, and yearnings of the person. The qualities of the biological core are not a priori "oughts" or "moral imperatives" in the old philosophical sense; rather, they are intrinsic to the nature of the individual. Denial and even absence of awareness of such a core leads to psychological illness, frustration, and disintegration. Thus, the task of psychotherapy is to train the person in authenticity, or to help the individual gain identity through discovery of the innate values that are part of his or her nature but unknown to him or her. Psychotherapy is, in other words, the search for and integration of one's own biologically intrinsic and authentic values. One's life problems, vocation, and decision making could be much easier if people knew what is easier for them to do—what, from the perspective of their organism, fits or suits them better. Psychotherapy is, in this sense, a process of recovery of "specieshood" or of "healthy animality," self-discovery, and integration leading toward greater authenticity of being and spontaneous expressiveness.[38]

Maslow and Rogers agreed that a significant facet of self-actualizing people is their spontaneous expressiveness, or authenticity of being. Both explained that such people consider their behavior and being as good, trustworthy, and ethical. They are alive, fully functioning, and true to their inner self; in other words, they are authentic to their nature. They held that the authenticity, values, and behavior of these people are descriptive qualities of psychological health. Since they are better perceivers and choosers, they naturally choose, in biological terms, what is growth-inducing and good for them. And, since they are human beings, it follows that their values could be the eternal verities—or, according to Maslow, the being-values of all people (i.e., what is good species-wide). If the values of self-actualizers induce growth and health in the best members of the species, then perhaps such values are ideals to be prescribed to the less fortunate. Knowledge of their ethics could serve as a beacon, or model, for the conduct, control, and improvement of our lives.[39]

In this context Rogers and Maslow had a new perspective on the age-old philosophical problem of freedom versus determinism. Fully functioning or self-actualizing people, they argued, are free people. In the process of choosing courses of action that are most satisfying, they exercise free will. Neurotics, on the other hand, are defensively organized; they follow settled, rigid patterns of feelings and behavior over which they have little or no control. They are said to be determined. Free will is, in this sense, a by-product of psychological health, of organismic awareness and choice. Conversely, absence of free will also explains the existence of evil. There is no such thing as an innate actualizing tendency toward destructiveness or fulfillment of an evil nature.[40]

Maslow's and Rogers's growth hypothesis version of authenticity and their discussion of freedom have close existential parallels in Rollo May, whose notion of freedom had a major role in his philosophy of human nature. May argued that any system of ethics leading to the full realization of one's potential must guarantee that freedom is not abdicated. Freedom, he argued, is the most basic prerequisite for our capacity to value. It is the source of all values, for the process of valuing depends on freedom. The intentionality of the human will in planning, imagining, and choosing values, the capacity to wonder, write poetry, and study nature presupposes freedom. Freedom is more precious than life itself, for some prefer to die for their own and their loved ones' freedom rather than give up their values. It is the source of human dignity, courage, honesty, and love. For example, love has value only if it is freely given, not because of dependency or conformity.[41]

May acknowledged, however, that people are not totally free from life-deterministic forces. No one is free from the determinations of their bodies or the historical realities of their psychological makeup and of their culture, to mention just a few factors. But, argued May, there is a margin of freedom within these realities. The more one is aware of the way in which one is determined, the more one is free to react to such deterministic forces. Freedom in this sense is a product of awareness and reaction to the deterministic realities of one's culture and psychological makeup. When one is not self-aware, one is determined by one's own instincts and the automatic development of history. The more anxieties, fears, inhibitions, repressions, and childhood conditioning unconsciously drive the individual, the more one is at the mercy of forces over which one has no control.[42]

People seek psychotherapy because they feel enslaved; they want to be set free and choose the values governing the unfolding of their potentials and future. Driven by unconscious motivation, they are unable to choose, unable to feel and know themselves and what they want; they are blocked off from large portions of their inner reality and have inaccurate perceptions of their surroundings. Indeed, they lack freedom to choose their values. Psychotherapy aims to reverse this process. Its purpose, according to May, is to set people free. One's increasing awareness of self-imposed determinations also increases the capacity to move one's world and shape one's destiny according to one's values. Increase in freedom and responsibility, in other words, relates directly to the increase of awareness of self-imposed and social deterministic forces. Thus, we may measure progress in psychotherapy in terms of the progress in consciousness of freedom and affirmation of values.[43]

Freedom, argued May, implies that we, as centered people, engage and act responsibly on both the personal and social levels. We are responsible for our convictions and the results of our actions. Mere centeredness, sincerity, and conviction are not enough. We can be sincere and firm but entirely wrong. Freedom and responsibility are related and cannot be separated. May called this "an ethic of intention," meaning that we must take responsibility for our intentions. In this context, May argued that the values of our intentions ought to have some universality (e.g., what is good for me ought to be good also for other people).[44]

Self-awareness, freedom, the valuing process, and centeredness are the subjective sources of human values. But Rollo May also acknowledged that human beings do not exist in a vacuum. They find themselves existing in a culture with a common history, aspirations, and values, the study of which (e.g., the humanities) is an important source of values. By looking unto the accumulated wisdom of history, we may rediscover the culturally inherited archetypes of human values as symbolically represented in our myths and symbols. The ethical dilemma, wrote May, is how to balance one's inherited traditions without compromising one's freedom and personal responsibility. We ought to live by our self-chosen values and at the same time not neglect the fact that we live in solidarity and identify with a particular group and the human race. He argued that the greater the self-awareness, the greater the capacity to merge into, experience, and discover oneself in all of one's uniqueness through the accumulated wealth of human traditions. Held in balance, they are the two sources of ethical creativity. We may even realize that we have chosen the same values that have been valued for centuries, although we have reached them in a very personal way.[45]

CONCLUSION

The humanistic views on ethics advocated by Allport, Maslow, Rogers, and May stemmed from a trust in the worthiness of human nature. They argued that when people are authentic, experience their inner worlds, and function freely from internal and external barriers, they value and choose what is good for them.

The growth hypothesis of Kurt Goldstein was a source of inspiration for Carl Rogers and Abraham Maslow, whose studies on self-actualization were an important pillar in the establishment of the humanistic movement in American psychology. Their versions of the growth hypothesis also dictated their understanding of human nature and naturalistic ethics. Maslow studied psychologically healthy people and the hierarchy of biological needs, and Rogers studied the process of growth experienced by patients in client-centered psychotherapy. Although the self-selected process and direction of becoming are subjective and, therefore, are relative from individual to individual, the choices of self-actualizing or fully functioning people embody the universally intrinsic values of human nature that are conducive to psychological health. Such values ought to be the guiding principles of human conduct for the less fortunate. Their choices and values ought to be the basis for a universal and naturalistic system of ethics. Such a system is not, they argued, a priori. Because these values can be tested, anyone scientifically studying the same people will arrive at similar conclusions. "To be that self which one truly is" (a phrase Rogers borrowed from Kierkegaard, one that is synonymous with authenticity) is the highest value in the naturalistic system of ethics advocated by Rogers and Maslow. In Maslow's words, authenticity was "truthfulness to one's own nature."

Another significant pillar in the establishment of humanistic psychology is the work of Rollo May. Although he is critical of the ethics of the growth hypothesis, he shares with Maslow and Rogers a belief in the significance of the concept of authenticity, discussion of which is found in his existential view of freedom.

According to May, values have an essential role in giving people their "sense of being" (he refers to man as "the ethical animal"). Values, he argues, do not arise from theoretical speculations. They are a product of subjective choice on one hand and, on the other hand, the collective levels or archetypes of human civilization symbolically represented in myths. In May's humanistic ethics, values are a product of a subjective process of courageous commitment of oneself to self-chosen centers of valuation that require consciousness of the body and feelings, intentionality, and responsibility. Such a process requires confrontation with anxiety and presupposes freedom from self-imposed and environmental constraints. Freedom, he argues, is the most essential prerequisite for the human capacity to value; thus, it is a universal value of major significance in psychotherapy. For May, the study of the humanities is also an important source of values. People exist within a culture with a common history, aspirations, and values. Study of this accumulated wisdom leads to the rediscovery of the universal archetypes of values symbolically represented in myths and symbols. Because these archetypes are subjectively present in each individual, they may be sought through studies of the humanities or our inner selves, or both.

Allport, another pillar of humanistic psychology, made some phenomenological observations on the schemata of values that he believed were essential in the organization of personality. Values, he argued, are personal subjective meanings and dispositions of addressing the future, and therefore they guide human motivation. Their intentional nature is responsible for the uniqueness of personality and the functionally autonomous process of becoming a person.

All four humanistic psychologists discussed in this chapter noted that an a priori understanding of human nature is essential in the making of psychology. They made their view of the person as a "being in the process of becoming" a cornerstone of their psychological thinking and humanistic systems of ethics. Personal values, they unanimously argued, are essential in the organization of personality because they hold the future-oriented subjective meanings and dispositions that guide the process of becoming a person. Thus, an ethical act gives the person a sense of being, or ontology, making him or her proactive, autonomous, intentional, and unique. For all these reasons, values presuppose a deep trust in our philosophy for the capacity and necessity of the person to value and determine the unfolding of his or her destiny. Authenticity, freedom, autonomy, commitment, and self-determination, not adjustment, are the keynotes of humanistic ethics in psychology.

NOTES

1. DeCarvalho's "The Ethics of the Growth Hypothesis of Abraham Maslow and Carl Rogers," *J. Ethical Stud.*, 1991, 16:3–17; "The Naturalistic Ethics of Carl Rogers," *Psy. Reports*, 1989, 65:1155–62; "The Growth Hypothesis and Self-Actualization: An Existential Alternative," *The Humanistic Psychologist*, 1990, 18:252–58.

2. M1959a:viii; M1964b:3,38,82; M1971a:377. R1961j; R1964b. Richard I. Evans, *Carl Rogers: The Man and His Ideas*, New York: Dutton, 1975, p. 101. MY1956b; MY1957b; MY1960b:41. A1950a:187; A1955d:154; A1960a:155.

3. A1955a:99.

4. MY1953a:174,180; MY1955c; MY1977b:303,309.

5. A1950a:144,187–97; A1954a:206; A1955a:14,17; A1961a:223; A1961h:6; A1967f:1; A1968a:305. Richard I. Evans, *Gordon Allport: The Man and His Ideas*, New York: Dutton, 1970, p. 44.

6. M1959b:viii. See also: M1964b:3,38,82; M1971a:377.

7. M1959a:127; M1959b:245; M1961f:8; M1962b:3–8,74,167,205; M1964b:82,97–102; M1971a:9–10,135–51. R1957d; R1957g; R1964b; R1978b.

8. See Chapter 9, "Human Nature in Humanistic Psychology." M1956d:23. R1955a:248; R1956f; R1961a:391. Evans, *Rogers*, p. 101.

9. M1954a:6–12; M1956d:17–33; M1962b:ch.1,189–214; M1971b:22–32. MY1967b:72.

10. For Goldstein, see Chapter 7, "Other Sources of Influence in Humanistic Psychology."

11. M1954a:107,146–54,183,379.

12. M1948c; M1955a:1–9; M1966b:119–27.

13. M1949b:179; M1955a:1–30; M1961f; M1962b:206; M1971b:32. T. B. Roberts, "Maslow's Motivation Needs Hierarchy: A Bibliography," *Research in Education*, 1972, ED–069–591.

14. R1951a:522; R1961j.

15. R1951a:139,141; R1964b:166.

16. R1943a:285; R1948e; R1950c:236; R1951a:71; R1961a:87.

17. R1947b:113; R1950d; R1951a:75,149,157,530; R1963d; R1972a:208.

18. MY1972a:254; MY1981a:21.

19. MY1956b:357; MY1972a:259; MY1977b:304.

20. MY1969a:265–71; MY1977d.

21. MY1953a:216; MY1977d.

22. MY1975a:12; MY1977b:302; MY1980b:242–48.

23. MY1967a:177.

24. MY1953a:175; MY1967a:ch.5,51.

25. MY1963d:206; MY1967a:80,178,184; MY1980b:246–47; MY1980b:246.

26. A1967a:21.

27. A1950a:65; A1955a:75–78; A1961a:236,303,543; A1967f:3; A1968a:164.

28. A1955a:88–93.

29. E. Spranger, *Types of Men*, trans. P. Pigors, New York: Stechert-Hafner, 1928. A1931a; A1933d; A1961a:296,450,543; A1968a:51. Evans, *Allport*, p. 84.

30. A1931a.

31. A1955a:88–93; A1961a:ch.10; A1968a:167.

32. A1937a:202; A1950a:86; A1967f:4; A1968a:43.

33. A1948b:105; A1955c:199; 1960a:ch.11; A1968a:ch.9. Evans, *Allport*, pp. 66,75.

34. A1960a:220,ch.13.

35. A1950b. Evans, *Allport*, pp. 67–73.

36. MY1953a:47,179; MY1981a:19.

37. R1961a:31,107; R1964b; R1978b. M1954a:291–304,379–90; M1959b:131; M1961a:179; M1971a:51–53,185–87.

38. M1954a:213,224–28,389; M1961c:5; M1962b:176–78; M1971a:186. R1961a; R1964b; R1978b.

39. M1954a:199–234; M1959a:119–36; M1962b:81–84; M1964b:91–96; M1965g:119–21; M1968b:3–5; M1968i:18–24; M1971a:43,122–25,133–35,192–95,299–340; M1971b:32. R1956g; R1957d; R1961a:163–82,183–98; R1963c; R1964b; R1972a:208.

40. R. Bayne, "An Encounter with Carl Rogers and R. D. Laing," *Bull. Brit. Psy. Soc.*, 1979, 32:99–100; M. Friedman, "Comment on the Rogers-May Discussion of Evil," *J. Hum. Psy.*, 1982, 22:93–96. R1948e; R1957d:192; R1961a:163,177,344; R1971c:89; R1982g:87. M1961f:8; M1962b:195; M1962c; M1968f:36; M1968g; M1971a:124.

41. MY1962c; MY1967a:73; MY1969a:268; MY1981a:3,6.

42. MY1953a:162; MY1967a:175.

43. MY1953a:160,188; MY1967a:174; MY1969a:268; MY1977b:298; MY1981a:19.

44. MY1967b:72; MY1972a:253; MY1973e:16.

45. MY1953a:187,206; MY1967a:51,177, MY1968c; MY1974f; MY1977a; MY1980b:244.

10

The Problem of Method in Humanistic Psychology

Although a positivistic methodology permeates most studies of human nature by American psychologists, it would be overly parochial to fail to recognize that in the non-English-speaking world the existential and phenomenological perspective prevails in such studies.

Seen from the perspective of Western civilization, twentieth-century psychology has been dominated by the experimental (or objective) and the experiential (or subjective) methodological paradigms. According to the objective paradigm, human nature is a natural phenomenon to be studied by the methods of the natural sciences. The philosophy of positivism, proposed by Auguste Comte at the beginning of the nineteenth century, was the first clear enunciation of this view in the human sciences. Working from the assumption that physical, biological, human, and social phenomena were equal in nature, he advocated introduction of the positivistic method to the human sciences. Comte's program was taken up a century later by J. B. Watson and his followers, who advocated the exclusive use of observation in the study of behavior. Watson thought that because there was no dividing line between people and animals, both could be studied with equal success under the same experimental conditions. Watson thus proposed a psychology that was a "purely objective experimental branch of natural sciences." Through the work of B. F. Skinner, this approach monopolized American psychology in the mid-decades of the twentieth century.[1]

Early in the twentieth century, the German phenomenologist Edmund Husserl criticized this positivistic attitude, or "psychologism." He thought that because human beings have unique ontological characteristics, students of human nature should not imitate the mechanistic model of the natural sciences but, rather, develop a science that is truthful to the uniqueness of the beings under study.

In 1925, Husserl termed this new science "phenomenological psychology," or the science of inner experience, subjectivity, and the mental.[2]

A decade later, reacting against Husserl's transcendental phenomenology and concept of the ego, Martin Heidegger and Jean-Paul Sartre argued that Husserl had gone too far in the search for transcendental concepts within the subjectivity of human experience, thus betraying his own phenomenological principle. By requesting a return to subjectivity, they created an existential current within phenomenological psychology. Sartre proposed an existential psychoanalysis, and Ludwig Binswanger and Medard Boss, elaborating on Heidegger's concept of Dasein, developed the Daseinsanalysis.[3]

Since Husserl's criticism of psychologism, the ideal of positivism in psychology has been considered philosophically immature by phenomenological and existential psychologists whose studies of consciousness and subjectivity have been viewed by experimental psychologists as poetic pursuits. Proponents of both paradigms accused one another of naively misunderstanding human nature and the epistemology of psychology. Seen from a nonparochial perspective, this is the most dramatic issue in the history of Western psychology. Americans, however, have had the privilege to have the tension between the experimental and experiential paradigms clarified in the work of humanistic psychologists.[4]

Some well-known American psychologists during the "golden age" of behaviorism following World War II, discontented with behaviorism's view of human nature and method, drew upon a long tradition linking psychology with humanities and, in a rebellious manner, institutionally founded humanistic psychology. They regarded themselves as a third force, thereby alluding to the fact that they were an alternative to the dominant behavioristic and psychoanalytical orientation in psychology. More specifically, this chapter examines the work of four prominent founders of humanistic psychology: Gordon Allport, Abraham Maslow, Carl Rogers, and Rollo May. They wrote eloquently on the philosophical tension between the objective and subjective methods of studying human nature. No other American psychologists since William James have personally lived the tension and understood the two paradigms better than they did; indeed, they represent a rare occurrence in the history of Western psychology. A discussion of their views on method is particularly suitable to clarification of the philosophical tension between the experimental and phenomenological paradigms, since they introduced their understanding of phenomenology and existentialism into the positivistic milieu that intellectually nurtured them.[5]

MASLOW'S STUDIES IN COMPARATIVE PSYCHOLOGY

Like Rogers and Allport, Maslow also made his reputation in psychology with quantitative studies, first of infra-human primates and later of New York City college women. Maslow encountered experimental psychology—behaviorism, more specifically—as a philosophy student at Cornell. His dislike of the speculative character of philosophical discourse attracted him to the empirical and physiological nineteenth-century psychology advocated in America by Tichener. The discovery of Watson's behavioristic program, he wrote many years later, produced such "an explosion of excitement" that he went "dancing down Fifth Avenue with exuberance." All you needed, he thought, was to work hard and everything could be changed and reconditioned. The techniques of conditioning promised to solve all psychological and social problems, and its easy-to-understand objective philosophy protected him from repeating the philosophical mistakes of the past. With such ideas in mind, Maslow joined the Department of Psychology at the University of Wisconsin–Madison. Here, in the primate laboratory of Harry Harlow, he was nurtured in the best behavioristic tradition of the 1930s and received a B.A. (1930), M.A. (1931), and Ph.D. (1934) in psychology. Thus, great familiarity with experimental psychology, behaviorism in particular, is evident in his critique of this model of psychological science.[6]

Maslow's research at Madison focused on classical laboratory research with dogs and apes. His M.A. thesis, an experimental study of the effect of varying simple external conditions on learning, initiated him into the science of prediction and control of behavior. His doctoral dissertation explored the role of dominance in the social and sexual behavior of primates; he argued that dominance among primates is established by visual contact rather than by fighting.[7]

Maslow's transition from the study of apes to the study of humans was related to his encounter with Alfred Adler soon after his departure from Madison. Adler read Maslow's dissertation and encouraged Maslow to write a summary for the *Journal of Individual Psychology*. In his essay, Maslow indirectly invited comparisons between the behavior of humans and apes by placing an asterisk next to statements about apes that had a close human parallel. "It remains true," he wrote, "now as always, that in the animal, it seems, we see ourselves writ small and clear." There was hope, he argued, that the study of animals would help understand humans. He thus advocated experimental studies of human subjects employing control groups of apes. The recourse to apes, he argued, simplified the problems and the development of experimental apparatus by giving him definite hints, hypotheses, methods, and objective criteria by which to judge human behavior.[8]

Maslow's research in comparative psychology focused on the relationship between dominance and sexual behavior and their correlation to self-esteem, both from biological and cultural points of view. He concluded that sexual attitudes and behavior were more closely related to personal and social dominance than to sexual drive. The only difference between apes and humans was the extent of internalization of social inhibitions present in humans. In the late 1930s, however, Maslow gradually concentrated on the study of college women. He developed experimental studies and inventories in social personality, measuring the correlation among feelings of security, self-esteem, and social and sexual dominance. Maslow's suspicion that these human conditions relate to mental health developed into a lifelong interest in the study of psychological health. Maslow's last experimental study measured the effects of beauty and ugliness upon people—more specifically, the short-term effects of three visual aesthetic conditions: beautiful, average, and ugly.[9]

MASLOW'S PSYCHOLOGY OF HEALTH AND GROWTH

A year after graduation, Maslow left behind the behavioristic approach of his teachers. In New York City, while teaching at Teachers College, Columbia University and Brooklyn College, Maslow read Sigmund Freud, the Gestalt psychologists, and the embryologist Ludwig von Bertalanffy. He became disillusioned with English philosophy, particularly as represented by Bertrand Russell. During World War II, when exiled German psychologists made New York City an intellectual capital, Maslow associated with Alfred Adler, Max Wertheimer, Erich Fromm, Karen Horney, Kurt Goldstein, and Ruth Benedict. Under their influence he replaced Harlow's primates with New York college women in his experimental studies of dominance and sexual behavior. In the context of this research, Maslow developed the theory of human motivation that made him famous.[10]

When Maslow began studying human subjects, he recognized that psychological research and personality theories relied almost exclusively on subjects who had turned to psychologists for pathological reasons. The view of human nature stemming from the study of the illnesses of these patients was inevitably distorted and pessimistic. "The study of crippled, stunted, immature, and unhealthy specimens," he wrote, "can yield a cripple psychology and a cripple philosophy." Maslow thus criticized orthodox psychologists for formulating their views of human nature primarily on the basis of pathological human subjects.[11]

Physiological and psychological health in these psychological systems is defined as the absence of illness, the relief of symptoms, or the cessation of any particular kind of misery. It meant the transformation of acute misery into normal suffering. Trying to remedy the situation, Maslow selected for study a small sample of the healthiest people he could find, a panel of students representing about one percent of the college population, and he studied them to know what they were like.[12]

Maslow's original criteria for "health" were the absence of neurosis, psychosis, and other symptoms of abnormal personality. In determining these, he employed the traditional personality tests and conducted extensive clinical interviews, looking for evidence of self-actualization such as the full use and exploitation of talents, capacities, potentialities, and the gratification of basic emotional, safety, belonging, and love needs. He wanted to know more about the higher levels of human nature, what qualities and values induce health, and what was the significance of all-too-human qualities such as the poetic, mythic, symbolic, and self-esteem.[13]

Maslow's pioneering study of psychological health posed many problems, and he had to develop new methods, concepts, and attitudes. In the first major work presenting this research, Maslow apologized to those who insisted on conventional reliability, validity, and procedural standards for the methodological short-comings of his research. He described his attempt as a primitive naturalistic and phenomenological pilot study, a private venture motivated by his own curiosity where he sought to learn rather than to prove or demonstrate.[14]

In doing so, Maslow believed that he had initiated a revolution in psychology, creating a new Zeitgeist, or humanistic Weltanschauung, in the human sciences. Colin Wilson concurred with Maslow's estimation of his own work. Wilson placed Maslow among the most original and influential thinkers in post-Freudian psychology.[15]

ALLPORT'S NOMOTHETIC AND MORPHOGENIC STUDIES

Like Maslow, Allport also received formal training in behavioristic psychology. It was, however, the postdoctoral fellowship in Germany that had a significant impact on the development of his own thinking on the nature and study of the uniqueness of personality. His education in Germany helped him to conceptualize a structural view of personality focused on organizational aspects rather than on the study of isolated psychological profiles. In this view, the self acts as a complex patterning agent that organizes stimuli and emits a response that is only indirectly related to the stimuli. The patterning follows the lines of subjective values that provide guidance and direction to life and make a person proactive, purposive, choice-oriented, autonomous, and above all, a unique being. An understanding of such intentional attitudes and motives is a prerequisite for the understanding of human behavior.[16]

Allport addressed the methodological problems of the study of subjective aspects of psychology in the context of what were in his terminology "morphogenic" or "idiographic" studies of the uniqueness of personality. He was critical of experimental psychologists' attempt to imitate the natural sciences and to study the uniform factors all humans share (*Scienta non est individuorum*). They seek "nomothetic" knowledge, or knowledge of the general laws governing human behavior, and in doing so they fail to account for what makes each human being a unique person. They purposely neglect everything that does not fit the method, explaining human nature exclusively on the basis of a single aspect that has been isolated for study. They fail to recognize that even a collection or catalog of all behaviors will fall short in describing human nature because personality is more than the sum of all its parts.[17]

Morphogenic or idiographic methods, on the other hand, seek to understand what makes every one of us a unique being. Allport clarified this distinction between the general and the unique with an example borrowed from biology. While molecular biology teaches that DNA molecules are the common building blocks of life, morphogenic biology teaches that all forms of life are strikingly unique. In biology as in psychology, the study of the unique lags behind the study of the general.[18]

Traditionally, the study of the uniqueness of personality has been the province of the poet. It was time, argued Allport, for psychologists to develop scientific methods appropriate for the study of the uniqueness of personality. Its conclusions should be testable and should have predictive power. Allport's eclectic attitude thus permeates his synthesis of quantitative and qualitative methods. On one occasion he wrote to deplore the "sharp separation of the 'insight of the artist' and the 'measurements of the scientist.' Cannot a psychology of personality in the future do a better job of understanding, prediction, and control by fusing the two modes of knowledge?"[19]

In his own work he aimed to show that personality testing and measurements, although nomothetic in principle, can also be morphogenic tools if they are focused on the unique organization of motives and traits within "the internal coherent system" of personality. When these factors are well known, as for example in clinical practice, they offer much more predictive power than knowledge of statistical frequencies about people. Thus, morphogenic methods should be admitted as valid scientific tools.[20]

Allport thought that we can understand, predict, and control human behavior nomothetically and idiographically. Distinguishing between actuarial and individual predictions, Allport argued that a statement like "72 percent of group A will behave in such a way given a certain stimulus" is an abstract generalization, or actuarial statement, that tells nothing about each individual member of group A. Although such statements are accurate in predicting trends that are often useful for public policy and the insurance industry, they are of little or no value in understanding and predicting the behavior of each person in group A. Knowledge of one's personality, on the other hand, is much more efficient in providing individual predictions. Better predictions ensue when there is knowledge of personal single trends, traits, or imperatives. Carl Rogers made a similar argument in the essay, "The role of self-understanding in the prediction of behavior."[21]

Two views permeate most of Allport's studies of personality: the view that personality is a unit that is more than the sum of its various traits, and the view that traits and personality should be studied nomothetically and idiographically. His earliest works experimentally classified and measured unique personal dispositions or personality traits and ascribed major roles to intuition and empathy in the synthesis of the various traits.[22]

Allport's *Study of Values* was developed out of the conviction that a more holistic logic of personality is a prerequisite to improve the classification, measurement, and testing of personal values. In this test the scores of the relative strength of six personal values interact with each other, giving a profile that is strictly personal and individual.[23]

In *Studies in Expressive Movement*, Allport objectively measured the consistency of expressive movements that were distinctive enough to differentiate one person from the other. He concluded that the unity found in human personality is reflected in the consistency of expressive acts and mannerisms.[24]

In the context of his views on personality and method, Allport evaluated personality from voice, measured morale, and rumors. He also studied love, hate, religious and political attitudes, prejudice, youth's outlook on the future, and personal crisis.

In addition to semi-nomothetic/semi-morphogenic methods, Allport extensively studied personal documents relevant to the understanding of the single life pattern such as letters, life-stories, diaries, and autobiographies. He defined personal documents as "any self-revealing record that intentionally or unintentionally yields information regarding the structure, dynamics, and functioning of the author's mental life." In his usual eclecticism, Allport critically reviewed in the 1960s morphogenic methods he regarded as being part of the emerging third force, or humanistic current, in psychology.[25]

ROGERS'S QUANTITATIVE STUDIES IN PSYCHOTHERAPY

As Rogers began writing on psychotherapy, he acknowledged that psychotherapy combines artistry with science and that experiential, not cognitive, learning is essential in training therapists. However, the proliferation of unchecked theories and techniques created a state of chaos, making psychotherapy a cult of personalities and systems. This situation, he argued, made inevitable the development of fact-finding empirical attitudes, objective measurements, and appraisals of the subjective aspects of psychotherapy. There was a need to clarify the goals of psychotherapy, evaluate outcomes, measure success and failure, validate theoretical assumptions, and determine what is a healing and destructive experience. Adopting Edward L. Thorndike's dictum that "anything that exists, exists in some quantity that can be measured," Rogers argued that if psychotherapeutic skills and the psychological processes they initiated can be observed in practical clinical experience, then experimental conditions can be developed that will measure, prove, disprove, or modify psychotherapeutic hypotheses.[26]

Rogers's raw data in the quantification of psychotherapy were phonographically recorded interviews. He was the first to employ the new audio recording technology in psychological research. His book *Counseling and Psychotherapy* (1942) presented for the first time a complete verbatim account of a successful counseling case study. *The Case Book of Non-Directive Counseling* presented five additional cases. By the early 1950s Rogers had recorded and transcribed eighty more cases. Based on these verbatim case studies, Rogers and his associates measured the changes in personality structure and behavior, the increase in attitudes of acceptance toward oneself and others, and the decrease in psychological tension that occurs in the process of psychotherapy.[27]

Rogers showed that in a field noted more for its art than its science, nondirective psychotherapy provided a simple, clear, and consistent hypothesis of the if-then type of invariance with an operational definition given to experimental testing. If the necessary and sufficient conditions are fulfilled, then there is a predictable chain of events. To be more precise, if the therapist is real and congruent in his relationship with the client and provides unconditional positive regard and empathy for the client's condition, then significant and constructive personality changes will occur. Since all the factors in the equation could be measured, Rogers and his associates at the Ohio State University and at the Counseling Center at the University of Chicago tested out this hypothesis.[28]

Clients at the Counseling Center were given the traditional batteries of personality tests and the Q-sort test before the first interview, two months later at the beginning of therapy, after its completion, and at a follow-up point six months to one year later. The Q-sort test implemented by William Stephenson of the Counseling Center was developed from the Q-technique of Victor Raimy, a close associate of Rogers at Ohio State University. The analysis of self-descriptive statements drawn from recorded interviews led to a sampling of 100 edited, unambiguous statements of ways people perceive themselves that were classified into positive, negative, and ambivalent categories. Printed on cards, the statements were given to the client, who then chose the cards that most accurately described himself or herself and represented the self he or she would like to be—that is, the ideal self.[29]

Administered at different stages in the process of therapy, the client's Q-sort, the traditional personality tests, and the Q-sort analyses performed by independent observers of the patient's self-reference statements showed that there were alterations in the person's concept of self. This confirmed the hypothesis of the client-centered approach: that changes in the picture of oneself—one's "internal frame of reference"—have a profound influence, leading to changes in personality and behavior. Other conclusions that Rogers believed to have experimentally tested were that (1) the perceived self-image of the client changes during therapy, (2) the perceived self is more positively valued after therapy, and (3) the perceived self is more congruent with the ideal self following therapy. After a successful therapy, self-confidence, self-reliance, self-understanding, and more satisfying relationships with others increase; feelings of guiltiness, resentfulness, and insecurity decrease.[30]

ROGERS ON SUBJECTIVE KNOWLEDGE

Maslow came to the study of the subjective aspect of psychology through his interest in psychological health, and Allport came to it through his study of the uniqueness of personality. Rogers, on the other hand, began studying the subjective aspects of psychotherapy primarily as a result of his discovery in the late 1950s of the writings of existentialists Soren Kierkegaard and Martin Buber.[31]

While he was in Chicago, Rogers read the writings of Buber and Kierkegaard. He did this because his thinking was becoming increasingly divided between the tenets of logical positivism and subjectivism, and because some theology students taking his classes insisted that he explore the two existentialists. The reading had a "loosening up" effect upon Rogers, encouraging him to trust and write about his own subjective experiences in the practice of psychotherapy. He thought that their insights and convictions expressed views he had held but was unable to formulate.[32]

One of these insights was Kierkegaard's statement that the aim of life is "to be that self which one truly is." Rogers interpreted the passage to mean that the most common despair results not from being responsible for becoming what one truly is, but from desiring to be something else. This idea had been a cornerstone of Rogers's thought on the self and person-centered psychotherapy. Rogers agreed with Kierkegaard that the goal of life was to move away from "oughts" and facades. In therapy, argued Rogers, when the person becomes what he or she is inwardly, he or she is able to hear the inner messages and meanings of the self. When this happens, a deep desire follows to be fully oneself in all one's complexity and richness, withholding and fearing nothing that is part of the inner self. Self-experience becomes a friendly resource, not a frightening enemy.[33]

The theology students at Chicago also introduced Rogers to the philosophy of the Hasidic philosopher Martin Buber. Rogers thought that in addition to unconditional positive regard and the immediacy and realness of the therapist, it was crucial that there be a deep sense of communication and unity between therapist and client. Psychotherapy was in this sense a genuine person-to-person experience, and this was exactly what Buber had described in the I-thou relationship. Buber thought that the deep mutual experience of speaking truly to one another without playing a "role"—the meeting between two persons at a deep and significant level—had a healing effect. Buber named this process "healing through meeting."[34]

Describing the essence of therapy in terms of his personal experience, Rogers explained that when he entered the therapeutic relationship he made a sincere attempt to understand and unconditionally accept the inner world of the other, hoping that doing so would lead to a significant personality change followed by a more authentic and satisfying process of becoming in the client. People come to therapy because they have grown alienated from their true selves and have lost contact with their organismic wisdom. The therapist's unconditional acceptance and interest in the inner self of the client invites him or her to follow the therapist's steps. In this process there is unity of experiencing, a trancelike situation in which both therapist and client slip together into a stream of subjective authentic becoming—a real I-thou relationship, as Buber had described.[35]

It is easy for the therapist to engage in this process because he has lived the experience many times, but as the client begins to recognize its healing effect he or she follows the role model of the therapist and learns to explore the healing potential of the intimate encounter. Once people learn to dip into their subjectivity and the intimacy of the therapeutic encounter, there is a gradual growth of trust and even affection for the awareness of their organismic wisdom. This is a sort of learning or process of self-discovery that cannot be taught; it can only be experienced subjectively. Even when learned, it cannot be symbolized or intellectually recreated. It has value and immediacy only when experienced. Once experienced it also has a significant life-lasting effect.[36]

ROGERS'S THREE MODES OF KNOWING

At first, Rogers understood that experimental and experiential are two legitimate approaches to the study of psychotherapy, each holding significant truths, but nonetheless antagonistic and irreconcilable points of view. He wrote about this conflict as a growing puzzlement "between the logical empiricism in which I was educated, for which I had a deep respect, and the subjectively oriented existential thinking which was taking root in me because it seemed to fit so well with my therapeutic experiences."[37]

By the mid–1960s, however, Rogers solved this conflict within himself. He proposed a humanistic psychology, integrating the objective and subjective modes of knowing with a third mode, the intersubjective or phenomenological. Rogers sought a nonmechanistic model of science developed from an existential orientation that preserved the values of logical positivism and placed human subjectivity at the heart of the system. He argued from the outset that there were three modes of knowing; the subjective or experiential, the objective or experimental, and a synthesis of the two, which he named interpersonal or phenomenological knowing.[38]

Subjective knowledge ensues from experience and the internal frame of reference of the person. Love, hate, joy, and similar subjective judgments are personal inner hypotheses that have meaning only in relation to our internal frame of reference. The sharper, more precise, differentiated, and accurate we are in relation to our inner and outer realities, the more correct our subjective hypotheses are. In psychotherapy, for example, one often searches for words and hypotheses that most accurately describe inner experiences, feelings, and ways of being. There is often a great sense of relief when specific knowledge of the inner self replaces vague knowing. In psychotherapy one often contradicts previously held hypotheses because of the increase in self-knowledge. The criteria are the internal frame of reference of the person and his or her stream of experiencing the world.[39]

Although it is fundamental in everyday living, subjective knowledge is just that, subjective. It has little or no significance except for the person, and for this reason modern psychological science has had little regard for it. However, when we test our inner hypotheses with other people or in modes of objective assessment, then, argued Rogers, we seek intersubjective verification and are in the domain of objective knowing.[40]

Objective knowledge relies upon an external frame of reference—observable events and operations. When independent observers who speak the same language and share similar values and contextual framework collect, examine, and test data, they arrive at similar conclusions and assume that such knowledge is independent of the observer and is objective. This method, according to Rogers, is restricted only to observable facts. It also transforms whatever it studies into objects to be manipulated and dissected.[41]

Interpersonal or phenomenological knowledge, Rogers's third mode of knowing, is a synthesis of the objective and subjective methods. In this mode of knowledge, there is an attempt to objectively know by available means the subjective hypotheses of the phenomenological frame of reference of a person. The goal is to penetrate the private world of the person and see if the therapist's hypotheses about the client—and the client's own hypotheses—are valid in relation to his or her internal frame of reference. The simpler, but not always accurate, way is to ask the person specific questions or to observe his or her behavior. In the case of client-centered therapy, the counselor creates a psychological climate that is safe and rewarding for the person to reveal the internal frame of reference so the therapist and the client's own hypotheses may be validated against it.[42]

Roger argued that people and scientists do not use one mode exclusively. We all trust to some extent our experience and intuition about people. Most of us also test our subjective knowledge with those or about those we care in empathic and phenomenological ways. Some of us even put our hypotheses to the most severe tests and remain open to either confirmation or denial of our tentative hypotheses.[43]

Gordon Allport was well aware of Rogers's personal dilemma over the nature of psychology and its proper methods; he totally agreed with Rogers's suggestion for a syncretism of phenomenological and experimental methods. Abraham Maslow had similar thoughts on the problem of method in psychology. He described Rogers's phenomenological process of knowing as "taoistic science."[44]

MASLOW'S TAOISTIC METHOD IN PSYCHOLOGY

In *The Psychology of Science* (1966), originally an invitational lecture of the John Dewey Society, Maslow elaborated on the philosophy of psychology first stated in *Motivation and Personality* (1954). The chapter "Taoistic Science" presented original thoughts on phenomenology and the problem of method in psychology. He described taoistic knowledge as an approach to learning that is meant to complement Western science. He argued that the organization, classification, and conceptualization methods of Western science removed our perception of reality to an abstract realm invented by the mind. This negative aspect should be balanced against taoistic non-intruding receptivity and contemplation of experience, or "getting back to things themselves," as Husserl had argued. He referred to this type of knowledge as "taoistic objectivity" as opposed to "classical objectivity."

Maslow had no doubts that the psychologists' attempt to imitate outdated models of the physical sciences had only depersonalized psychology and made it atomistic and mechanistic. A science of human nature where the observer is also the observed has to be a unique science. Recognizing that the empiricism of logical positivism and the private subjective world of existential mysticism should be balanced, Maslow proposed a philosophy of psychology that synthesized both methods. Like Rogers, he also termed the new endeavor humanistic psychology.[45]

Maslow argued that every knowledge is a product of experiencing. At some point in the process of experiencing, one senses the emergence of a pattern, rhythm, or relationship. "Some things just come to mind," wrote Maslow. He learned that when the organism operates freely and nondefensively it is able to sense a pattern even before it can consciously formulate it. But this sensing is not enough. By itself it is as unacceptable as the rigidity of a behavioral psychologist. The subjective hypothesis ought to be put, first, to a rough and then to a rigorous testing that will confirm, modify, or disconfirm the hypothesis. Arguing that there is no special virtue in any particular testing procedure, he thought that the method of testing should be appropriate to the nature of the hypothesis. The statistical method, for example, should not be used to test subjective phenomena.[46]

Maslow's discussion of taoistic science pointed out the significance of phenomenological knowledge. All knowledge pertaining to human life must first be known by direct and intimate experience. There is no substitute for experience. Conceptual, theoretical knowledge is useful only when people already know experientially. Words fail when there is no experience and are good when people share similar experiences.[47]

These first efforts in psychological research are inelegant, imprecise, and crude. They require honest and authentic knowing, surrender, identification, and unselfish fusion with the object under study. They require the researcher to observe, listen, and absorb—wholly, passively, and receptively—without presupposing, classifying, improving, evaluating, or approving. They assume fearless respect for the object as it is and suspension of judgment. Psychologists should relax, let go, melt away with the object of study; they should experience it receptively, taoistically, and contemplatively, not intruding or interfering with the order of things.

Maslow described this first stage as "taoistic nonintruding receptivity to the experience"; it is an attitude rather than a technique. At this level of study experience just happens as it is, not according to the psychologists' expectations of control and prediction. However, as researchers begin to organize, classify, and abstract their phenomenological accounts of the object under study, they move away from reality as it is and document it as their own hypothetical constructions determine their perception of experience.[48]

ALLPORT'S SYSTEMATIC ECLECTICISM

Although not explicitly stated, the proposals of Rogers and Maslow for a humanistic methodology in psychology were eclectic in nature. In the case of Allport, however, he deliberately sought to synthesize the bits and pieces of truth he found in the history and systems of psychology. Human personality and behavior have many causes acting separately and conjointly, and each current of psychology chooses to focus exclusively on any one particular aspect. The goal of the third force psychology, as Allport understood it, was to integrate the partial truths of each system under a systematic eclecticism.

Whether consciously stated or not, each system in psychology has a particular view of human nature that organizes the collection of data and legitimates its methodology. For example, the views of behaviorism and psychoanalysis on human nature as a response to stimulus or as a product of unconscious forces, respectively, dictate the methodology that both disciplines follow to articulate their theories. In this sense all psychological theories are skilled and famous for the elegance and sophistication of their self-validating methods. They focus exclusively on one or a few selected aspects of human nature, pressing forward their investigation only in that direction. Each system is thus meritorious in its own terms because it describes restricted truths about human nature. These systems are pragmatic and rational because their validating logic is derived from the logical consistency of the internal structure of their arguments. For this reason, argued Allport, they are closed, reductionistic, nontheoretical, and anti-eclectic systems. A closed system accepts neither facts nor internal logic, nor is it given to evaluation on the bases of the criteria set by another system. Advocates of each system authoritatively avoid or deny what they deliberately have chosen to neglect in their views of human nature. The opposite of a closed system is a random collection of all knowledge about human nature, an open-ended eclecticism.[49]

"Systematic eclecticism," on the other hand, argued Allport, avoids the pitfalls of open-ended eclecticism and closed systems. Systematic eclecticism seeks to solve fundamental problems in psychology by selecting and binding together what it regards as meaningful in all specialized psychological particularism. It aims to attain a comprehensive metatheory of human nature that will accommodate all valid partial data: subjective and objective, conscious and unconscious, mechanistic and holistic, social and personal. It excludes no valid inference about human nature for as long as the inference relates to concrete human experience.[50]

Systematic eclecticism, argued Allport, has the pluralistic characteristic of an open system of personality. By admitting all closed systems, it provides an inclusive variety of views of human nature. "We shall have defined our subject matter in such a way," wrote Allport, "that any and all valid data and all verified processes can be woven into our central conception of man as an open system."[51]

Unlike open-ended eclecticism, however, Allport's proposal was systematic because it posed some basic prerequisites for the assimilation of knowledge about human nature. While in closed systems every knowledge relates to the internal theoretical framework of the system (or particular view of human nature), in the case of systematic eclecticism knowledge has ultimately to be truthful to the human condition. Like existentialism, systematic eclecticism rejects nothing that is true about human nature, and it studies the person in relation to his or her outer environment (*Umwelt*), other persons (*Mitwelt*), and his or her own self

(*Eigenwelt*). Both existentialism and systematic eclecticism refuse to relate the study of people to nonhuman models, such as the animal or the mechanical. Only the totality of human existence serves as the unifying point of reference, center of gravity, or rationality for the admission of knowledge.[52]

Allport illustrated how the variety of psychological systems could be integrated in a systematic eclecticism in the discussion of the book *Letters from Jenny* (1965). He analyzed Jenny from the point of view of Jungian, Adlerian, Freudian, dynamic, and ego-psychologies, in the perspective of the humanist and the existentialist, arguing that the true understanding of Jenny was a synthesis of the partial truths stated by each system. In a restricted sense they were all true because they ultimately referred to some human aspect of Jenny.[53]

TOWARD A MORE HUMANISTIC PSYCHOLOGY

Allport, Rogers, and Maslow had no doubt that the attempt of the experimental psychologists—behaviorists in particular—to imitate what they thought were outdated models of the physical sciences had only made psychology mechanistic and depersonalized. A science of human nature where the observer is also the observed had to be a unique science. Thus, recognizing that the empiricism of positivistic psychology and the private subjective world of existential mysticism had to be balanced, Allport, Rogers, and Maslow developed a philosophy and methodology of science that combined quantitative and phenomenological methods and recognized the centrality of human subjectivity. Indeed, this was a rare if not unique occurrence in the history and systems of psychology. They termed the new endeavor humanistic psychology, which was first coined by Allport in 1930.[54]

Specifically addressing the behavioristic psychology in vogue at the time, Allport, Rogers, and Maslow argued that exclusive focus on external behavior, disregard for the rich world of personal meanings, and avoidance of human subjectivity places a human being in the same line of ontological existence as rats and pigeons. The whole range of human experience and the subjective world of the person, they argued, should be taken into consideration. In doing so, they were confident that humanistic psychology would invigorate the field of psychology by broadening its restrictive scope into the study of control and prediction of behavior. Allport, Rogers, and Maslow believed they were laying the seeds of a newer philosophy of psychology that was not fearful of studying the person, who happens to be both the observer and the observed, in his or her subjective and objective existence. Utilizing "all" channels of knowing, humanistic psychology would open psychology to "all" significant human problems.[55]

In their proposal for a humanistic psychology, Allport, Maslow, and Rogers argued as much as the Continental phenomenologists and existentialists did that psychological research should begin with a "getting back to the things themselves." Study of human nature should begin with phenomenological knowledge and only then should be submitted to objective, experimental, and behavioral laboratory methods of study. In Allport's words,

The only reasonable thing to do if one wishes to study a phenomenon is to put a specimen before one's eyes and look at it repeatedly until its essential features sink indelibly into one's mind. Later, dissection and ablation may be used to gain acquaintance with details. But unless the fundamental interrelations are first grasped, analysis is likely to be aimless.[56]

Rogers advanced a similar argument when he proposed that all knowledge is a product of experiencing, thus rewriting the Cartesian dictum as "I experience–therefore I exist." "All knowledge, including all scientific knowledge," he wrote, "is a vast inverted pyramid resting on this tiny, personal, subjective base." When one studies human nature, one should trust one's intuition and be guided by the experiences that subjectively move us to question, be perplexed, and study that particular phenomenon. One should, therefore, first and foremost immerse and experience from within the particular human phenomenon one is studying. One should be open to all subtleties of experience, tolerate ambiguity and contradiction, be personally involved, and truly "indwell" in the feelings, attitudes, and perceptions of the people under study. In Rogers's words, "it means soaking up experience like a sponge so that it is taken in all its complexity, with my total organism freely participating in the experiencing of the phenomena, not simply my conscious mind." Maslow termed this attitude "taoistic receptivity," and Allport, the "idiographic method."[57]

At some point in the process of "soaking up experience," "taoistic receptivity," or "intuition," Allport, Maslow, and Rogers similarly argued that one senses the emergence of a pattern, rhythm, or relationship: "Some things just come to mind." They were confident that when one operates freely and non-defensively one is able to sense a pattern even before one can consciously formulate it. Intuition alone, however, is as unacceptable as the rigidity of behavioral studies. Personal insights must be submitted to the rigors of the experimental method which should help to sharpen the final formulation of our knowledge.[58]

Allport, Maslow, and Rogers never totally denied the value of quantitative methods in the human sciences. The experiential and experimental modes of knowing, they argued, are not dichotomously antagonist; it is not the case of experience versus abstracting, cautious versus bold knowledge. Both forms complement each other. Abstract knowledge dichotomized from experiential knowledge is dangerous and false. It should be hierarchically integrated with a contextual base of experiential knowledge. Without foundations in concrete living experience, abstract knowledge becomes functionally autonomous and divorced from the empirical foundations or the experience it attempts to explain and organize.[59]

Allport, Maslow, and Rogers advocated the hierarchical integration of phenomenological and experimental methods in order to enlarge, not replace, either method. Experiential knowledge occurs prior to conceptual knowledge, but in itself it is as useless as an isolated objective knowledge. Employing Buberian terminology, Maslow and Rogers argued that the study of human nature should begin with "I-thou" experiential or subjective knowledge, and only then through ordering and systematization should this knowledge be translated into spectator "I-it" knowledge—a verifiable, more reliable level of knowledge. In Maslow's words,

It [science] need not abdicate from the problems of love, creativeness, value, beauty, imagination, ethics and joy, leaving these altogether to "non-scientists," to poets, prophets, priests, dramatists, artists, or diplomats. All of these people may have wonderful insights, ask the questions that need to be asked, put forth challenging hypotheses, and may even be correct and true much of the time. But however sure they may be, they can never make man-kind sure. They can convince only those who already agree with them, and a few more. Science is the only way we have of shoving truth down the reluctant throat. Only science can overcome characterological differences in seeing and believing. Only science can progress.[60]

From this perspective, they argued, knowledge of human phenomena occurs in stages or levels. Starting with simpler, tentative, and exploratory boldness, the psychologist moves up to careful technical work and refinement of statement. The experimental method is definitely not the beginning but the end of the process of knowledge acquisition. The controlled, predesigned crucial experiment is the last or highest step in this progressive accumulation of knowledge, not the beginning. In doing so, Allport, Rogers, and Maslow argued that humanistic psychologists will make the study of human nature a more inclusive science, encompassing positivistic and phenomenological psychologies.[61]

Not all humanistic psychologists, however, were as accommodating and eclectic as Allport, Maslow, and Rogers. Seeking instead philosophical legitimization in Continental existentialism and phenomenology, members of the existential current within humanistic psychology denied the positivistic method in the human sciences any significant value. Rollo May was the most outspoken member of this group.

ROLLO MAY AND EXISTENTIALISM IN AMERICA

Allport, Rogers, Maslow, and May agreed that existentialism had a significant influence on the formulation of their views in psychology. Humanistic psychology, however, was not an import of the Continental tradition. When humanistic psychologists discovered existentialism in the late 1950s, they already had formulated most of their original ideas. It was only in the mid–1960s that this homegrown existentialism was termed humanistic psychology. The idea of philosophical parallelism is thus historically more accurate than the root analogy.[62]

Existence: A New Dimension in Psychiatry and Psychology, edited in 1958

by Rollo May, Ernest Angel, and Henri F. Ellenberger, was the milestone of the introduction of existential psychiatry and psychology to the United States. *Existence* presented American readers for the first time with translations of the writings of leading European phenomenological and existential psychologists. May wrote two epoch-making introductory chapters, which were no less influential than the rest of the volume. Thereafter, May was viewed as the spokesman for the existential approach in American psychology.[63]

Following the publication of *Existence*, May was active in the growing existential movement in American psychology. In 1958 and 1959, he organized two symposia on existential psychology, one at the recently formed American Academy of Psychotherapists and the other at the APA meeting in Cincinnati. The Cincinnati symposium attracted a great deal of interest. May, Maslow, and Rogers presented papers, and Allport wrote a "comment on earlier chapters" for the book *Existential Psychology*, edited by May, which published the symposium papers. The symposia and the volume cemented the identification of May, Rogers, Maslow, and Allport with an American brand of existential psychology.[64]

Rollo May accepted the claim of most existentialists that an understanding of human nature should rely on the immediate experience of the individual. Like the existentialists, May argued that one ought to understand the individual as he or she truly is, rather than as filtered through one's theories. Like them he also studied the central role of freedom, choice, decision, and responsibility in human existence, arguing that these themes should be at the center of psychology.[65]

Nonetheless, May was critical of some trends in existentialism. More specifically, he was critical of Sartre's statement that "freedom is existence, and in it existence precedes essence." May agreed with Sartre that "man is his project." It is commitment and determination, will and responsibility that make oneself. But he also thought that Sartre had gone too far in assuming that a person is a "non-substantial absolute" or "nothingness." May pointed out that one's power to create oneself is already a human essence. Moreover, there is no freedom without some structure in which one acts; freedom necessarily implies some kind of structure. He was also critical of what he considered to be the undesirable anti-scientific and anti-genetic dimensions in existentialism. Like Allport, Maslow, and Rogers, May was as critical of despairing nihilism (Nietzsche), nothingness (Sartre), and absurdism (Camus) as he was of behaviorism's S-R philosophy and the psychic determinism of psychoanalysis. Thus, he was closer to the Kierkegaardian, Buberian, and Tillichian theological brand of existentialism.[66]

In his doctoral dissertation May explained that the experience of anxiety relates to the development of the self, thereby linking two major themes in the literature of existentialism. This idea also ran through most of May's writings. Viewing anxiety initially from the perspective of the individual, he discussed anxiety in relation to the human predicament, love, power, and aggression. In various forms he described modern people living in an age of anxiety and loneliness caused by the dichotomy between reason and emotion, isolation from the community, and the tragic loss of a center of values. But it is also exactly this predicament that sets us in search of ourselves. He thought that personal integration in a disintegrated world was possible only if we find a center of strength within ourselves. All of May's major writings clarified the dilemmas of the human predicament in an age of anxiety. He persistently alerted his generation to the dangerous shaping of human nature upon the image of the machine and the resulting increased feeling of hopelessness and loss of a sense of significance.[67]

MAY'S CRITIQUE OF POSITIVISM IN PSYCHOLOGY

People turn to psychology, wrote May, seeking to clarify their most oppressing problems of love, hope, despair, and anxiety related to the meaning of their lives. However, psychologists systematically avoid confronting these human dilemmas. They explain love as sexual urges, turn anxiety into physical stress, rule out hope as illusion, explain despair as depression, trivialize human passion into satisfaction of needs, and make relaxation the release of tension. When, in total despair, people courageously and passionately act on their destiny, psychologists call it nothing but a response to a stimulus. Modern psychology, argued May, not only suppressed but also trivialized the essential aspects of human experience. Under the gospel of technique, psychologists avoid confrontation with the real and most essential aspects of being human, which are somehow lost in the reductionistic tendencies of objective test measurements. What does not fit the technique is automatically discarded. Because psychologists focus on the study of things that happen to the person, the person to whom the things happen is lost in the process.[68]

May traced the obsessive concern of modern psychology with method to the Cartesian split between object and subject, which culminated in the theory of modern man's mastery over nature. The mechanical psychology and mathematical method were relatively successful in the study of the physical world. Mind and subjectivity, however, were left out, because they could not be submitted to the rigors of the newly found method. As a result, today we know a lot about people as biological entities but very little about what it means to be a human being. May pointed out that there was not only a radical split between the person as object and subject, but also an almost total concentration on the biological side and an avoidance of spiritual aspects. The "I" became an "It." If psychology cannot deal with the whole range of human experience and dilemmas, argued May, then perhaps the notion of psychology as a science was one big mistake.[69]

The obsessive concern of modern psychology with manipulation and prediction of behavior was, according to May, also a form of puritanism inherited from Victorian moralism. The emphases on pragmatic rationalism and practical controls are defense mechanisms against the subjective and irrational human elements that modern psychologists and the Victorians were so afraid to confront. In both cases, the worship of technique reflects a need for intellectual security, reliability, and belief that manipulation either destroys or subdues the human uncertainties. The control and prediction of the S-R formula fulfilled the undeclared war upon the self of the Victorian ideal of "conquering ourselves."[70]

The human condition of freedom, argued May, implies responsibility for and commitment to one's attitudes, values, and beliefs. Often this responsibility leads to anxiety, which in turn forces us to abdicate freedom and responsibility to the control of someone, the state or science. Psychologists and their patients, he thought, turn to behavioral therapy to escape this anxiety and feeling of helplessness. Skinner's behavioristic utopia of *Walden Two* had its strongest appeal to those who hoped for a scientific substitute for personal values, choices, and commitment.[71]

May severely criticized the notion that scientific research is objective because it is open to study the data as they truly are and it assumes no presuppositions. Rather, he was convinced that every approach in science—psychology in particular—assumes presuppositions that are prior and that transcend research. Such presuppositions determine and select the data to be studied, and where and how to be studied, thereby dictating the findings. If some sort of objectivity is sought, there is no escape from the need to clarify our presuppositions or biases. In the case of psychology, the crucial presupposition is the model or conception of human nature held by the psychologist.[72]

MAY'S PHENOMENOLOGICAL METHOD

In his proposal for a humanistic psychology May argued that psychologists should clarify and give up all pretenses for the manipulation and prediction of behavior. They should not avoid human subjectivity and dilemmas merely because they do not have an animal counterpart or do not fit their models. A science that avoids the problems that do not fit its methods is a defensive science. Any psychological study of human nature must focus on the whole person, not animals, machines, reduced and isolated behaviors, or diagnostic categories with no center whatsoever. A science of human nature, he argued, ought to follow a human model and study the unique features of human beings ("the ontological characteristics of human existence")—for example, their capacity to relate to themselves as subjects and objects, their potential for freedom and ethical action, their ability to create symbols, reason, and participate in the historical development of their communities.[73]

Psychology, according to May, should adopt the phenomenological approach and study the person as given. It should study people as they really are, not as projections of our own theories about human nature. Phenomenological knowledge of the person ought to precede methodological and theoretical presuppositions. In this context May distinguished between "describing what" and "explaining why." Psychologists should describe rather than explain. Causological explanations of the origins or causes of any particular event fail to describe what the event is. To explain how a thing, anxiety for example, came to be does not say what anxiety is as experienced by the person. Psychology should study the phenomenology of human conditions rather than seek causological explanations.[74]

Psychology should cut through the split between object and subject. As objects people understand themselves following the expectations and customs imposed by their immediate human environment. As subjects, however, people act according to their values, feelings, and wishes. They are, in other words, proactive. The human dilemma arises, argued May, out of the capacity to experience oneself simultaneously as subject and as object, and psychologists should focus their studies on this condition. Students of human nature should also assume from the very beginning that people are centered in themselves and need to preserve their centeredness by self-affirmation no matter how distorted that center is in conflict and illness.[75]

Students of human nature should take into consideration the historical dimension of the culture in which people live. They should study myths, symbols, and literature—classical literature in particular. According to May, because literature is the self-interpretation of humans throughout history, it expresses the perdurable crosscultural and historical essences of human experience.[76]

In summary, May thought that psychology has more affinity with the humanities than with the physical and biological sciences. However, most psychologists of his time—behaviorists in particular—regarded May's psychology and the existential wing within humanistic psychology that he represented as poetic or philosophical psychology.

CONCLUSION

Although Allport, Maslow, and Rogers were well versed in experimental psychology, as soon as they began exploring the subjective aspects of human psychology they recognized the restrictive nature of behavioral studies and the experimental method. Their suggestion to integrate positivistic psychology with their understanding of phenomenology and existentialism ostracized them, primarily Maslow and Rogers, from mainstream American psychology. Their proposal did not fare any better with the phenomenologists. Their suggestion to submit the phenomena of subjectivity to objective, quantitative, experimental, and behavioral scrutiny (in the cases of Rogers and Maslow) and synthesis in a systematic eclecticism (in the case of Allport) was equally anathema in phenomenological and existential circles. Totally in the context of the humanistic current in psychology, Rollo May, on the other hand, departed from his colleagues, possibly because of his affinity with Continental existentialism and phenomenology. He thought that although the positivistic method had a major role in explaining the biological aspect of the human organism, it had little or no significance in understanding the ontological characteristics of human existence.

In an age when most American psychologists understood human nature as a mere response to stimulus, worshipped experimentalism, and studied psychologically maladjusted persons, Allport, Maslow, Rogers, and May advocated a humanistic psychology that studied the subjective aspects of becoming a person, sought to improve human nature and society, and trusted and placed the uniqueness of each person at the core of its concerns. With the partial exception of May, their critique of experimental psychology (behaviorism in particular), views on the proper method of psychology, and proposal for the humanistic psychology they helped to establish in the 1960s constituted a rare if not unique clarification and syncretism of the experimental and phenomenological paradigms in the history and systems of psychology. The views of Allport, Maslow, Rogers, and May on the proper methods of psychology and of understanding human nature were an original American expression of existentialism and phenomenology— or, as they are best known in the history and systems of psychology, their views were major pillars of the humanistic current in psychology.

NOTES

1. D. Polkinghorne, *Methodology for Human Sciences*, Albany: State University of New York, 1983; J. B. Watson, "Psychology as the Behaviorist Views It," *Psy. Rev.*, 1913, 20:158–77.

2. E. Husserl, *Phenomenological Psychology*, trans. J. Scanlon, The Hague: Nijhoff, 1977 (original work published in 1925).

3. E. Craig, "Psychotherapy for Freedom," *The Humanistic Psychologist*," 1988(16) (special issue).

4. T. W. Wann, *Behaviorism and Phenomenology*, Chicago: Jeremy Tarcher, 1964.

5. DeCarvalho's "Carl Rogers' Naturalistic System of Ethics," *Psy. Rep.*, 1989, 65:1155–62; "A History of the 'Third Force' in Psychology," *J. Hum. Psy.*, 1990, 30:22–44; "Abraham H. Maslow (1908–1970): An Intellectual Biography," *Thought Quart. Rev.*, 1991, 66:32–50; "The Ethics of the Growth Hypothesis of Abraham Maslow and Carl Rogers," *J. Ethical Stud.*, 1991, 16:3–17; "The Growth Hypothesis and Self-Actualization," *The Humanistic Psychologist*, 1990, 18:252–58.

6. See Chapter 4, "Humanistic Psychology and Behaviorism." W. Frick, *Humanistic Psychology*, Columbus, Ohio: Merrill, 1971, p. 19. M1968f:37,55; M1966b:7.

7. M1931a.

8. M1935b. See also: M1936a:336; M1935b:47; M1937a:487–89.

9. M1956a:247; M1942e; M1954a:61. R. Lowry, *Dominance, Self-Esteem, Self-Actualization*, Monterey, Calif.: Brooks/Cole, 1973.

10. M1954a:ix. R. J. DeCarvalho, "Abraham H. Maslow," in E. Hoffman, ed., *The Right to be Human*, Los Angeles: Jeremy Tarcher, 1988.

11. M1954a:234,353–63.

12. M1959b; M1954a:199–234; M1961c:3.

13. M1954a:199–234; M1956b; M1962b:189.

14. M1954a:ch.12.

15. M1961f; M1962b:i–v; M1970a:x–xii; M1971a:4. C. Wilson, *New Pathways in Psychology*, London: Gollancz, 1972.

16. A1930c; A1947e; A1948b:81.

17. A1942a:56, 146; A1962a; A1965a:158.

18. A1962a Richard I. Evans, *Gordon Allport: The Man and His Ideas*, New York: Dutton, 1970, p. 99.

19. A1946e:67; A1950a:198–209; A1961a:389.

20. A1924a; A1961a:x.

21. R1948e. A1940b; A1942a:149; A1946a; A1940a.

22. A1921a; A1921b; A1924a; A1929a; A1930a.

23. A1931a. Evans, *Allport*, p. 80.

24. A1933a:171.

25. A1942a:xii; compare A1968a:171; A1954d; A1964c; A1942a:60–64.

26. R1948c:99; R1957e; R1946c:588; R1963e:9,15; R1954e:13.

27. W. U. Snyder, ed., *Case Book of Non-Directive Counseling*, Boston: Houghton Mifflin, 1947. R1951a:13; compare R1954e:27; R1951b:20.

28. R1942e; R1946c; R1949b:150; R1957a:100; R1951b:12; R1961a:225–42.

29. R1954e:413–34; compare R1946c:583; R1977k:137. W. Stephenson, *The Study of Behavior*, Chicago: University of Chicago Press, 1953; Victor Raimy, *The Self-Concept as a Factor in Counseling and Personality Organization*, unpublished doctoral dissertation, Ohio State University, 1943.

30. R1954e:55,350,429; R1959h; R1952a; R1953b.

31. R1967a.

32. R1961a:200; R1952c:342.

33. R1961a:163.

34. R1960a.

35. R1960a; R1963b:73; R1961a:66.

36. R1955c:290.

37. R1961a:199; compare R1959g:100.

38. R1955c; R1959h:251.

39. R1955c; R1965j.

40. R1955c.

41. R1963g:75.

42. R1955c; R1963g:77; R1965j.

43. R1965j.

44. A1957a:20.

45. M1956d.

46. M1961f:1.

47. M1966b:ch.10.

48. M1966b:100.

49. A1962a; A1962b; A1964b; A1964c.

50. A1964b; A1967f; A1968a:116. Evans, *Allport*, pp. 19,54.

51. A1968a:117; compare A1960f.

52. A1962a; A1964b; A1964c; A1967f.

53. A1965a:211.

54. A1930a:127. R1955a:299; R1967b:22; R1971c:107; R1974b; R1985b. M1942e:260; M1961f; M1966b:ch.10; M1971a:16–19. R1968f:154. A1946e:66; A1950a:198.

55. R1963g:81,90; R1966b; R1965g:2. M1946b; M1961c:13; M1966d:107.

A1943g:452; A1947e. Richard I. Evans, *Carl Rogers: The Man and His Ideas*, New York: Dutton, 1975, pp. 147–76.

56. A1942a:143.

57. R1965j:186. A1950a:198.

58. R1965j:187; compare R1968f:ch.4. M1961f:1. A1929a; A1930a:127; A1933b:264; A1942a:143.

59. M1945a; M1945c; M1970:ix. A1933b:263; A1961h.

60. M1962b:viii. A1931a; A1964e:67. Evans, *Allport*, p. 44. M1960b; M1966b:ch.11. R1960a.

61. M1966b:107,ch.10; M1970a:16–19. R1961a:ch.21; R1965g. A1962b; A1964b; A1964c; A1933a; A1961h:11.

62. A1955a:81; A1957a:11; A1962c:373; A1964c:135; A1965a:174. R1954c; R1960c:96; R1961a:200; R1967a:378; R1974i:11. M1959e:20; M1960b:59; M1962b:ix,xi,174; M1965g:127; M1966b:52,102. MY1958c; MY1958b; MY1967a:ch.8; M1959e:87; MY1967g:25; MY1968f:191; MY1963b:75.

63. MY1958a; MY1958b; MY1958c.

64. See Chapter 6, "Humanistic Psychology, Existentialism, and Phenomenology." MY1960a.

65. DeCarvalho, "A History of the 'Third Force'."

66. A1955a:81; A1957a:11; A1962c:73; A1964e:135; A1965a:174, A1967f:1. M1962a:190; M1962b:167,174; M1964b:xvi; M1970a:xvii; M1971a:186,315,349. R1971cc:87; R1973b:45; R1979a. MY1958b:11; MY1953a:165; MY1953c; MY1961e:34; MY1962e; MY1967a:135; MY1968f:212; MY1969a:157. Evans, *Allport*, p. 55; Frick, *Humanistic Psychology*, p. 22.

67. MY1950a; MY1953a; MY1967a; MY1969a; MY1972a.

68. MY1967a:ch.1; MY1969:18.

69. MY1967a:64; MY1958c:76.

70. MY1967a:64.

71. MY1960c:12; MY1962c; MY1963b:205; MY1963d; MY1967a:ch.12–14; MY1968f:187; MY1972a:22,106; MY1981a:137,194. B. F. Skinner, *Walden Two*, New York: MacMillan, 1948; compare R1956f.

72. MY1958b:8; MY1959e; MY1967g.

73. MY1967a:ch.13.

74. MY1959e; MY1958b.

75. MY1967a:ch.3; MY1958b:11; MY1958a:39.

76. MY1967a:vix; MY1982b.

11

Summary and Conclusion

Seen from a nonparochial perspective, modern Western psychology has been dominated by the experimental and experiential paradigms of method and understanding of human nature. In the experimental attitude, psychological methods imitate the model of the natural sciences and study human nature as a natural phenomenon.[1] In the experiential attitude, phenomenological methods study the unique ontological characteristics of human beings.[2] While phenomenological and existential psychologists consider the ideal of positivism in psychology to be philosophically immature, their studies of consciousness and subjectivity have been viewed by experimental psychologists as poetic pursuits. Proponents of both paradigms accuse one another of naively misunderstanding human nature and the epistemology of psychology. Americans, however, have had the privilege to have the tension between experimental and experiential paradigms clarified in the work of humanistic psychologists.

Well-known American psychologists during the golden age of behaviorism following World War II, discontented with behaviorism's view of human nature and method, drew upon a long tradition linking psychology with humanities and, in a rebellious manner, institutionally founded humanistic psychology. They regarded themselves as a third force, an alternative to the dominant behavioristic and psychoanalytical orientations in psychology. The founders of humanistic psychology wrote eloquently on the philosophical tension between objective and subjective methods of studying human nature. A discussion of their views on psychology is particularly suitable to clarification of the philosophical tension between the experimental and experiential paradigms, because they introduced their understanding of phenomenology and existentialism into the positivistic milieu that intellectually nurtured them.

THE INSTITUTIONALIZATION OF HUMANISTIC
PSYCHOLOGY

In order to further their thoughts as a movement, thinkers need grants, research facilities, and intellectual stimulation by means of seminars, conferences, and journals; they need, in other words, institutions. The institutionalization of humanistic psychology was in great part a product of the work of Abraham Maslow and Anthony Sutich.[3]

Although he was a talented psychologist, colleagues avoided Maslow in the early 1950s because of his unorthodox interests. Blaming this state of affairs on the dominance of behaviorism in psychology, Maslow contacted other discontented psychologists and, around 1954, compiled a list of 125 names in order to facilitate communication among them. In the mid–1960s, the individuals on this list became the first subscribers to the *Journal of Humanistic Psychology* (*JHP*) and the first members of the Association for Humanistic Psychology (AHP). Over the next decade Maslow's colleagues emerged as a distinct group with a separate body of theory and research within the field of psychology. One of the names on Maslow's list was Anthony Sutich.

In their first encounter in 1949, Maslow and Sutich expressed a common anger over the dominating behavioristic presence in psychology.[4] Six years later, they were exchanging correspondence on the inefficiency of the mailing list. They soon delineated the statement of purpose of the Journal, assembled a board of editors, and began the search for a title. Upon Maslow's insistence, the president of Brandeis University, A. L. Sachar, agreed to sponsor the venture—with no financial participation, however.[5]

The title *Journal of Humanistic Psychology* was first suggested by Stephen Cohen, a senior psychology student at Brandeis and Maslow's son-in-law. With Sutich as editor, the first issue of the *JHP* appeared in the spring of 1961. The Journal's publication spurred an increase in the number of discontented psychologists, and Sutich and Maslow recognized that it was time to found an association for humanistic psychology. They appointed James Bugental as president pro tem of the future association. The first national and founding meeting took place in Philadelphia in the summer of 1963.[6] With over a hundred participants, the Philadelphia meeting was highly spirited. Maslow's opening comments on the narrowness and exclusiveness of behaviorism and psychoanalysis stimulated a discussion that went on into the night. By the following day, there was already a feeling of "belonging to a group." By the second annual meeting in Los Angeles, the number of members had doubled.[7]

The culminating event in establishing humanistic psychology in American psychology was a conference held in November 1964 in a country inn at Old Saybrook, Connecticut. Attendance at the conference by Allport and Rogers finally made their support for the humanistic psychology public. Bugental, Maslow, and May were also present. So were, among others, Jacques Barzun, Charlotte Buhler, George Kelly, Clark Moustakas, Gardner Murphy, and Henry

Murray. The presentations dealt with the theoretical issues implied by the "new psychology."[8]

At first, the AHP was a protest group against behaviorism and psychoanalysis, merely advocating the introduction of humanistic values into mainstream psychology. But as the membership of AHP grew (from 100 members in 1963 to 500 in 1966), so did the need for more precise statements on the policy, aims, and methods of humanistic psychology. Thus, in 1965 Charlotte Buhler, the newly elected president, took on the challenge of confronting "the great deal of confusion regarding the objective and methods of a humanistic psychology." Four years later, the president, Floyd W. Matson, stated that the Association was no longer a protest group but a firmly established "third force" in psychology with an identity of its own. In 1969 the AAHP dropped the first "A" (standing for American) from its title mainly because its activities had become international.[9]

One of the primary concerns of the early AHP was the introduction of humanistic psychology into mainstream psychology. For this purpose, in 1964 the AHP began cosponsoring symposia at the American Psychological Association meetings. In 1971, 347 members of both the APA and the AHP requested the creation of APA Division 32 on humanistic psychology. At the same time, the AHP became a network of networks: a system of diffusing information about humanistic-oriented groups, practitioners, growth centers, and education in humanistic psychology.[10]

The eclectic melting pot of the founding members of the AHP and the absence of a single founder or humanistic orthodoxy in psychology make an intellectual account of the history of humanistic psychology extremely difficult to undertake. The 200 members of the AHP in 1963 and the 500 in 1965 included psychologists sympathetic to the orientations of classical phenomenologists; European theorists of Geisteswissenschaften; dialogical-religious, secular, and psychological emphases of existentialism; Gestalt psychology, person-oriented neo-Freudians; the organismic psychology of Kurt Goldstein; personality theorists who advocated an active and interactive self; and the more contemporary contributions of American personality psychologists. Finally, to make the picture even more confusing, we find traces of the hippy counterculture, the human potential movement, and the Big Sur–Esalen phenomena, from whom the more academically oriented humanistic psychologists sought to distance themselves. The only common ground the founding members shared was a willingness to do something about their deep dissatisfaction with the domineering presence of behaviorism and psychoanalysis in mid-century American psychology.

When the movement came to maturity, however, affirmative statements replaced mere protest, and few humanistic psychologists stood out either because of their leadership roles or because they were sought for intellectual inspiration and legitimization. We refer to this group as the founders of humanistic psychology: Gordon Allport, Abraham Maslow, Carl Rogers, Rollo May, and James Bugental. In order to avoid the pitfall of intellectual histories that assign ideas ontological reality with the human protagonists playing a puppetlike role, we focus on these five founders assuming that their thoughts share crucial similarities, thus emphasizing individual nuances over the abstract synthesis of their thoughts.

HUMANISTIC PSYCHOLOGY AND BEHAVIORISM

Humanistic psychology was primarily an outcry against the atomistic and behavioristic image of human nature.[11] For the behaviorists, they argued, a person was an inanimate, purely reactive organism, a passive helpless thing not responsible for its own behavior; nothing but a collection of responses to stimuli and a mere collection of independent habits. In contrast, humanistic psychologists argued that people are proactive and that even if a complete catalog of behaviors were possible, it would fail to describe human nature because a person is more than the additive sum of isolated behaviors.

Both Allport and Maslow received the best behavioristic education of their time; both had a romantic encounter with behaviorism while they were in college followed by a tragic divorce soon after receiving their doctoral degrees.[12] The belief that a crucial "o" (for organism) stands between stimulus and response permeates their critique of behaviorism. The study of isolated and single behaviors was misleading because behavior is more than a mere linear connection between stimuli and response. Personality was, rather, the primary determinant of the response to stimuli.[13]

Considering Rogers's critique of behaviorism, one is reminded of his debate with B. F. Skinner in the 1950s and 1960s on freedom and the control of human behavior. During the 1960s May and Bugental also criticized behaviorism on the issue of freedom and control of behavior. Bugental blamed behaviorists for being unable to confront their own subjectivity; their objective studies were a pathological defense mechanism.[14]

Humanistic psychologists were critical of behaviorism's attempt to imitate the methods of the exact sciences—biology in particular—from which it inherited the animal model. Behaviorists focused on animal research, they said, because animal data and the ritual of method deceitfully gave them the scientific legitimacy they so obsessively sought. Behaviorism was in this sense a prejudiced empiricism derived from extreme metaphysical nominalism and fidelity to method. The excessive stress on quantitative methods, they thought, excluded everything that did not fit the technique, thus leaving for study the simple, preselected problems. What was not physiological and quantifiable—such as human values, consciousness, freedom, and responsibility—they accused behaviorism of pushing aside and denying the existence of altogether.[15]

Behaviorists such as Skinner argued that it was time for social scientists to seize the political institutions and rule by objective and rational norms established by scientific means, thus advocating a rational redesign of the environment. Allport, Maslow, Rogers, May, and Bugental were unanimously critical of Skinner's behavioral engineering. May interpreted Skinner's advocacy of behavioral control in his discussion of the dilemmas of the modern age. Anxiety resulting from the confrontation with freedom forces the abdication of responsibility to someone; in Skinner's case, it was to the behavioral engineer. Therefore, according to May, behaviorism was a pseudoscientific substitute for the problems of modern age on freedom, responsibility, and power. May also argued that behavioral psychotherapy was a mere mechanical mode of relieving symptoms without treating the underlying problem. Rogers made a similar argument.[16]

Like May, Rogers focused his critique of behaviorism on the subject of freedom and choice in human motivation. He criticized Skinner's assumption that people do not have the capacity for meaningful subjective appraisal, choice, and responsibility and that they should rely on experts for evaluation and conduct. In this process, argued Rogers, people are transformed into objects to be measured and regulated, thereby degrading their sense of freedom and dignity. Rogers also asked how the experts were to be selected, and toward what end or value the control. May asked identical questions.[17]

Maslow and Allport, on the other hand, argued that the coping type of behavior studied by Skinner is functional, instrumental, and adaptive, acquired as a conditioned response for survival or coping reasons. If not rewarded or bombarded with stimuli, it dies out. Coping behavior is consequently not a reflection of human personality but, rather, of the animal-like aspect of the human species.[18]

All five humanistic psychologists pointed out that while people resent external control, they are gratified when, through self-knowledge, they control and predict their own behavior. Thus, the best frame of reference for the study, control, and prediction of behavior was not single and isolated behaviors or external scientific control but, rather, personality and one's self-understanding.[19]

The founders of humanistic psychology criticized behaviorism's view of human nature. For the behaviorists, a person was a collection of independent habits acquired through reward and punishment with no organizational interference by the organism—indeed, a passive, helpless empty organism not responsible for its existence. In reply, the humanistic psychologists argued that the person was a unit, gestalt, or whole. In their view the self was a complex patterning agent that sought out and selected stimuli, organized them, and emitted responses that were only indirectly related to the stimuli. A single behavioral act had many different components that could not be studied in isolation from the subjective meaning of the self-defining organism.[20] Nevertheless, none of the five humanistic psychologists entirely denied the value of behavioral studies because these studies describe facts useful to understanding of the person. Having granted this, they also argued that behavioral studies did not warrant the behaviorists' neglect of all other aspects of the human personality that did not fit the experimental and animal model.[21]

HUMANISTIC PSYCHOLOGY AND PSYCHOANALYSIS

Humanistic psychologists often set their views in contrast to Freudian psychoanalysis, arguing that humanistic psychology was also a protest against the determinism, reductionism, dogma, and medicalization of psychoanalysis. Perhaps ambivalently, humanistic psychologists also paid a tribute of reverence to Sigmund Freud. They often referred to their approach as complementing rather than replacing Freud's observations by providing a broader phenomenological and existential conception of human nature.[22]

Of the five, only Allport met Freud, an encounter he described as a "traumatic developmental episode."[23] According to the existing evidence, Maslow, May, and Bugental were psychoanalyzed—Maslow three times, and Bugental during the first years of practice of psychotherapy. May was probably analyzed by Erich Fromm in the practicum of psychoanalysis.[24]

Their critique of psychoanalysis distinguished between Freudian psychoanalysis and that of the neo-Freudians. In the case of Maslow, Rogers, and May, they derived more from the neo-Freudians than is generally realized; Bugental and Allport, on the other hand, had little contact with them. Bugental was the youngest and was already under the spell of May, Maslow, and Rogers; and Allport himself inspired psychoanalysts of ego-psychology leanings.

Maslow's encounters with the neo-Freudians—Alfred Adler, Erich Fromm, and Karen Horney—took place in New York City during the 1930s and 1940s. Adler encouraged young Maslow to replace primates with human subjects in the study of dominance. As for Fromm and Horney, Maslow often had discussions with them, acknowledging that he learned psychoanalysis from them and that his psychology was an effort to integrate the partial truths of their theories.[25]

In the case of Rogers, it was Otto Rank who had a significant impact on him during the formative years of the client-centered therapy. Client-centered therapy was based on Rank's description of reflective, passive therapy and his belief that it should focus on the person's intuitive insight rather than on intellectual analysis.[26] Like Otto Rank, young May also pointed out that psychology was not a natural science and that personality was not deterministic and mechanical. May also borrowed from Carl Jung the concept of the "play of opposites" in personality; from Alfred Adler, whose seminars he attended in Vienna, he borrowed the idea that human motivation was teleological. May's doctoral dissertation on anxiety also included discussions of Karen Horney and Erich Fromm.[27]

Regarding classical psychoanalysis, the five humanistic psychologists accused Freud of emphasizing the unconscious in human motivation. In reply, they distinguished between conscious and unconscious motivations, and they blamed Freud for generalizing the pathological trends of unconscious neurotic personality to all human motivation. In healthy people, they argued, motivation is much less unconscious, compulsive, instinctual, and past-oriented than it is among neurotic people. Among healthy people, motivation is functionally autonomous; it is continuously changing and growing in the course of life. Maslow, for example, argued that unconscious regression was not exclusively unhealthy; it could serve as revelations of the inner core of human nature.

According to May, psychoanalysis failed to solve the problem of balancing the id's wish against the conscious will mainly because Freud had mistakenly assumed they were independent and autonomous entities. A wish, according to May, was not only a regressive pole demanding the satisfaction of biological needs, but it was also symbolic of the intention of one's motivation. Wish blended with will carries meaning; it selects and molds one's actions and destiny.[28]

Rogers criticized psychoanalysis for the same reason Rank parted ways with Freud, over the critique of the psychoanalytical "assimilated intellectual interpretation." Both thought that behavior changes because of intuitive insight, not because of intellectualized analysis. Freud used directives and manipulative psychotherapeutic techniques, argued Rogers, because he did not trust the individual's capacity for self-understanding and direction in life. In this context Allport criticized the psychoanalytical view of the ego as a helpless passive agent vulnerable to conflicting pressures of the id and the superego. For Allport, the ego was conflict free and proactive.[29]

Humanistic psychologists referred to Freud's pessimism, fatalism, and frequent attention to the dark side of human nature. For Freud, they argued, nothing but destruction, incest, and murder would follow if one's basic nature was allowed full expression. A person, in Freud's view, was never free from the primitive and ferocious passions originating in childhood fixations. One was nothing but a product of powerful and dangerous biological drives dictated by the individual's past history. No wonder, they pointed out, the entire Freudian dynamics of personality aimed at holding the id's forces in check, seeking their sublimation and a precarious equilibrium between pain and pleasure.[30]

As in the critique of behaviorism, the humanistic psychologists countered Freud with a proactive and teleological view of human nature. They trusted the capacity of the individual for shaping, directing, and being responsible for his or her existence. With few exceptions they regarded human personality as essentially positive, social, and realistic. They thought that only when the inner core of human nature was released from internal and external controls and allowed full expression would one become fully functioning (Rogers), self-actualizing (Maslow), functionally autonomous (Allport), and authentic (May and Bugental).

HUMANISTIC PSYCHOLOGY AND EXISTENTIALISM

The founders of humanistic psychology agreed that the idiosyncratic Continental tradition of existentialism was a major source of inspiration in humanistic psychology. It was, however, historically inaccurate to interpret humanistic psychology as an import of European existentialism. The idea of parallelism was more accurate than the root analogy. In most cases when humanistic psychologists, including participants of the Saybrook Conference, discovered existentialism in the late 1950s, they had already formulated the core of their psychological thought.[31]

With the exception of short references to Victor Frankl and Paul Tillich, Allport rarely mentioned the existentialists by name, using instead the generic and often misleading term "existentialism." He thought that American psychology needed a "blood transfusion" or a "generous injection" of existentialism mainly because of the neglected study of subjectivity. Maslow also never discussed the literature of existentialism, although he occasionally referred to Jean-Paul Sartre, who he thought was "flat-wrong," and Martin Buber, whose I-thou relationship he considered a prime example of the humanistic paradigm. When he studied this literature, he pragmatically asked, "What's in it for me as a psychologist?" Like Allport, he concluded that it would enrich American psychology.[32]

Rollo May introduced existential psychology and psychiatry to the United States. *Existence*, the book that May co-edited in 1958, presented to Americans translations of leading European thinkers for the first time. The two introductory chapters written by May were no less influential than the rest of the volume. May was also instrumental at the end of the 1950s in the organization of the first symposium on existential psychology and the birth of two journals on existential psychology. Paul Tillich and Soren Kierkegaard had the greatest impact on May's thinking.[33]

The founders of humanistic psychology shared with the existentialists the vague concepts often used to characterize this group of thinkers. They were all perplexed by the uniqueness of people and argued that one ought to understand the person with the fewest possible preconceptions. They equally denied determinism in human destiny and focused on the authentic or inner self and not on objectivities, oughts, or facades. In different ways, they all understood the significance of intentionality in the study of personality. Their favorite themes of study were anxiety, choices, freedom, responsibility, and human meanings.

Both Maslow and Rogers wrote about Kierkegaard's statement that the aim of life is "to be that self which one truly is." Client-centered therapy, wrote Rogers, merely provides an environment that promotes the ability to hear the inner self so that one may become fully oneself. In a similar manner, Maslow argued that self-actualizing people choose what is good for them because they are in touch with who they truly are. Both Maslow and Rogers often mentioned Martin Buber's I-thou relationship. Rogers recognized there was a parallel between "unconditional positive regard" and Buber's description of the I-thou relationship. In both cases, there was an effect of "healing through meeting." Maslow referred to the I-thou relationship as part of the emerging humanistic paradigm in psychotherapy, often contrasting it to the I-it relationship of the medical paradigm.[34]

The similarities between Bugental's thought and the existentialism of Sartre are striking. Both argued that existential anxiety generated by the world's contingencies and responsibility for our lives makes us authentic people. The failure to respond authentically ("bad faith"), however, leads to refuge in objectivizations or "real" meanings that in turn become the source of neurosis.[35]

Humanistic psychologists were, however, critical of the anti-scientific and anti-biological dimensions of existentialism. They were as critical of existentialism's focus on despairing nihilism (Nietzsche), nothingness (Sartre), and absurdity (Camus) as they were of behaviorism's S-R philosophy and Freud's psychic determinism. In this sense they were certainly closer to the theological brand of existentialism represented by Kierkegaard, Buber, and Tillich.

The most persistent critique of existentialism by the founders of humanistic psychology addressed Sartre's famous statement that "freedom is existence, and in it existence precedes essence." Humanistic psychologists agreed with Sartre that "man is his own project." It is freedom, commitment, will, and responsibility that make oneself. But they equally thought that Sartre had gone too far in assuming that we are a "nothingness" and that the process of becoming has no biological basis.[36] Therapy for Rogers and Maslow, for example, aims to help "discover" the true identity rather than to "create" one. Allport and Rogers also wrote on therapy as a process of "discovering" the self rather than of building one. May, on the other hand, pointed out that one's ability to create oneself is already an innate part of human nature or essence.[37]

OTHER SOURCES OF INFLUENCE IN HUMANISTIC PSYCHOLOGY

Often, humanistic psychologists referred to Kurt Goldstein's work as an integral part of the emerging humanistic paradigm in psychology. Rogers and Maslow made the growth hypothesis the cornerstone of their thinking. This concept, however, was first coined by Goldstein in *The Organism* to denote the reorganizational capability of the organism after injury. Allport and Bugental identified Goldstein in the late 1950s and 1960s with the emerging humanistic paradigm, and May had many stimulating hours of discussion with Goldstein while writing his doctoral dissertation, in which he included extensive digressions on Goldstein's views.[38]

Historically, humanistic psychology was closer to personality theory than to any other school of psychology. Maslow and Rogers are often discussed in most psychology textbooks as personality theorists. As for the key humanistic psychologists such as Allport, Henry Murray, and Gardner Murphy, their writings are still today at the forefront of the field of personality theory. Among the personality theorists, Allport felt intellectually closest to William Stern, Maslow had professional contacts with Gardner Murphy, and Rogers praised George Kelly. Kelly was also one of Bugental's dissertation advisors.[39]

Gestalt psychology was another important source of inspiration. Statements equating a person to an irreducible unit where everything is related to everything; claims that the individual's field of experience determines behavior and that behavior is intentional; and the idea of one's reaction to "reality-as-perceived" were typical of humanistic psychologists and were borrowed from Gestalt psychologists. Among the Gestalt psychologists, Max Wertheimer had a substantial influence on Maslow, Allport, and Rogers; Kurt Lewin on Allport and Rogers. Allport often praised and referred to Kurt Lewin as a first cousin of his thought. Rogers also regarded his thought to be very close to Kurt Lewin's. He acknowledged that his assumption that the present field of experience determines behavior derived from Lewin's Gestalt psychology. Maslow's discussion of the "syndrome" in his holistic dynamic theory of personality is an example of borrowing from the Gestalt psychology he learned from Kurt Koffka and Max Wertheimer.[40]

THE PROBLEM OF METHOD IN HUMANISTIC PSYCHOLOGY

Allport, Rogers, and Maslow had no doubt that the attempt of experimental psychologists—behaviorists in particular—to imitate outdated models of the physical sciences had only mechanized and depersonalized psychology. Like the German phenomenologist Edmund Husserl, they argued that a science of human nature where the observer is also the observed had to be a unique science. Recognizing that the empiricism of positivistic psychology and the private subjective world of existential mysticism had to be balanced, Allport, Rogers, and Maslow developed a philosophy of science that combined quantitative and phenomenological methods and recognized the centrality of human subjectivity. This was a rare if not unique occurrence in the history and systems of psychology.[41] In doing so they were confident that by broadening the restrictive scope of psychology as the study of control and prediction of behavior, humanistic psychology would invigorate the field of psychology. Utilizing "all" channels of knowing, they thought that humanistic psychology would open psychology to "all" significant human problems.[42]

In their proposal for a humanistic psychology, Allport, Maslow, and Rogers argued that psychological research should begin with a "getting back to the things themselves." Study of human nature should begin with phenomenological knowledge and only then be submitted to objective, experimental, and behavioral laboratory methods of study. In Allport's words, "the only reasonable thing to do if one wishes to study a phenomenon is to put a specimen before one's eyes and look at it repeatedly until its essential features sink indelibly into one's mind."[43] Rogers advanced a similar argument when he proposed that all knowledge is a product of experiencing.[44] In Rogers's words, "it means soaking up experience like a sponge so that it is taken in all its complexity, with my total organism freely participating in the experiencing of the phenomena, not simply my conscious mind." Maslow termed this attitude "taoistic receptivity," and Allport, the "idiographic method."[45]

At some point in the process of "soaking up experience," "taoistic receptivity," or "intuition," Allport, Maslow, and Rogers argued that one senses the emergence of a pattern, rhythm, or relationship; "Some things just come to mind." Intuition alone, however, is as unacceptable as the rigidity of behavioral studies. The subjective hypothesis ought to be put to a rigorous testing that will confirm, modify, or disconfirm it. The experiential and experimental modes of knowing, they argued, are not dichotomously antagonist; it is not the case of experience versus abstracting, cautious versus bold knowledge. Both forms complement each other.[46] In doing so, Allport, Rogers, and Maslow argued that humanistic psychologists would make the study of human nature a more inclusive science, encompassing positivistic and phenomenological epistemologies.[47]

Not all humanistic psychologists, however, were as accommodating and eclectic as Allport, Maslow, and Rogers. Seeking instead philosophical legitimization in Continental existentialism and phenomenology, members of the existential current within humanistic psychology denied the positivistic method in the human sciences any significant value. Rollo May was the most outspoken member of this group.

People turn to psychology, wrote May, seeking to clarify their most oppressing problems related to the meaning of their lives. However, psychologists under the gospel of technique trivialize the essential aspects of being human, which are somehow lost in the reductionistic tendencies of objective test measurements. Since they focus on the study of things that happen to the person, the person to whom the things happen is lost in the process.[48]

May traced the obsessive concern of psychology with method to the Cartesian split between object and subject. The mechanical philosophy and mathematical method were relatively successful in the study of nature. Mind and subjectivity, however, were left out because they could not be submitted to the rigors of the newly found method. If psychology cannot deal with the whole range of human experience and dilemmas, argued May, then perhaps the notion of psychology as a science was one big mistake.[49]

Psychology, according to May, ought to follow a human model and study the unique features of human beings, "the ontological characteristics of human existence."[50] Phenomenological knowledge of the person ought to precede our methodological and theoretical presuppositions. In this context distinguishing between "describing what" and "explaining why," May argued that psychologists should describe rather than explain. Causological explanations of the origins or causes of any particular event fail to describe what the event is. To explain how a feeling—anxiety, for example—came to be does not say what anxiety is as experienced by the person at the present moment.[51]

The study of human nature should consider human history, culture, myths, symbols, and classical literature, since they express the perdurable crosscultural and historical essences of human experience. In summary, May thought that psychology has more affinity with the model of the humanities than with the model of the physical and biological sciences. However, most psychologists of his time, behaviorists in particular, regarded May's psychology and the existential wing within humanistic psychology as poetic or philosophical psychology.[52]

UNDERSTANDING HUMAN NATURE

The founders of humanistic psychology were certain that the crucial element in the making of any current of psychology was the view of human nature. Any psychology deserving the name entails an a priori view of human nature, they argued. Such a view determines the focus of research, the gathering and interpretation of data, and above all, the construction of theories. Every one, including the most experimentally oriented psychologist, has, whether consciously stated or not, an understanding of people. The founders of humanistic psychology thought that it was impossible for a psychologist to be objective and not to have a view of human nature. They fervently argued that the most significant value in psychology was a well-articulated view of human nature.[53]

Humanistic psychologists shared a conviction that a person is a "being-in-the-process-of-becoming." A person at his or her best, they said, is proactive, autonomous, choice-oriented, adaptable, and mutable. Each human being, they argued, is a unique organism with the ability to direct, choose, and change the guiding motives or "project" of life's course. In the process of becoming, one must assume the ultimate responsibility for the individualization and actualization of one's own existence. To reach the highest levels through the process of becoming, an individual must be fully functioning (Rogers) or functionally autonomous (Allport); the self must be spontaneously integrated and actualizing (Maslow); there must be self-awareness, centeredness (May), and authenticity of being (Bugental). Humanistic psychologists believed that the process of becoming was never simply a matter of genetics, biology, or the contingencies of external reinforcement, and they were convinced that the rejection of becoming was a psychological illness that should be the main concern of psychotherapy.

Although agreeing that the process of becoming characterizes human nature, humanistic psychologists disagreed on the causes of that process. Maslow, Rogers, and to a lesser degree Allport believed that the process of becoming had a biological basis, but they were extremely careful not to revert to simple biological determinism. Maslow thought that human beings had an instinctoid inner core that contained potentialities pressing toward actualization. In a similar vein, Rogers argued that the human organism had a directional and actualizing tendency toward the fulfillment of an inner potential. May and Bugental, however, regarded all biological assumptions as overly vague. They explained the process of becoming as a product of self-awareness and affirmation in the face of anxiety when dealing with existential contingencies. Allport, Maslow, and Rogers believed that human nature was inherently good when given the proper environment and opportunity for growth and self-actualization. May, on the other hand, believed that evil and anxiety had a major role as motivators of choice, responsibility, meaning, and authenticity.

In the cases of Maslow and Rogers, the cornerstone of their views on human nature was the growth hypothesis. Maslow, for example, explained that an instinctoid inner core of human nature contains potentialities pressing for actualization.[54] Rogers argued that the human organism has a directional or "formative tendency" toward the fulfillment of inner potential.[55] Both were inspired by Kurt Goldstein, the German-born Jewish psychiatrist and World War II émigré who first coined the term self-actualization to denote the reorganizational capability of the organism after injury.

Allport's own principle explaining the "formative tendency" was "the functional autonomy of motives." Allport thought that in a nonpathological personality the structural dispositions of the self undergo a continuous metamorphic process of transformation and alteration in the motives of action. Adult motives, noted Allport, are radically different from childhood motives. Adult motives, newer systems of motivation, are not the same as the older systems (childhood motives) out of which they emerged. In spite of continuity in personality development, motives in adult life supplant and are different from the motives of infancy. In other words, the tensions involved in any acquired system of motivation are not of the same kind as the antecedent tensions from which that acquired system developed. There is a progressive internal organization of the person's motives. This is the reason, argued Allport, why healthy personality and motivation are a never-ending process of becoming.[56]

May's view of human nature is closer to Allport's functional autonomy than to the growth hypothesis of Rogers and Maslow. May argued, for example, that people's morals and lives do not grow in the same way technology or the economy grows. In human terms growth does not imply right growth. Growth can also be evil; cancer, for example, is a growth.[57]

The process of becoming a person, according to May, results from the intentional act of asserting oneself. It is the affirmation of the self ("I can" rather than "I think") that builds identity and individualizes oneself. Throughout the 1960s May rewrote the Cartesian formula in different ways, but the conceived idea remained the same. We find it as "I think–I can–I am," "I–am, therefore, I–think, I–feel, I–do," and "I conceive–I can–I will–I am." In this sense, argued May, the process of becoming relates to the capacity to experience the self as a valuing source and to affirm personal goals and values. Becoming is a process of centering oneself around self-chosen values. The significance is not on values but on the process of centering oneself on centers of valuation that vary not only among people but within the person as well. These centers change over time and circumstances; they are, in other words, functionally autonomous, as Allport had argued. May's understanding of the process of becoming resembles the growth hypothesis of Rogers and Maslow. It is exempted, however, from the biological reductionism implied by his colleagues and is permeated by the notion of the intentionality of consciousness.[58]

HUMANISTIC ETHICS IN PSYCHOLOGY

No other group of thinkers in the history and systems of psychology have been as concerned with problems of values as the humanistic psychologists have. They pointed out that we live in an age where the ultimate disease is the lack of something to believe and be devoted to. They blamed this uncertainty in value orientation on the anachronism between rigid ethical systems of the past and the relativistic world view of science.[59]

Psychology, according to the founders of humanistic psychology, had a role in the clarification and treatment of modern ethical dilemmas, enlarging people's moral sense and guiding the neutralism of science and technology with human values. A valueless or value-free psychology, they argued, is neither desirable nor a possibility. A psychology obsessed with techniques unconsciously embraces a "directionless and conscienceless scientism," which is also a value.[60]

Every major work of Rollo May was an elucidation of ethics. Values, he argued, were essential in understanding human nature because they give humans—whom he once called the ethical animals—their "sense of being" and ontology. Values are a product of subjective choice exercised in the process of commitment to self-chosen centers of valuation and the collective levels or archetypes of civilization symbolically represented in myths. Values require awareness of the body and feelings, courage to affirm convictions, responsibility, and confrontation with the anxiety associated with this process. For all these reasons, values presuppose freedom.[61]

Like May, Allport also studied the process of valuing. He thought that a person's schemata of value are essential in the organization of personality. Values, he argued, are personal subjective meanings and dispositions of addressing the future that guide human motivation. Their intentional nature is responsible for the uniqueness of personality and the functionally autonomous process of becoming a person.[62]

As for Maslow and Rogers, they thought that the solution to the ethical dilemmas of modern age was to find a "true" ethical system independent of subjective values. They complained that the study of ethics had always been within the domain of philosophy, insisting that it was now the turn of psychologists to initiate scientific studies of values. Both Rogers and Maslow concluded that there are universal values that are an integral part of human nature and that are experienced when the individual is in touch with his or her own organism. Organismic awareness, in their opinion, could help the individual to find within himself or herself a system of universal ethics that would answer the most perplexing value questions of our age. Such values are synonymous with psychological or physical health and are concrete observable facts, not mere subjective phenomena.[63]

The founders of humanistic psychology argued that in the attempt to evade the modern predicament of valuelessness and instead of looking inward unto themselves, people cling instead to authority as a source of security and persist to find and fulfill "scientific" or "objective" external ethical criteria. In doing so, there is a tendency toward conformity, passivity, apathy, obedience, and adjustment to the anonymous authority of public opinion. This tendency to melt down in the "collectivist pot of conformity" results, first, from the absence of a center of values in society and, second, from the loss of self-awareness and an effective center of motivation within the individual. The only alternative, they argued, is to develop a deeper understanding of ourselves, rediscover an inner ethical center of strength and integrity, and stage a courageous confrontation with our historical situation and traditions.

The version of the growth hypothesis put forward by Rogers and Maslow also refers to the ability of self-actualizers to transcend the environment. Like May, in this context they also criticized the identification of psychological health with the concept of adjustment. They thought that it is misleading to define a healthy person in environment-centered terms of adjustment to a reality or society, and they argued that mental health should be defined instead in terms of the individual's autonomy and transcendence of the environment. Healthy people are, in this sense, according to Maslow and Rogers, said to be authentic, original, and creative, but not well adjusted.[64]

For the founders of humanistic psychology, authenticity, not adjustment, was the main value of psychotherapy. For Rogers and Maslow, the goal of psychotherapy was not to create but to reveal and facilitate integration with the biological core, or inborn preferences, talents, and yearnings of the person. Denial and even absence of awareness of such a core lead to psychological illness, frustration, and disintegration. One's life problems, vocation, and decision making could be much easier if people knew what is easier for them to do, what fits or suits them better from the perspective of their organism.[65]

May, on the other hand, argued that any system of ethics leading to the full realization of one's potential must guarantee that freedom is not abdicated. Freedom, he argued, is the most basic prerequisite for our capacity to value. May acknowledged, however, that people are not totally free from life's deterministic forces. No one is free from the determinations of their bodies or the historical realities of their psychological makeup and of their culture, to mention just a few factors. But, argued May, there is a margin of freedom within these realities. The more one is aware of the way one is determined, the more one is free to react to such deterministic forces. Freedom, in this sense, is a product of awareness and reaction to the deterministic realities of one's culture and psychological makeup. When one is not self-aware, one is determined by one's own unconscious instincts and the automatic development of history.[66]

May also acknowledged that human beings do not exist in a vacuum. They find themselves existing in a culture with common history, aspirations, and values, the study of which (e.g., the humanities) is an important source of values. By looking unto the accumulated wisdom of history, we may rediscover the culturally inherited archetypes of human values as symbolically represented in myths and symbols. The ethical dilemma, wrote May, is how to balance one's inherited traditions without compromising one's freedom and personal responsibility. Greater self-awareness allows one to merge into experience and discover oneself in all of one's uniqueness through the accumulated wealth of human traditions. We may even realize that we have chosen the same values that have been valued for centuries, although we may have reached them in a very personal way.[67]

CONCLUSION

At first an eclectic melting pot of nonbehavioristic and nonpsychoanalytical European and American psychological orientations, as the humanistic current in psychology matured and affirmative statements replaced protest, few humanistic psychologists stood out either because of their leadership role or because they were sought for intellectual legitimization and inspiration. We have referred to them as the founders of humanistic psychology.

An examination of the psychological systems of the founders reveals that despite philosophical similarities between Continental existentialism and phenomenology, humanistic psychology was an American phenomenon primarily because it was a response to the mechanical and atomistic experimental philosophy of behaviorism. But since in addition to existentialism the founders' other sources of inspiration (Goldstein, the neo-Freudians, Gestalt and personality psychologies) were also of European origin, this history has placed humanistic psychology in the context of the history and systems of psychology.

The founders of humanistic psychology recognized the restrictive nature of behavioral studies and the experimental method in the study of subjective aspects of human existence. Their suggestion to integrate positivistic methods with their understanding of phenomenology and existentialism was not well received in mainstream American psychology. Their proposal did not fare any better with the phenomenologists. Their suggestion to submit the phenomenon of subjectivity to objective, quantitative, experimental, and behavioral scrutiny (in the cases of Rogers and Maslow) and synthesis in a systematic eclecticism (in the case of Allport) was equally anathema in phenomenological and existential circles. Totally in the context of the humanistic current in psychology, Rollo May, on the other hand, departed from his colleagues, possibly because of his affinity with Continental existentialism and phenomenology. He thought that although the positivistic method had a major role in explaining the biological aspect of the human organism, it had little or no significance in the understanding of the ontological characteristics of human existence.

The keynote in the revolt and establishment of humanistic psychology was the understanding of human nature. The view of the person as a being in the process of becoming permeated the founders' critique of behaviorism and psychoanalysis and dictated their views on method and psychotherapy. An a priori understanding of human nature, whether consciously stated or not, was essential in the making of any psychology, they argued. For this reason most psychologists of the time, especially behaviorists, regarded humanistic psychology as a philosophy or poetic psychology.

No other group of thinkers in the history of psychology was as concerned with ethics as were the humanistic psychologists. The founders' views on ethics stemmed from a trust of the worthiness of human nature. They argued that when people are authentic, experience their inner worlds, and function freely from internal and external barriers, they value and choose what is good for them from an organismic point of view. Personal values, they unanimously argued, are essential in the proposition of personality because they hold the future-oriented subjective meanings and dispositions that guide the process of becoming a person. An ethical act gives the person a sense of being, or ontology, making him or her proactive, autonomous, intentional, and unique. For all these reasons, values presuppose a deep trust in our philosophy for the capacity and necessity of the person to value and determine the unfolding of his or her destiny. Authenticity, freedom, autonomy, commitment, and self-determination (not adjustment) are the keynotes of humanistic ethics in psychology.

In an age when most American psychologists understood human nature as a mere response to stimulus, worshiped the experimental models of the physical and biological sciences, and studied psychologically maladjusted persons, the founders of humanistic psychology advocated a humanistic psychology that studied the subjective aspects of becoming a person, sought to improve human nature and society, and placed the uniqueness of each person at the center of its concerns. With the partial exception of May, their critique of experimental psychology, (behaviorism in particular), views on the proper method of psychology, and proposal for the humanistic psychology they helped to establish constituted a rare if not unique occurrence of clarification and syncretism of experimental and phenomenological paradigms in the history and systems of psychology. The psychological systems of the founders of humanistic psychology were an American epistemological expression of existentialism and phenomenology—or, as they are best known in the history and systems of psychology, major pillars of the humanistic current in psychology.

Although it is still regarded today by most experimental psychologists as poetic or philosophical psychology, the impact of humanistic psychology on the field of psychology is often underestimated. Most of the negative reputation of humanistic psychology stems from the 1960s and 1970s extremists of the hippy, human potential, and feminist movements who attached themselves to humanistic psychology. The more moderate humanistic psychologists, and the founders of humanistic psychology among them, sought to distance themselves from these extremists.

The persistent and, at times, fierce criticism of behaviorism by humanistic psychologists had a share in dismantling the monopoly that behaviorism enjoyed in American psychology for most of the middle twentieth century. Outside of the United States, primarily in South America, humanistic psychology has been as popular as behaviorism has been inside the United States. Humanistic psychologists' claim that most psychological research and views of human nature overly relied on the study of mental illness—and their alternative studies of psychological health, growth, and self-actualization—have earned them a place in the history and systems of psychology. When one is perplexed by the meaning of existence and death, values, human wonder, psychological health, self-esteem, self-actualization, the process of creativity, altered states of mind, personal mythology, and other human issues, there is no other available literature than the writings of humanistic psychologists. In education, humanistic psychology was a paradigm maker. Most educators are aware of Maslow's notions of intrinsic learning and self-actualization, and many have even tested the student-centered approach of Carl Rogers. Psychotherapy in its most fundamental bases remains

Rogerian in character. There is no psychotherapist who is not, to some extent, Rogerian. The "encounter group" form of psychotherapy also owes its foundations to humanistic psychology. These were, no doubt, significant and often underestimated contributions of humanistic psychologists to the field of psychology.

Today, although European existential and phenomenological psychologists persist in not assimilating the methods and concepts of the natural sciences, some humanistic psychologists do attempt such integrations. The Saybrook Institute, for example, a leading program and research center in humanistic psychology, is committed to the teaching of a variety of research methods including the experimental approach. The notion of humanistic psychology as a school of psychology is outdated. Humanistic psychology has found its way into the "human sciences"; it is an eclectic approach to the study of human nature that, excluding no valid method of study, employs experimentalism, hermeneutics, heuristics, phenomenology, systems research, and other minor esoteric approaches. Some humanistic psychologists, for example, have considered the techniques of the natural sciences of general systems theory. In this case, the subjective aspects of humanistic psychology—its therapeutic practices in particular—and the methodology of general systems theory have combined in order to provide a framework for the development and evaluation of theories, methods, and research in humanistic psychology.[68]

NOTES

1. D. Polkinghorne, *Methodology for Human Sciences*, Albany: State University Press, 1983; J. B. Watson, "Psychology as the Behaviorist Views It," *Psy. Rev.*, 1913, 20:158–77.

2. E. Graig, "Psychotherapy for Freedom," *The Humanistic Psychologist*, 1988, 16(1); E. Husserl, *Phenomenological Psychology*, trans. J. Scanlon, The Hague: Nijhoff, 1977 (Original work published in 1925). MY1958a.

3. Anthony Sutich, *The Founding of Humanistic and Transpersonal Psychology: A Personal Account*, unpublished doctoral dissertation, Humanistic Psychology Institute, 1976.

4. Ibid., pp. 7–51.

5. Ibid., pp. 65–88.

6. Tom Greening, "The Origins of the Journal of Humanistic Psychology and the Association for Humanistic Psychology," *J. Hum. Psy.*, 1985, 25:7–11.

7. Sutich, *The Founding of Humanistic and Transpersonal Psychology*, p. 118; *AHP Newsletter*, December 1963; November 1965. The *AHP Newsletter* is available in microfilm.

8. Sutich, *The Founding of Humanistic and Transpersonal Psychology*, pp. 127–39; B1965d:180–81.

9. *AHP Newsletter*, December 1963; November 1965; April 1968; October 1969. Information was also drawn from an interview by the author with Dr. Bugental on March 8, 1985. For the dropping of the first "A" from the Association's title, see Sutich, *The Founding of Humanistic and Transpersonal Psychology*, pp. 94–95. For the internation-

alization of the AHP, see *AHP Newsletter*, October and December 1969; April, Summer, and November 1970.

10. As early as 1966 we find an ad in the *AHP Newsletter* seeking humanistically oriented personnel (July 1966). See also *AHP Newsletter*, July 1968; December 1971; February and Summer 1972. For the educational concern, see July and October 1966; June and October 1967; April 1968; January, April, and July 1969; February, April, and October 1970. For the initiatives in master's degree programs in humanistic psychology, see April and July 1966; April 1969; April 1970. Throughout the 1970s the *AHP Newsletter* had a special column on the Humanistic Psychology Institute (now Saybrook Institute)— see especially October 1970; April, June, Summer, October, and December 1971; February, March, June, and Summer 1972; February 1974.

11. See, for example, R1965g:1–5; B1965f; B1967a:vii,2,5–11,223; Richard I. Evans, *Carl Rogers: The Man and His Ideas*, New York: Dutton, 1975, pp. 115,130–35; *AHP Newsletter*, December 1963; April 1968.

12. For Allport, see Richard I. Evans, *Gordon Allport: The Man and His Ideas*, New York: Dutton, 1970, pp. 13,17–19; A1967a; A1968a:30–32. For Maslow, see his unpublished master's thesis (M1931a) and his doctoral dissertation (M1936a–d); see also M1966b:7; M1968f:37,55; W. Frick, *Humanistic Psychology*, Columbus, Ohio: Merrill, 1971, pp. 19–20.

13. A1940a:1–28; A1947e:182–92. M1937c:404–29; M1939a:30–31,38; M1954a:22–62,291–304; M1961e:572–73; M1964b:326–31; M1966b:40–44.

14. R1955a:247–49; R1956c:316–22; R1961a:ix,363–402; R1964a:37–40; R1976b. Evans, *Rogers*, p. 114. For a discussion of Rogers versus Skinner in the light of Kuhn's paradigm debate, see Patrick K. Dooley, "Kuhn and Psychology," *J. for the Theory of Soc. Beh.*, 1982, 12:275–89. See also MY1967a:182–200; B1962c:38–46; B1967a:7; B1971b:34,95; B1976a:191,193–94,197,233; B1976b:55–59.

15. A1940a; A1940b; A1947e; A1950a:198–209. M1946b; M1961e. R1955c:267–78; R1961a:363–402; R1963g:72–92; R1965j:182–94. MY1956b:352–53; MY1958b:13–14; MY1967a. B1963c:563–67; B1964h:19–26; B1967a:5–11.

16. MY1962c;   MY1963b:205;   MY1963d;   MY1963e;   MY1967a:130–33; MY1968f:187; MY1972a:22,106; MY1981a:194–203. R1955a; R1948b:209–19.

17. R1956f:1057–66; R1955c:298; R1962a:17. Evans, *Rogers*, p. 114. MY1962c; MY1963d:205; MY1981a:194–203.

18. M1943b:130,370–96;   M1949b:261–72;   M1954d:291–304;   M1966b:40–44. A1940a; A1940b; A1946a:185; A1950a:vi; A1961a:ch.19.

19. A1940a; A1940b; A1950a:vi. M1966b:40–44. R1948e:174–86. Evans, *Rogers*, p. 63. B1971b:34,95; B1971d.

20. A1940a; A1940b; A1947e; A1955a:7–12; A1961a:27–28,314–19; A1961h:2–4; A1962c:373–81; A1968a:68–70. M1951a:350–51; M1954a:55,72(note 2); M1966b:55; M1968b:2;   M1968c:64–79.   R1946d:422;   R1947c:367;   R1948e;   R1951a:ch.11; R1961a:chs.20–21; R1970b:521–23. MY1940a:32; MY1943a:144,147; MY1943a:56; MY1956b:352–56; MY1958b:13–14; MY1967a. B1963c; B1964h; B1965f:11,97; B1966a:223–39; B1967a:5–11; B1976b:48–61.

21. A1964b:19–23;   A1967a:23;   A1968a:12,45;   A1968b:1–2.   MY1971a:20–49. R1973a:83–84.   Evans,   *Rogers*,   pp. 115,130–35.   MY1940a:32;   MY1943a:147; MY1972a:76. B1964h:25; B1966a:235; B1967a:7; B1971b:20,49.

22. On the humanistic psychologists' protest against psychoanalysis, see, for example, A1933b:264; A1955a:37; A1967a:7–8; A1967f:1. Evans, *Allport*, pp. 3–12. M1939a:4–

5; M1956d:21; M1959c:141; M1962b:60; M1964b:6,8; M1968b:2–3; M1968c:65; M1970a:xi. R1937b:56,323; R1951a:4; R1954a:32; R1963g:72; R1974c:23. MY1939a:45–49; MY1958b:6–7; MY1959e:87; MY1961c:641; MY1964b:111–15; MY1966a:55–60; MY1981a:22–23. B1964h:22,25; B1965f:10,16; B1966a:223–24.

23. A1967a:7–8. Evans, *Allport*, pp. 3–6. See also M. D. Faber, "Allport's Visit with Freud," *Psychoanalytic Rev.*, 1970, 57:60–64; Allan C. Elms, "Allport, Freud, and the Clean Little Boy," *Psychoanalytic Rev.*, 1972–1973, 59:627–32.

24. M1954a:x; M1962v:xi; M1966b:xix. B1976a:281. MY1967g:72.

25. M1954a:ix. Maslow mentioned Adler in writing at least seventy-seven times; see Jenny Scheele, *Register Referring to the Complete Published Works by A. H. Maslow*, Delft, The Netherlands: Delft University of Technology, 1978, pp. 411,455,444. M1935b:47; M1941a:xii–xiii; M1943b:90–91; M1943e:401; M1954a:x; M1956d:21; M1962c:34–35; M1962f:125; M1970a:xi; M1971b:20. Heinz L. Ansbacher, "Alfred Adler and Humanistic Psychology," *J. Hum. Psy.*, 1971, 11:53–63.

26. R1937a:239,241–42; R1937b:56–57; R1939b:338,346; R1954a:32; R1961a:9; R1967a:356–60; R1977k:128–29.

27. MY1939a:7–10,19,44–77,227fn2;MY1940a:20–26,39–43,148–51,187–88,244–59; MY1943a:146–50; MY1950a:133–70,191–239,247; MY1951a:304; MY1953a:13–14,266; MY1953b:16–17; MY1958b:7; MY1961e:31; MY1964b:113; MY1967g:25.

28. MY1953a:248–53; MY1958b:6–7,32–36; MY1959e:98–108; MY1960c:18,34–35; MY1961a:11–30; MY1961b:31–40; MY1961c:641; MY1963b:77–81; MY1963g:41–50; MY1965g:125–27; MY1966a; MY1967d; MY1968a:3–14; MY1969a:48–52,81–88,chs.7–10; MY1972a:212–13; MY1981a:84. Clement Reeves, *The Psychology of Rollo May*, San Francisco: Jossey-Bass, 1977, ch. 4, pp. 147–221,264–309.

29. A1935b:4–5; A1936a:10; A1937a:12–15,181–89; A1937b; A1947e:118–19; A1950f:204; A1953b; A1955a:37,45,49,65; A1957a:10; A1958a:37; A1961a:103,149–55,202–9,216,229; A1961h:4; A1965a:176–89; A1967a:7–8; A1967f:2–5; A1968a:71–73. Evans, *Allport*, pp. 3–12,79. R1940a:163; R1942a:25–28,151; R1942e:430; R1945e:141;R1946d:418–19;R1947b:112–13;R1951a:197–218;R1953c:81–82. Evans, *Rogers*, pp. 30–31.

30. B1962g:244;   B1964h:22,25;   B1965f:16,59,63,71,89,93,142–43,332; B1966a:224, 228; B1978b:64–65. M1939a:4–5; M1943a:66–67,77,79; M1943b:90–91, 101; M1949b:193–98; M1951b:636–37; M1956c:56–57; M1959c:141–42; M1961a:182–83; M1962a:196; M1962b:56–57,207–10; M1964b:6–8. A1935b:4–5; A1937a:12–15,181–89; A1937b; A1950f:204; A1953b; A1955a:65–66; A1961a:103,149–55, 202–3, 206–9, 229; A1965a:176–89; A1967a:7–8; A1967f:4–5; A1968a:71–73. Evans, *Allport*, pp. 3–12,79. B1965f:59, 63, 89, 93, 332; B1976a:291.

31. A1955a:81; A1957a:11; A1962c:73; A1964e:135; A1965a:174; A1967f:1. Evans, *Allport*, pp. 55–58. MY1959e:87; MY1968f:191; MY1963b:75. R1959i:196; R1960c:96; R1961a:200; R1967a:378; R1974j:256; R1974i:11–12. Evans, *Rogers*, p. 70.

32. M1959e:20–21; M1960b; M1962b:ix,xi; M1962h:127–32; M1964d. A1955a:79, 83; A1955c:195; A1957a:19; A1959b:ix–xii; A1960d:305; A1961a:x,217, 282, 555–64, 560; A1964b:17–18; A1964e:134; A1965a:174,175. Evans, *Allport*, pp. 57,133.

33. MY1951a:306–22; MY1953a:ch.3; MY1958a; MY1958c:46; MY1960b; MY1961a:2,4; MY1961e:31–40; MY1962c:14–19; MY1962d:19; MY1963b:74–81; MY1966a:68. MY1969a:243. Interview with Dr. Bugental in San Francisco on March 8, 1985. Mahrer's letter to the author, October 25, 1985. R1961b:164.

34. R1950d:26; R1952c:342; R1955c:199–200,290; R1956g:198; R1957d:172;

R1960a:208,273; R1960d; R1961a:166,199,200; R1961b:175; R1961f:5–6; R1965e:26; R1973e:12. M1962b:168; M1968h:186. Evans, *Rogers*, pp. 25,69. Soren Kierkegaard, *Fear and Trembling and the Sickness unto Death*, trans. Walter Lowrie, Garden City, NY: Doubleday, 1954, p. 29.

35. B1965f:102; B1967c:286; B1967e:629; B1976a:54,99–100; B1978a:184.

36. For Sartre's discussion of this issue, see Jean-Paul Sartre, *Being and Nothingness*, trans. Hazel E. Barnes, New York: Washington Square Press, 1956, p. 725.

37. M1959a:131; M1962a:190–91; M1962b:167,174–75; M1964b:xvi; M1964e:128; M1968h:186; M1970a:xvii–xviii; M1971a:315–16,349; M1971b:22–23. R1971c:87–90; R1973b:45–46; R1979a. MY1953a:165–67; MY1953c; MY1961e:34–36; MY1962e:147–57; MY1967a:135–37; MY1968f:212–17; MY1969a:157.

38. Joseph I. Meiers, *Kurt Goldstein Bibliography 1903–1958*, Washington, D.C.: American Documentation Institute, Doc. 5816; "Papers in Honor of Kurt Goldstein," *J. Indiv. Psy.* 1959, 15:1–19; Marianne L. Simmel, ed., *The Reach of Mind: Essays in Memory of Kurt Goldstein*, New York: Springer, 1968; Herbert Spiegelberg, *Phenomenology in Psychology and Psychiatry*, Evanston, Ill.: Northwestern University Press, 1972, pp. 301–18. M1941a:xiii; M1951b:645; M1954a:ix, 27, 36, 80, 89, 91, 95, 109, 116, 124, 161, 166, 192, 206, 262, 286, 287, 291, 296, 342, 383; M1955a:2, 5, 13; M1959e:19; M1961f:7; M1962b:ii, v, ix, xi, 118; M1962h:247; M1965b:v; M1966b:23, 42, 69; M1968f:55; M1969d:132; M1971a:119, 252. R1951a:481, 489; R1959a:193; R1963a:3; R1979a:100. MY1950a:xi,62–70,96–100,108,115,120,122, 161,167,213,221,225,286,376,383,384,390. Evans, *Allport*, p. 54. A1955a:16,50,80; A1960a:107,166,303; A1960d:302,305; A1961a:212,215,269,348,558,569; A1961h:8; A1968a:73. B1966a:224.

39. A1930c; A1931a; A1937c; A1938b; A1943g; A1967a:10–11; A1967f; A1968a:271–97. Evans, *Allport*, p. 18. See, for example, M1936a:261; M1941a; M1948c:116; M1951b; M1954a: M1955a. R1947c; R1951a:481–533; R1956d; R1956g; R1961e:35; R1963e:11; R1973h; R1974j. B1948c:188; B1952a:435; B1962g:245; B1965f:xvi,403; B1969a:96; B1970a:286; B1971a:37; B1976a:320; B1982b:47; B1984a:549.

40. A1923b; A1929a; A1930c:695; A1930d; A1937a:15–17,343–65; A1947a:100; A1948a:vii–xiv; A1955a:12–19; A1967a:10; A1968a:360–70. Evans, *Allport*, p. 18. M1941a:xii,xiii; M1943b:97,80; M1943d:31–37; M1956d:32; M1961d:215; M1961f:7; M1962i:23; M1963c:117–19; M1965b:v; M1967g:42; M1968f:55; M1971a:42,118; M1971b:21. R1947c:366; R1951a:57,481–533; R1967a:366,383; R1974j:256. Evans, *Rogers*, p. 28. MY1943a:144–45.

41. R1955a:299; R1967b:22; R1971c:107; R1974b; R1985b. M1942e:260; M1961f; M1966b:ch.10; M1971a:16–19. R1968f:154. A1946e:66; A1950a:198.

42. R1963g:81,90; R1965g:2; R1966b. M1946b; M1961c:13; M1966d:107. A1943g:452; A1947e. Evans, *Rogers*, pp. 147–76.

43. A1942a:143.

44. R1965j:198.

45. A1940a; A1940b; A1942a:xii,60–64,149; A1946a; A1946a:67; A1950a:198–209; A1954d; A1957a:20; A1959g:100; A1960f; A1961a:x,199,389; A1962a; A1962b; A1964b; A1964c; A1965a:211; A1967f; A1968a:116,171. Evans, *Allport*, pp. 19,54,80,99. R1948e; R1955c; R1959h:251; R1963g:75,77; R1965j. M1956d; M1961f:1; M1966b:100,ch.10.

46. R1965j:187; R1968f:ch.4. M1961f:1. A1929a; A1930a:127; A1933b:264; A1942a:143.

47. A1931a; A1933a; A1933b:263; A1961h:11; A1962b; A1964b; A1964c; A1964e:67. Evans, *Allport*, p. 44. M1945a; M1945c; M1960b; M1962b:viii; M1966b:chs.10–11; M1970a:ix,16–19. R1960a; R1961a:ch.21; R1965g.

48. MY1967a:ch.1; MY1969:18.

49. MY1958b:8; MY1958c:76; MY1959e; MY1960c:12; MY1962c; MY1963d; MY1967a:64,chs.12–14;   MY1967g;   MY1968f:187;   MY1972a:22,106; MY1981a:137,194. Compare M1963b:205; R1956f.

50. MY1967a:ch.13.

51. MY1958a:39; MY1958b:11; MY1959e; MY1967a:ch.3.

52. MY1967a:vix; MY1982b.

53. A1967a:14,15,23; A1967c:271; A1967f:1; A1962c. M1954f:353; M1956d:23; M1962a:189; M1962b:220; M1968c:64; M1971b:20,49. R1946d:418–19; R1948b:17; R1950d:26; R1952c:352; R1957b. MY1956c; MY1959e:87,90–91; MY1963b:75; MY1967a:3–22; MY1978d:vii. B1951c:194–200; B1964h:23; B1965f:142,193; B1966a:228; B1967b:7.

54. M1943b;   M1954a:9,80,106,116,124,139,145,153,183,345–49,379–90; M1955a:3; M1957a:116; M1961c:3; M1962a; M1962b:3–4,81,130,138,167–85,222; M1964b:xvi; M1968b:3; M1968c:64–65; M1968g:36; M1968h:186; M1968k:211,223; M1970a:xvii,xxvil; M1971a:101,148,186,223; M1971b:22–24,28.

55. R1948a:29–30; R1951a:522; R1954a:33–36; R1956g:206; R1957a; R1957d:186– 87; R1960a:171; R1961a:27,60; R1963a; R1963b:17–26; R1963g; R1965e; R1971c:87– 89; R1974c:23; R1977k; R1979a:98–99,103; R1984b:26–27.

56. Evans, *Allport*, pp. 13–15,22–43. A1937b; A1950f:204; A1953b; A1953d:352– 53;   A1955a:vii,35,37,45–46,49,65–68;   A1957a:10;   A1958a:37;   A1960a:v–vi; A1960d:303; A1961a:103,149–55,202–3,206–9,216–17,229,345,347; A1961h:2–4,11– 12; A1962b; A1964b; A1965a:176–89; A1965c:43; A1967a:7–8; A1967f:2,3,4–5; A1968a:45,68–70,71–73.

57. MY1940a:58–60,114–27,249–51;   MY1952a;   MY1956b:355–57;   MY1963d; MY1963f:216; MY1963g:45; MY1964b:116; MY1966c:21; MY1967a:xi,3–20,215,217; MY1967g:28,29,73;   MY1969a:112,123–29,278,311,chs.5–6;   MY1972a:54,75,110, 122,217,238,254;   MY1973c:48,95–96,121,239;   MY1973e:17;   MY1974e:16,55,61; MY1975a:20;   MY1976d:27;   MY1976e:48;   MY1977b:304;   MY1981a:xi,66; MY1982a:19. See also MY1967a:ix,17,19,216; MY1972a:255–80.

58. MY1951a:306–22;   MY1958b;   MY1958c:46;   MY1961a:2;   MY1961b; MY1961e:31–40; MY1962c:14–19; MY1962d:19; MY1963b:74–81; MY1964b:117; MY1966a: MY1967a:ix,94,108–9; MY1969a:chs.7–10; MY1982a:19.

59. For additional analysis of humanistic ethics in psychology, see DeCarvalho's "The Ethics of the Growth Hypothesis of Abraham Maslow and Carl Rogers," *J. Ethical Stud.*, 1991, 6(3):3–17; "Carl Rogers' Naturalistic System of Ethics," *Psy. Reports*, 1989, 65:1155–62; "The Growth Hypothesis and Self-Actualization: An Existential Alternative," *The Humanistic Psychologist*, 1990, 18:252–58.

60. M1959a:viii; M1964b:3,38,82; M1971a:377. R1961j; R1964b. Evans, *Rogers*, p. 101. MY1956b; MY1957b; MY1960b:41. A1950a:187; A1955a:99; A1955d:154; A1960a:155.

61. MY1953a:174,180; MY1955c; MY1977b:303,309.

62. A1931a;   A1933d;   A1937a:202;   A1948b:105;   A1950a:65,86,144,187–97;

A1954a:206;   A1955a:14,17,77,88–93;   A1955c:199;   A1960a:ch.11;
A1961a:223,236,296,303,450,543,ch.10;   A1961h:6;   A1967a:21;   A1967f:1–3;
A1968a:43,51,164–67,305,ch.9. Evans, *Allport*, pp. 44,66,75,84.

63. M1959a:127;   M1959b:viii,245;   M1961f:8;   M1962b:3–8,74,167,205;
M1964b:3,38,82,97–102;   M1971a:9–10,135–51,377.   R1957d;   R1957g;   R1964b;
R1978b.

64. M1948c; M1949b:179; M1954a:107–22,146–54,183,379; M1955a:1–30; M1961f;
M1962b:206;   M1966b:119–27;   M1971b:32.   R1943a:285;   R1947b:113;   R1948e;
R1950c:236; R1950d; R1951a:71,75,139,141,149,157,522,530; R1961a:87; R1961j;
R1963d; R1964b:166; R1972a:208.

65. M1954a:199–234,213,224–32,389; M1959a:119–36; M1959b:119–36; M1961c:5;
M1961f:8; M1962b:81–84,176–78,195; M1962c; M1964b:91–96; M1965g:119–21;
M1968b:3–5;   M1968f:36;   M1968g;   M1968i:18–24;   M1971a:43,122–25,133–
35,186,192–95,299–340; M1971b:32. R1948e; R1956g; R1957d; R1961a:163–82,183–
98,344;   R1963c;   R1964b;   R1971c:89;   R1972a:208;   R1978b;   R1982g:87.
MY1953a:160,162,188; MY1962c; MY1967a:73,174; MY1969a:268; MY1977b:298;
MY1981a:3,6,19.

66. MY1953a:175,216; MY1956b:357; MY1963d:206; MY1967a:51,80,177,184,
ch.5;   MY1969a:265–71;   MY1972a:254,259;   MY1975a:12;   MY1977b:302,304;
MY1977d; MY1980b:242–48; MY1981a:21.

67. MY1953a:187,206;   MY1967a:51,177;   MY1968c;   MY1974f;   MY1977a;
MY1980b:244.

68. S. Krippner et al., "Toward the Application of General Systems Theory in Humanistic Psychology, *Systems Research*, 1985, 2:105–15.

Appendix: Chronological Bibliographies

Because of extensive discussion of the works of the five humanistic psychologists, we have developed a special reference format. Notes referring to the chronological bibliographies listed in the Appendix include the year of publication and item letter, followed by the page number. The codes used were: "A" for Allport, "M" for Maslow, "R" for Rogers, "MY" for May, and "B" for Bugental. "A1923a:64," for example, refers to Allport's chronological bibliography, year 1923, item "a" (e.g., "Germany's state of mind"), page 64. Many of the writings of the five were reprinted in different places and years. The following bibliographies refer only to the essay's original publication. In cases where our quotation comes from a different source, a second reference follows. For detailed information, see Allport's *The Person in Psychology* (A1968a:410–30); Maslow's *The Farther Reaches of Human Nature* (M1971a:391–407); Rogers's *A Way of Being* (R1980a:357–79); and for May see C. Reeves, *The Psychology of Rollo May*, San Francisco: Jossey-Bass, 1977, pp. 311–29. The bibliographies of Rogers, May, and Bugental for the late 1980s are incomplete.

A. GORDON W. ALLPORT

1921

a. "Personality traits: Their classification and measurement" (with F. H. Allport), *J. Abnorm. Soc. Psy.*, 1921–1922, 18:6–40.

b. "Personality and character," *Psychol. Bull.*, 1921, 18:441–55.

c. Review of W. H. Pyle, *The Psychology of Learning, J. Abnorm. Soc. Psy.*, 1921–1922, 16:414–15.

d. Review of M. S. Pittman, *The Value of School Supervision*; W. S. Herzog, *State Maintenance for Teachers in Training*; A. G. Peaks, *Periodic Variations in Efficiency*, *J. Abnorm. Soc. Psy.*, 1921–1922, 16:415.

1922

a. Review of L. Berman, *The Glands Regulating Personality*, *J. Abnorm. Soc. Psy.*, 1922, 17:220–22.

b. Review of E. S. Bogardus, *Essentials of Social Psychology*, *J. Abnorm. Soc. Psy.*, 1922, 17:104–6.

1923

a. "Germany's state of mind," *New Republic*, 1923, 34:63–65.

b. "The Leipzig congress of psychology," *Amer. J. Psy.*, 1923, 34:612–15.

1924

a. "The study of the undivided personality," *J. Abnorm. Soc. Psy.*, 1924, 19:132–41.

b. "Eidetic imagery," *Brit. J. Psy.*, 1924, 15:99–120.

c. "Die theoretischen Hauptstromungen in der amerikanischen Psychologie der Gegenwart," *Zeitschrift f. Padagog. Psychol.*, 1924, 4:129–37.

d. "The standpoint of Gestalt psychology," *Psyche*, 1924, 4:354–61.

e. Review of M. P. Follett, *Creative Experience*, *J. Abnorm. Soc. Psy.*, 1924, 19:426–28.

f. Review of W. W. Smith, *The Measurement of Emotion*; H. Eng, *Experimentelle Untersuchungen uber das Gefuhlsleben des Kindes im Vergleich mit dem des Erwachsenen*, *J. Abnorm. Soc. Psy.*, 1924, 18:414–16.

1925

a. Review of W. B. Munro, *Personality in Politics*, *J. Abnorm. Soc. Psy.*, 1925, 20:209–11.

1926

a. Review of K. Dunlap, *Social Psychology*, *J. Abnorm. Soc. Psy.*, 1926, 21:95–100.

b. Review of O. Selz, *Uber die Personlichkeitstypen und die Methoden ihrer Bestimmung*, *Amer. J. Psy.*, 1926, 37:618–19.

1927

a. "Concepts of trait and personality," *Psychol. Bull.*, 1927, 24:284–93.

b. Review of A. A. Roback, *A Bibliography of Character and Personality*, *Psychol. Bull.*, 1927, 24:309–10.

c. Review of A. A. Roback, *Psychology of Character, Psychol. Bull.*, 1927, 24:717–23.

d. Review of W. S. Taylor (Ed.), *Readings in Abnormal Pschology and Mental Hygiene, J. Abnorm. Soc. Psy.*, 1927, 21:445–48.

1928

a. *A-S Reaction Study* (with F. H. Allport), Boston: Houghton Mifflin, 1928.

b. "The eidetic image and the after-image," *Amer. J. Psy.*, 1928, 40:418–25.

c. "A test for ascendance-submission," *J. Abnormal. Soc. Psy.*, 1928, 23:118–36.

1929

a. "The study of personality by the intuitive method: An experiment in teaching," from *The Locomotive God, J. Abnorm. Soc. Psy.*, 1929, 24:14–27.

b. "The composition of political attitudes," *Amer. J. Sociol.*, 1929, 35:220–38.

c. Review of E. T. Clark, *The Psychology of Religious Awakening, Psychol. Bull.*, 1929, 26:710–11.

d. Review of W. McDougall, *The Group Mind, J. Abnorm. Soc. Psy.*, 1929, 24:123–26.

e. Review of H. Meltzer and E. Bailor, *Developed Lessons in Psychology, Dartmouth Alumni Bull.*, 1929.

f. Review of T. Munro, *Scientific Method in Aesthetics, Psychol. Bull.*, 1929, 26:711.

g. Review of C. Murchison, *Social Psychology, Psychol. Bull.*, 1929, 26:709–10.

h. Review of M. Prince, *Clinical and Experimental Studies in Personality, Psychol. Bull.*, 1929, 26:711–12.

i. Review of L. T. Troland, *Fundamentals of Human Motivation, J. Abnorm. Soc. Psy.*, 1929, 23:510–13.

1930

a. "Some guiding principles in understanding personality," *The Family*, 1930, 11:124–28.

b. "The neurotic personality and traits of self-expression," *J. Soc. Psy.*, 1930, 1:514–27.

c. "The field of personality" (with P. E. Vernon), *Psychol. Bull.*, 1930, 27:677–730.

d. "Change and decay in the visual memory image," *Brit. J. Psy.*, 1930, 21:133–48.

e. Review of J. E. Downey, *Creative Imagination, Psychol. Bull.*, 1930, 27:408–10.

f. Review of K. Young, *Social Psychology, Psychol. Bull.*, 1930, 27:731–33.

1931

a. *A Study of Values* (with G. Lindzey and P. E. Vernon), Boston: Houghton Mifflin, 1931; rev. ed. 1951, 1960.

b. "What is a trait personality?" *J. Abnorm. Soc. Psy.*, 1931, 25:368–72.

c. "A test for personal values" (with P. E. Vernon), *J. Abnorm. Soc. Psy.*, 1931, 26:231–48.

1932

a. Review of W. Boven, *La Science du Caractère, Amer. J. Psy.*, 1932, 44:838–39.

b. Review of J. C. Flugel, *The Psychology of Clothes, Psychol. Bull.*, 1932, 29:358–59.

c. Review of D. Katz and F. H. Allport, *Students' Attitudes, Psychol. Bull.*, 1932, 29:356–58.

d. Review of F. Kunkel, *Vitale Dialektik, Psychol. Bull.*, 1932, 29:371–73.

e. Review of A. A. Roback, *Personality, Psychol. Bull.*, 1932, 29:359–60.

f. Review of J. J. Smith, *Social Psychology, Psychol. Bull.*, 1932, 29:360.

g. Review of P. M. Symonds, *Diagnosing Personality and Conduct, J. Soc. Psy.*, 1932, 3:391–97.

1933

a. *Studies in Expressive Movement* (with P. E. Vernon), New York: Macmillan, 1933.

b. "The study of personality by the experimental method," *Char. & Pers.*, 1933, 1:259–64.

c. "The determination of personal interests by psychological and graphological methods" (with H. Cantril and H. A. Rand), *Char. & Pers.*, 1933, 2:134–51.

d. "Recent applications of the study of values" (with H. Cantril), *J. Abnorm. Soc. Psy.*, 1933, 28:259–73.

e. Review of C. Buhler, *Der Menschliche Lebenslauf als Psychologisches Problem, Sociologus*, 1933, 9:336–38.

f. Review of N.D.M. Hirsch, *Genius and Creative Intelligence, Psychol. Bull.*, 1933, 30:365–66.

g. Review of L. Klages, *The Science of Character* (trans. W. H. Johnston), *Psychol. Bull.*, 1933, 30:370–71.

h. Review of M. A. McLaughlin, *The Genesis and Constancy of Ascendance and Submission as Personality Traits, Amer. J. Psy.*, 1933, 45:779–80.

1934

a. "Judging personality from voice" (with H. Cantril), *J. Soc. Psy.*, 1934, 5:37–55.

b. Review of A. Goldenweiser, *History, Psychology, and Culture, Psychol. Bull.*, 1934, 31:363–64.

c. Review of A. A. Roback, *Self-Consciousness and Its Treatment, Psychol. Bull.*, 1934, 31:370.

1935

a. *The Psychology of Radio* (with H. Cantril), New York: Harper, 1935.

b. "Attitudes," in C. C. Murchison (Ed.), *A Handbook of Social Psychology*, Worcester: Clark University Press, 1935, ch. 17; A1950a:1–47.

c. "The radio as a stimulus situation," *Acta Psychol.*, 1935, 1:1–6.

d. "The nature of motivation," *Understanding the Child*, Jan. 1935, pp. 3–6.

1936

a. *Trait-Names: A Psycho-Lexical Study* (with H. S. Odbert), *Psychol. Monogr.* 1936, 47:1–171, no. 211.

b. "Are attitudes biological or cultural in origin?" (with R. L. Schanck), *Char. & Pers.*, 1936, 4:195–205.

c. Review of G. K. Zipf, *The Psycho-Biology of Language, Psychol. Bull.*, 1936, 33:219–22.

1937

a. *Personality: A Psychological Interpretation*, New York: Holt, 1937.

b. "The functional autonomy of motives," *Amer. J. Psy.*, 1937, 50:141–56; A1950a:76–91.

c. "The personalistic psychology of William Stern," *Char. & Pers.*, 1937, 5:231–46.

1938

a. "The Journal of Abnormal and Social Psychology: An editorial," *J. Abnorm. Soc. Psy.*, 1938, 33:3–13.

b. "William Stern: 1871–1938," *Amer. J. Psy.*, 1938, 51:770–74.

c. "Personality: A problem for science or a problem for art?", *Revista de Psihologie*, 1938, 1:1–15; A1950a:198–209.

d. Review of L. B. Murphy, *Social Behavior and Child Personality, J. Abnorm. Soc. Psy.*, 1938, 33:538–43.

1939

a. "Dewey's individual and social psychology," in P. A. Schlipp (Ed.), *The Philosophy of John Dewey*, Evanston and Chicago: Northwestern University Press, 1939, ch. 9; A1968a:326–54.

b. "Recent applications of the A-S reaction study" (with R. Ruggles), *J. Abnorm. Soc. Psy.*, 1939, 34:518–28.

c. "The education of a teacher," *The Harvard Progressive*, 1939, 4:7–9.

1940

a. "The psychologist's frame of reference," *Psychol. Bull.*, 1940, 37:1–28; A1950a:48–75.

b. "Fifty years of change in American psychology" (with J. S. Bruner), *Psychol. Bull.*, 1940, 37:757–76.

c. "The psychology of newspapers: Five tentative laws" (with J. M. Faden), *Publ. Opin. Quart.*, 1940, 4:687–703.

d. "Motivation in personality: Reply to Mr. Bertocci," *Psychol. Rev.*, 1940, 47:533–54; A1950a:92–113.

e. "Liberalism and the motives of men," *Frontiers of Democracy*, 1940, 6:136–37.

f. Foreword to H. Werner, *Comparative Psychology of Mental Development* (trans. E. B. Garside), New York: Harper, 1940.

1941

a. "Liabilities and assets in civilian morale," *Ann. Amer. Acad. Pol. Soc. Sci.*, 1941, 216:88–94.

b. "Psychological service for civilian morale," *J. Consult. Psy.*, 1941, 5:235–39.

c. "Personality under social catastrophe: Ninety life-histories of the Nazi revolution" (with J. S. Bruner and E. M. Jandorf), *Char. & Pers.*, 1941, 10:1–22.

d. "Morale: American style," *Christian Sci. Monitor* (Weekly Magazine Section), April 26, 1941, pp. 1–2,13.

e. Review of J. M. MacKaye, *The Logic of Language, J. Abnorm. Soc. Psy.*, 1941, 36:296–97.

1942

a. *The Use of Personal Documents in Psychological Science*, Bull. 49, New York: Social Science Research Council, 1942.

b. "The nature of democratic morale," in G. Watson (Ed.) *Civilian Morale*, Boston: Houghton Mifflin, 1942, ch. 1, pp. 3–18.

c. "Defense seminars for morale study and morale building," *J. Soc. Psy.*, 1942, 15:399–401.

d. "Report on the third front: At home," *Christian Sci. Monitor* (Weekly Magazine Section), Sept. 5, 1942, pp. 6,14.

e. "Morale and its measurement," in *Public Policy*, Cambridge: Littauer School of Public Administration, 1942, 3:3–17.

f. Review of F. C. Bartlett, *Political Propaganda, Sat. Rev. Lit.*, 1942, 25:18.

1943

a. "The productive paradoxes of William James," *Psychol. Rev.*, 1943, 50:95–120; A1968a:298–325.

b. "Test tube for rumors," *Coronet*, 1943, 14:136–40.

c. "Psychological considerations in making the peace: Editorial note," *J. Abnorm. Soc. Psy.*, 1943, 38:131.

d. "This clinical supplement: Editorial note," *J. Abnorm. Soc. Psy.*, 1943, 38:3–5.

e. "Do rosy headlines sell newspapers?" (with E. C. Winship), *Publ. Opin. Quart.*, 1943, 7:205–10.

f. "Social psychology and the civilian war effort" (with H. R. Veltfort), *J. Soc. Psy.*, 1943, 18:165–233.

g. "The ego in contemporary psychology," *Psychol. Rev.*, 1943, 50:451–78; A1950a:114–41.

h. "Morale research and its clearing" (with G. R. Schmeidler), Psychol. Bull., 1943, 40:65–68.

i. "Restoring morale in occupied territory," *Publ. Opin. Quart.*, 1943, 7:606–17.

j. Review of E. P. Aldrich (Ed.), *As William James Said, J. Abnorm. Soc. Psy.*, 1943, 38:119–20.

k. Review of M. D. Allers, *The Psychology of Character, Amer. Sociol. Rev.*, 1943, 8:735–36.

l. Review of M. A. May, *A Social Psychology of War and Peace, Ann. Amer. Acad. Pol. Soc. Sci.*, 1943, 229:186–87.

m. Review of A. A. Roback, *William James: His Marginalia, Personality and Contribution, New England Quart.*, 1943, 16:143–44.

n. Review of C. Schrodes, J. van Gundy, and R. W. Husband (Eds.), *Psychology through Literature, J. Abnorm. Soc. Psy.*, 1943, 38:203, no. 2, Clin. Suppl.

o. Review of E. C. Tolman, *Drives toward War, J. Abnorm. Soc. Psy.*, 1943, 38:293–96.

1944

a. *A Tentative and Partial Manual for Police Training on the Subject of Police and Minority Groups*, Boston: Headquarters of the Boston Police Dept., 1944.

b. Prefaces to *Educational Opportunities in Greater Boston*, Cambridge: Prospect Union Educational Exchange, 1944 and annually thereafter.

c. "The quest of Nellie Wise Allport," privately printed, 1944.

d. "The roots of religion," *Advent Paper*, No. 1, Boston: Church of the Advent, 1944.

e. *ABC's of Scapegoating* (editor and author of foreword), Chicago: Central YWCA College, 1944.

f. "This clinical number: Editorial," *J. Abnorm. Soc. Psy.*, 1944, 39:147–49.

g. "Social psychology and the civilian war effort" (with G. R. Schmeidler), *J. Soc. Psy.*, 1944, 20:145–80.

h. "The bigot in our midst," *Commonweal*, 1944, 25:582–86; rev. ed., New York: Community Relations Service, 1950.

1945

a. "The psychology of participation," *Psychol. Rev.*, 1945, 52:117–32; A1950a:142–57.

b. "Human nature and the peace," *Psychol. Bull.*, 1945, 42:376–78.

c. "Catharsis and the reduction of prejudice," *J. Soc. Issues*, 1945, 1:3–10.

d. "The basic psychology of rumor" (with L. Postman), *Trans. N.Y. Acad. Sci.*, section on psychology, 1945, 8:61–81.

e. "Is intergroup education possible?" *Harv. Educ. Rev.*, 1945, 15:83–86.

f. Review of G. Gallup, *A Guide to Public Opinion*, *J. Abnorm. Soc. Psy.*, 1945, 40:113–14.

1946

a. "Personalistic psychology as science: A reply," *Psychol. Rev.*, 1946, 53:132–35.

b. "Controlling group prejudice" (editor and author of foreword), *Ann. Amer. Acad. Pol. Soc. Sci.*, 1946, vol. 244.

c. "Psychology and social relations at Harvard University" (with E. G. Boring), *Amer. Psychol.*, 1946, 1:119–22.

d. "Some roots of prejudice" (with B. M. Kramer), *J. Psy.*, 1946, 22:9–39; rev. ed., *Roots of Prejudice*, New York: American Jewish Congress, Pamphlet Series, Jewish Affairs, 1946, 1:13.

e. "Geneticism versus ego-structure in theories of personality," *Brit. J. Educ. Psy.*, 1946, 16:57–68; A1950a:158–67.

f. "Effect: A secondary principle of learning," *Psychol. Rev.*, 1946, 53:335–47.

g. Preface to E. Simmel (Ed.), *Anti-Semitism: A Social Disease*, New York: International Universities Press, 1946, pp. vii–ix.

h. "The priest and the psychologist," *Bull. of General Theological Seminary*, Sept. 1946.

i. "An analysis of rumor" (with L. Postman), *Publ. Opin. Quart.*, 1946–1947, 10:501–17; A1960a:311–26.

j. Introduction to Swami Akhilananda, *Hindu Psychology*, New York: Harper, 1946.

k. Review of A. H. Leighton, *The Governing of Men, J. Abnorm. Soc. Psy.*, 1946, 41:89–92.

1947

a. *The Psychology of Rumor* (with L. Postman), New York: Holt, 1947.

b. "Guidelines for research in international cooperation," *J. Soc. Issues*, 1947, 3:21–37.

c. Introduction to M. I. Rasey, *Toward Maturity, The Psychology of Child Development*, New York: Hinds, Hayden, and Eldredge, 1947.

d. "The genius of Kurt Lewin," *J. Pers.*, 1947, 16:1–10; A1968a:360–70.

e. "Scientific models and human morals," *Psychol. Rev.*, 1947, 54:182–92.

1948

a. Foreword to K. Lewin (G. W. Lewin, Ed.), *Resolving Social Conflicts*, New York: Harper, 1948, pp. vii–xiv.

b. "Psychology," in *College Reading and Religion*, New Haven: Yale University Press, 1948. ch. 3, pp. 81–114.

c. "The religion of the post-war college student" (with J. M. Gillespie and J. Young), *J. Psy.*, 1948, 25:3–33.

d. Review of D. Jacobson, *The Affair of Dame Rumor, Boston Sunday Post*, Oct. 24, 1948.

e. Review of E. Mayo, *Some Notes on the Psychology of Pierre Janet, Survey Graphic*, 1948, 37:5,267.

f. Review of A. Schweitzer, *The Psychiatric Study of Jesus, Christian Register*, April 1948.

1949

a. "Psychology and the fourth R," *New Republic*, Oct. 17, 1949, pp. 23–26.

b. Editorial note, *J. Abnorm. Soc. Psy.*, 1949, 44:439–42.

1950

a. *The Nature of Personality: Selected Papers*, Reading, Mass.: Addison-Wesley, 1950.

b. *The Individual and His Religion*, New York: Macmillan, 1950.

c. Foreword to M. G. Ross, *Religious Beliefs of Youth*, New York: Association Press, 1950.

d. "How shall we evaluate teaching?" in B. B. Cronkhite (Ed.), *A Handbook for College Teachers*, Cambridge: Harvard University Press, 1950. ch. 3.

e. "The role of expectancy," in H. Cantril (Ed.), *Tensions that Cause Wars*, Urbana: University of Illinois Press, 1950; A1960a:327–46.

f. "A psychological approach to the study of love and hate," in P. A. Sorokin (Ed.), *Explorations in Altruistic Love and Behavior*, Boston: Beacon Press, 1950, ch. 5; A1960a:199–216.

g. "Prejudice: A problem in psychological and social causation," *J. Soc. Issues*, 1950, Suppl. Series.

h. Review of S. A. Stouffer, et al., *The American Soldier* (2 vols.), *J. Abnorm. Soc. Psy.*, 1950, 45:168–73.

i. Review of M. Horkheimer and S. H. Flowerman, (Eds.), *Studies in Prejudice* (5 volumes), New York: Harper, 1950, *Sci. Amer.*, 1950, 182:56–58.

1951

a. "The situation we face: A psychological analysis," in A. W. Loos (Ed.), *Religious Faith and World Culture*, New York: Prentice-Hall, 1951, pp. 35–48.

b. "Basic principles in improving human relations," in K. W. Bigelow (Ed.), *Cultural Groups and Human Relations*, New York: Teachers College–Columbia University, 1951, ch. 2, pp. 8–28.

c. Foreword to M. H. Wormser and C. Selltiz, *How to Conduct a Community Self-Survey of Civil Rights*, New York: Association Press, 1951.

d. Foreword to H. E. Kagan, *Changing the Attitude of Christian toward Jew*, New York: Columbia University Press, 1951.

e. Foreword to E. Powers and H. Witmer, *An Experiment in the Prevention of Delinquency*, New York: Columbia University Press, 1951.

f. Review of J. La Farge, S. J., *No Postponement, Thought*, 1951, 26:471–72, No. 102.

1952

a. "An evaluation of AFSC volunteer work service camps in Germany," in H. W. Riecken, *The Volunteer Work Camp: A Psychological Evaluation*, Cambridge: Addison-Wesley, 1952, Appendix A, pp. 185–220.

b. "Resolving intergroup tensions, an appraisal of methods," in L. A. Cook (Ed.), *Toward Better Human Relations*, Detroit: Wayne University Press, 1952, ch. 3.

c. "The individual and his religion," *The Andover Newton Bull.*, 1952, 44:3–10.

d. "The resolution of intergroup tensions," an *Intergroup Education Pamphlet*, New York: National Conference on Christians and Jews, 1952.

e. "The mature personality," *Pastoral Psychol.*, 1952, 2:19–24.

f. "What is on the student's mind?" Proceedings of the *Thirtieth Annual Meeting of the American College Health Association*, Bulletin, No. 32, Stanford: Stanford University Press, 1952.

g. "Why do people join?" Interview in *Adult Leadership*, 1952, 1:10–12.

h. "Reading the nature of prejudice," *Claremont College Reading Conference*, Seventeenth Yearbook (Claremont, Calif.), 1952, pp. 51–64.

1953

a. *An Evaluation of Present Methods for Selecting Postulants in the Episcopal Diocese . . .* (with J. Fairbanks), Boston: The Diocese of Massachusetts, 1953.

b. "The trend in motivational theory," *Amer. J. Orthopsychiat.*, 1953, 25:107–19; A1960a:107–19.

c. "The teaching-learning situation," *Publ. Hlth. Rep.*, 1953, 68:875–79.

d. "The psychological nature of personality," *The Personalist*, 1953, 34:347–57.

e. Review of H. G. Trager and M. R. Yarrow, *They Learn What They Live, The Child*, 1953, 18:30.

1954

a. *The Nature of Prejudice*, Reading, Mass.: Addison-Wesley, 1954.

b. "Techniques for reducing group prejudice," in P. A. Sorokin (Ed.), *Forms and Techniques of Altruistic and Spiritual Growth*, Boston: Beacon, 1954, ch. 24.

c. "The historical background of social psychology," in G. Lindzey (Ed.), *Handbook of Social Psychology*, Cambridge: Addison-Wesley, 1954, vol. 1, ch. 1.

d. Introduction to J. Evans, *Three Men*, New York: Knopf, 1954.

e. "A psychologist views the Supreme Court ruling on segregation," *Nieman Reports*, 1954, 8:12–13.

f. Comments on J. L. Moreno, "Transference, counter transference and tele: Their relation to group research and group psychotherapy," *Group Psychother.*, 1954, 7:307–8.

1955

a. *Becoming: Basic Considerations for a Psychology of Personality*, New Haven: Yale University Press, 1955.

b. *Youth's Outlook on the Future* (with J. M. Gillespie), New York: Doubleday, Papers in Psychology, 1955 (distributed by Random House).

c. "The limits of social service," in J. E. Russell (Ed.), *National Policies for Education, Health and Social Services*, New York: Doubleday, 1955, pp. 194–213.

d. Review of R. B. Perry, *Realms of Value: A Critique of Human Civilization, J. Abnorm. Soc. Psy.*, 1955, 50:154–56.

e. Review of S. A. Stouffer, *Communism, Conformity, and Civil Liberties, Sat. Rev. Lit.*, 1955, 28:14–15.

1956

a. "Prejudice in modern perspective," *The Hoernle Memorial Lecture*, 1956, Durban, South Africa: The South African Institute of Race Relations, 1956.

b. "The participant citizen," *The Sixth Annual George Denny Lecture*, September 4, 1956, Durban, South Africa: Natal Technical College.

c. Review of M. Freedman, *A Minority in Britain: Social Studies of the Anglo-Jewish Community, Amer. Anthrop.*, 1956, 58:401–2.

1957

a. "European and American theories of personality," in H. P. David and H. von Bracken (Eds.), *Perspectives in Personality Theory*, New York: Basic Books, 1957, ch. 1.

b. "Cultural influence on the perception of movement: The trapezoidal illusion among Zulus" (with T. F. Pettigrew), *J. Abnorm. Soc. Psy.*, 1957, 55:104–13.

c. Review of P. A. Bertocci, *Free Will, Responsibility, and Grace, Religion in Life*, 1957, 26:612–13.

1958

a. *The Nature of Prejudice*, abridged ed., Garden City: Doubleday Anchor, 1958.

b. "What units shall we employ?" in G. Lindzey (Ed.), *Assessment of Human Motives*, New York: Rinehart, 1958, ch. 9.

c. Foreword to G. V. Coelho, *Changing Images of America: A Study of Indian Students' Perceptions*, Glencoe, Ill.: The Free Press, 1958.

d. Foreword to E. Mira y Lopez (L. Bellak, et al., Eds.), M.K.P. Myokinetic Psycho-diagnosis (trans.) New York: Logos Press, 1958.

e. "Perception and public health," *Health Education Monographs*, Oakland, Calif.: Society of Health Educators, 1958, No. 2, pp. 2–15; A1960a:295–310.

f. "Binocular resolution and perception of race in South Africa" (with T. F. Pettigrew and E. O. Barnett), *Brit. J. Psy.*, 1958, 49:265–78, part 4.

g. "Personality: Normal and abnormal," *The Sociological Review*, 1958, 6:167–80; A1960a:155–68.

h. Review of P. Lafitte, *The Person in Psychology: Reality or Abstraction?, Contemp. Psy.*, 1958, 3:105.

1959

a. "Normative compatibility in the light of social science," in A. H. Maslow (Ed.), *New Knowledge in Human Values*, New York: Harper, 1959, pp. 137–50.

b. Preface to the English translation of V. E. Frankl, *From Death-Camp to Existentialism*, Boston: Beacon Press, 1959.

c. "Religion and prejudice," *The Crane Review*, 1959, 2:1–10; A1960a:257–67.

1960

a. *Personality and Social Encounter*, Boston: Beacon Press, 1960.

b. "Uniqueness in students," in W. D. Weatherford, Jr. (Ed.), *The Goals of Higher Education*, Cambridge: Harvard University Press, 1960, pp. 57–75.

c. "Psychology and religion," in J. Clark (Ed.), *The Student Seeks an Answer*, ch. 2. Ingraham Lectures in Philosophy and Religion, Waterville, Maine: Colby College Press, 1960, pp. 35–49.

d. "The open system in personality theory," *J. Abnorm. Soc. Psy.*, 1960, 61:301–10.

1961

a. *Pattern and Growth in Personality*, New York: Holt, Rinehart and Winston, 1961.

b. Introduction to W. James, *Psychology: The Briefer Course*, New York: Harper Torchbooks, 1961, pp. xiii–xxiii.

c. Foreword to C. E. Lincoln, *The Black Muslims in America*, Boston: Beacon Press, 1961, pp. ix–xi.

d. Comment in R. May (Ed.), *Existential Psychology*, New York: Random House, 1961, ch. 6, pp. 94–100.

e. "William Douglas (the man of the month)," *Pastoral Psychol.*, 1961, 12:6,66.

f. "Approach to mental health," reprint of portions of *The Individual and His Religion* (1950), *Sci. of Mind*, 1961, 34:6–11,37–42.

g. "Values and our youth," *Teachers Coll. Rec.*, 1961, 63:211–19; A1968a:155–57.

h. "The psychologist's image of man," in *Proceedings of the Summer Conference*, Bellingham, Wash.: *Western Washington State College Bull.*, 1961, 14:1–12.

i. "Prejudice in perspective" (Lucile P. Morrison Lecture), La Jolla, Calif., Western Behavioral Sciences Institute, *Report No. 1*, 1961.

1962

a. "The general and the unique in psychological science," *J. Per.*, 1962, 30:405–22; A1968a:81–102.

b. "Prejudice: Is it societal or personal?" *J. Soc. Issues*, 1962, 18:120–34; A1968a:187–207.

c. "Psychological models for guidance," *Harv. Educ. Rev.*, 1962, 32:373–81; A1968a:67–81.

d. Review of G. C. Zahn, *German Catholics and Hitler's Wars, Unitarian-Universalist Register-Leader*, 1962, 143:21.

1963

a. "Behavioral science, religion, and mental health," *J. Relig. & Health*, 1963, 2:187–97; A1968a:141–54.

b. Foreword to N. L. Farberow (Ed.), *Taboo Topics*, New York: Atherton Press, 1963.

1964

a. ''Crises in normal personality development,'' *Teachers Coll. Rec.* 1964, 66:235–41; A1968a:171–83.

b. ''The fruits of eclecticism: Bitter or sweet?'' *Acta Psychol.*, 1964, 23:27–44; A1968a:3–27.

c. ''Imagination in psychology: Some needed steps'' (York University Lecture Series), in *Imagination and the University*, Toronto: University of Toronto Press, 1964, 63–82; A1968a:103–19.

d. ''Peter Bertocci: Philosopher-psychologist,'' *The Philosophical Forum* (Boston University), 1963–1964, 21:3–7.

e. ''Mental health: A generic attitude,'' *J. Relig. & Health*, 1964, vol. 4; A1968a:123–40.

1965

a. *Letters from Jenny*, New York: Harcourt, Brace and World, 1965.

b. ''Abraham Aaron Roback: 1890–1965,'' *Amer. J. Psy.*, 1965, 88:689–90.

c. ''Traits revisited,'' *Psy. Today* (Journal of the Dept. of Psychology of the University of Newcastle on Tyne), 1965, pp. 57–76; A1968a:43–66.

1966

a. Foreword to Van Ness Bates, *Christianity and World Civilization*, Boston: Christopher Press, 1966.

b. ''Can prejudice be reduced?'' *East-West Center Today*, 1966, 6:3–6.

c. ''Prejudice and the individual,'' in John P. Davis (Ed.), *The American Negro Reference Book*, Englewood Cliffs, N.J.: Prentice-Hall, 1966, ch. 17, pp. 706–13; A1968a:208–17.

d. ''The religious context of prejudice,'' *The Graduate J.* (of the University of Texas), 1966, 7:115–30; A1968a:218–36.

e. ''The spirit of Richard Clarke Cabot,'' *J. Pastoral Counsel.*, 1966, 20:102–4.

f. ''William James and the behavioral sciences,'' *J. Behavioral Sciences*, 1966, 2:145–47.

g. Review of Karl Buhler, *Die Krise der Psychologie, J. General Psy.*, 1966, 75:201–4; A1968a:355–59.

h. Review of A. Koestler, *The Act of Creation, Contemp. Psy.*, 1966, 11:49–51.

1967

a. ''Gordon W. Allport,'' in E. G. Boring and G. Lindzey (Eds.), *A History of Psychology in Autobiography*, Vol. 5, New York: Appleton-Century-Crofts, 1967, 1–25.

b. "Personal religious orientation and prejudice" (with J. Michael Ross), *J. Pers. and Soc. Psy.*, 1967, 5:432–43; A1968a:237–63.

c. "The personalistic psychology of William Stern," in B. B. Wolman (Ed.), *Historical Roots of Contemporary Psychology*, New York: Harper and Row, 1967; A1968a:271–97.

d. "The problem, the mystery: Some reflections on theological education," *The Bull. of the Episcopal Theological School*, 1967, 59:15–18.

e. "Six decades of social psychology," in Sven Lundstedt (Ed.), *The Preparation of Social Psychologists*, ch. 1, Cleveland: Western Reserve University Press, 1967; A1968a:28–42.

f. "A unique and open system," *International Encyclopedia of the Social Sciences*, Vol. 12, pp. 1–5.

1968

a. *The Person in Psychology: Selected Essays*, Boston: Beacon Press, 1968.

B. ABRAHAM H. MASLOW

1931

a. *The Effect of Varying External Conditions on Learning, Retention and Reproduction*, unpublished master's thesis, University of Wisconsin–Madison, 1931.

1932

a. "Delayed reaction tests on primates from the lemur to the orangutan" (with Harry Harlow and Harold Vehling), *J. Comparative Psy.*, 1932, 13:313–42.

b. "Delayed reaction tests on primates at Bronx Park Zoo" (with Harry Harlow), *J. Comparative Psy.*, 1932, 14:97–101.

c. "The emotion of disgust in dogs," *J. Comparative Psy.*, 1932, 14:401–7.

1933

a. "Food preference of primates," *J. Comparative Psy.*, 1933, 16:187–97.

1934

a. "Influence of differential motivation on delayed reactions in monkeys" (with Elizabeth Groshong), *J. Comparative Psy.*, 1934, 18:75–83.

b. "The effect of varying external conditions on learning, retention and reproduction," *J. Comparative Psy.*, 1934, 17:36–47.

c. "The effect of varying time intervals between acts of learning with a note on proactive inhibition," *J. Experimental Psy.*, 1934, 17:141–44.

1935

a. "Appetites and hungers in animal motivation," *J. Comparative Psy.*, 1935, 20:75–83.

b. "Individual psychology and the social behavior of monkeys and apes," *International J. Individual Psy.*, 1935, 1:47–59.

1936

a. "The role of dominance in the social and sexual behavior of infra-human primates: I. Observations at Vilas Park Zoo," *J. Genetic Psy.*, 1936, 48:261–77.

b. "II. An experimental determination of the dominance behavior syndrome" (with Sydney Flanzbaum), *J. Genetic Psy.*, 1936, 48:278–309.

c. "III. A theory of sexual behavior of infra-human primates," *J. Genetic Psy.*, 1936, 48:310–38.

d. "IV. The determination of hierarchy in pairs and in groups," *J. Genetic Psy.*, 1936, 49:161–98.

1937

a. "The comparative approach to social behavior," *Social Forces*, 1937, 15:487–90.

b. "The influence of familiarization on preferences," *J. Experimental Psy.*, 1937, 21:162–80.

c. "Dominance-feeling, behavior and status," *Psychol. Rev.*, 1937, 44:404–29.

d. "Personality and patterns of culture," in Ross Stagner, *Psychology of Personality*, New York: McGraw-Hill, 1937, pp. 408–28.

e. "An experimental study of insight in monkeys" (with Walter Grether), *J. Comparative Psy.*, 1937, 24:127–34.

1939

a. "Dominance, personality and social behavior in women," *J. Soc. Psy.*, 1939, 10:3–39.

1940

a. "Dominance-quality and social behavior in infra-human primates," *J. Soc. Psy.*, 1940, 11:313–24.

b. "A test for dominance-feeling (self-esteem) in college women," *J. Soc. Psy.*, 1940, 12:255–70.

1941

a. *Principles of Abnormal Psychology: The Dynamic of Psychic Illness* (with Bela Mittelmann), New York: Harper, 1941.

b. "Deprivation, threat and frustration," *Psychol. Rev.*, 1941, 48:364–66; M1954a:155–58.

1942

a. "Liberal leadership and personality," *Freedom*, 1942, 2:27–30.

b. *Manual for Social Personality Inventory for College Women*, Stanford, Calif.; Stanford University Press, 1942.

c. "The dynamics of psychological security-insecurity," *J. Pers.*, 1942, 10:331–44.

d. "A comparative approach to the problem of destructiveness," *Psychiatry*, 1942, 5:517–22; M1954a:168–78.

e. "Self-esteem (dominance-feeling) and sexuality in women," *J. Soc. Psy.*, 1942, 16:259–94.

1943

a. "A preface to motivation theory," *Psychosomatic Medicine*, 1943, 5:85–92; M1954a:63–79.

b. "A theory of human motivation," *Psychol. Rev.*, 1943, 50:370–96; M1954a:80–100.

c. "Conflict, frustration and the theory of threat," *J. Abnorm. Soc. Psy.*, 1943, 38:81–86; M1954a:158–67.

d. "The dynamics of personality organization: I & II,"*Psychol. Rev.*, 1943, 50:514–39,541–58; M1954a:22–62.

e. "The authoritarian character structure," *J. Soc. Psy.*, 1943, 18:401–11.

1944

a. "What intelligence tests mean," *J. Genetic Psy.*, 1944, 31:85–93.

1945

a. "A clinically derived test for measuring psychological security-insecurity" (with E. Birsh, M. Stein, and I. Hanigman), *J. General Psy.*, 1945, 33:21–41.

b. "A suggested improvement in semantic usage," *Psychol. Rev.*, 1945, 52:239–40.

c. "Experimentalizing the clinical method," *J. Clinical Psy.*, 1945, 1:241–43.

1946

a. "Security and breast feeding" (with I. Szilagyi-Kessler), *J. Abnorm. Soc. Psy.*, 1946, 41:83–85.

b. "Problem-centering vs. means-centering in science," *Philosophy of Science*, 1946, 13:326–31; M1954a:13–21.

1947

a. "A symbol for holistic thinking," *Persona*, 1947, 1:24–25.

1948

a. " 'Higher' and 'lower' needs," *J. Psy.*, 1948, 25:433–36; M1954a:146–54.

b. "Cognition of the particular and the generic," *Psychol. Rev.*, 1948, 55:22–40; M1954a:261–90.

c. "Some theoretical consequences of basic need-gratification," *J. Pers.* 1948, 16:402–16; M1954a:107–22.

1949

a. "Our maligned animal nature," *J. Psy.*, 1949, 28:273–78; M1954a:123–45.

b. "The expressive component of behavior," *Psychol. Rev.*, 1949, 56:261–72; M1954a:179–98.

1950

a. "Self-actualizing people: A study of psychological health," *Personality Symposia: Symposium No. 1 on Values*, New York: Grune and Stratton, 1950, pp. 11–34; M1954a:199–234.

1951

a. "Social theory of motivation," in Maurice J. Shore (Ed.), *Twentieth Century Mental Hygiene*, New York: Social Science Publishers, 1951, pp. 347–57.

b. "Personality" (with D. MacKinnon), in Harry Helson (Ed.), *Theoretical Foundations of Psychology*, New York: Van Nostrand, 1951, pp. 602–55.

c. "Higher needs and personality," *Dialectica* (University of Liege), 1951, 5:257–65.

d. "Resistance to acculturation," *J. Soc. Issues*, 1951, 7:26–29.

e. *Principles of Abnormal Psychology* (with B. Mittelman), rev. ed., New York: Harper, 1951.

1952

a. "Volunteer-error in the Kinsey study" (with J. Sakoda), *J. Abnorm. Soc. Psy.*, 1952, 47:259–62.

b. *The S-I Test* (A measure for psychological security and insecurity), Palo Alto, Calif.: Consulting Psychologists, 1952.

1953

a. "Love in healthy people," in A. Montagu (Ed.), *The Meaning of Love*, New York: Julian Press, 1953, pp. 57–93; M1954a:235–60.

b. "College teaching ability, scholarly activity and personality" (with W. Zimmerman), *J. Educational Psy.*, 1953, 47:185–89.

1954

a. *Motivation and Personality*, New York: Harper, 1954. Includes various papers published previously and items M1954c-g.

b. "The instinctoid nature of basic needs," *J. Pers.*, 1954, 22:326–47; M1954a:123–45.

c. "Normality, health and values," M1954a:335–52.

d. "Unmotivated and purposeless reactions," M1954a:291–304.

e. "Psychotherapy, health and motivation," M1954a:305–34.

f. "Toward a positive psychology," M1954a:353–63.

g. "Elements of a psychological approach to science," M1954a:1–12.

h. "Abnormal psychology," *National Encyclopedia*.

1955

a. "Deficiency motivation and growth motivation," in M. R. Jones (Ed.), *Nebraska Symposium in Motivation*, Lincoln: University of Nebraska Press, 1955, pp. 1–30.

b. "Comments on Prof. McClelland's paper," in M. R. Jones (Ed.), *Nebraska Symposium in Motivation*, Lincoln: University of Nebraska Press, pp. 65–142.

c. "Comments on Prof. Old's paper," in M. R. Jones (Ed.), *Nebraska Symposium in Motivation*, Lincoln: University of Nebraska Press, pp. 143–47.

1956

a. "Effects of esthetic surroundings: I. Initial effects of three esthetic conditions upon perceiving 'energy' and 'well-being' in faces" (with N. L. Mintz), *J. Psy.*, 1956, 41:247–54.

b. "Personality problems and personality growth," in C. Moustakas (Ed.), *The Self*, New York: Harper, 1956; M1962b:3–8.

c. "Defense and growth," *Merrill-Palmer Quart.*, 1956, 3:36–47; M1962b:44–59.

d. "A philosophy of psychology," *Main Currents*, 1956, 13:27–32; Frank T. Severin (Ed.), *Humanistic Viewpoints in Psychology*, New York: McGraw-Hill, 1965, pp. 17–33.

1957

a. "Power relationships and patterns of personal development," in A. Kornhauser (Ed.), *Problems of Power in American Democracy*, Detroit: Wayne University Press, 1957.

b. "Security of judges as a factor in impressions of warmth in others" (with J. Bossom), *J. Abnorm. Soc. Psy.*, 1957, 55:147–48.

c. "Two kinds of cognition and their integration," *General Semantics Bull.*, 1957, 20–21:17–22.

1958

a. "Emotional blocks to creativity," *J. Individual Psy.*, 1958, 14:51–56; M1971a:81–95.

1959

a. "Psychological data and human values," M1959b:119–36.

b. Editor of *New Knowledge in Human Values*, New York: Harper, 1959.

c. "Creativity in self-actualizing people," in H. H. Anderson (Ed.), *Creativity and Its Cultivation*, New York: Harper, 1959; M1962b:135–45.

d. "Cognition of being in the peak experiences," *J. Genetic Psy.*, 1959, 94:43–66; M1962b:71–102.

e. "Mental health and religion," in *Religion, Science and Mental Health*, Academy of Religion and Mental Health, Albany: New York University Press, 1959, pp. 16–22.

f. "Critique of self-actualization: I. Some dangers of being-cognition," *J. Individual Psy.*, 1959, 15:24–32; M1962b:115–25.

1960

a. "Juvenile delinquency as a value disturbance" (with R. Diaz-Guerrero), in J. Peatman and E. Hartley (Eds.), *Festschrift for Gardner Murphy*, New York: Harper, 1960; M1971a:369–78.

b. "Remarks on existentialism and psychology," *Existentialist Inquiries*, 1960, 1:1–5; M1962b:9–17.

c. "Resistance to being rubricized," in B. Kaplan and S. Wagner (Eds.), *Perspectives in Psychological Theory, Essays in Honor of Heinz Werner*, International Universities Press, 1960; M1962b:126–31.

d. "Some parallels between the dominance and sexual behavior of monkeys and the fantasies of patients in psychotherapy" (with H. Rand and S. Newman), *J. Nervous and Mental Diseases*, 1960, 131:202–12; M1971a:351–68.

1961

a. "Health as transcendence of the environment," *J. Hum. Psy.*, 1961, 1:1–7; M1962b:179–85.

b. "Peak experiences as acute identity experiences," *Amer. J. Psychoanalysis*, 1961, 21:254–60; M1962b:103–14.

c. "Eupsychia—The good society," *J. Hum. Psy.*, 1961, 1:1–11.

d. "Are our publications and conventions suitable for the personal psychologies?" *Amer. Psychologist*, 1961, 16:318–19; M1962b:215–19.

e. "Comments on Skinner's attitude to science," *Daedalus*, 1961, 90:572–73.

f. "Some frontier problems in mental health," in A. Combs (Ed.), *Personality Theory and Counseling Practice*, Gainesville: University of Florida Press, 1961.

1962

a. "Some basic propositions of a growth and self-actualization psychology," in A. Combs (Ed.), *Perceiving, Behaving, Becoming, 1962 Yearbook of Association for Supervision and Curriculum Development*, Washington, D.C.: ASCD, 1962.

b. *Toward a Psychology of Being*, New York: Nostrand, 1962; 2d ed., 1968.

c. Review of John Schaar, *Escape from Authority, The Humanist*, 1962, 22:34–35.

d. "Lessons from the peak-experiences," *J. Hum. Psy.*, 1962, 2:9–18.

e. "Notes on being-psychology," *J. Hum. Psy.*, 1962, 2:47–71; M1971a:126–48.

f. "Was Ader a disciple of Freud? A note," *J. Individual Psy.*, 1962, 18:125.

g. "Summary comments: Symposium on human values," in L. Solomon (Ed.), *WBSI Report No. 17*, pp. 41–44; *J. Hum. Psy.*, 1962, 2:110–11.

h. *Summer Notes on Social Psychology of Industry and Management*, Del Mar, Calif.: Nonlinear Systems, Inc., 1962; rev. ed. in M1965g.

i. "A dialogue with Abraham H. Maslow" (transcript by M. Hardeman at The New School for Social Research in 1962), *J. Hum. Psy.*, 1979, 19:23–28.

1963

a. "The need to know and the fear of knowing," *J. General Psy.*, 1963, 68:111–25; included in M1962b:60–67.

b. "The creative attitude," *The Structurist*, 1963, 3:4–10; M1971a:57–71.

c. "Fusion of facts and values," *Amer. J. Psychoanalysis*, 1963, 23:117–31; M1971a:105–25.

d. "Criteria for judging needs to be instinctoid," *Proceedings of 1963 International Congress of Psychology*, Amsterdam: North-Holland, 1964, pp. 86–86; M1971a:379–90.

e. "Further notes on being-psychology," *J. Hum. Psy.*, 1963, 3:120–35.

f. "Notes on innocent cognition," in L. Schenk-Danzinger and H. Thomas (Eds.), *Gegenwartsprobleme der Entwicklungspsychologie: Festschrift fur Charlotte Buhler*, Gottingen: Verlag fur Psychologie, 1963; M1971a:251–59.

g. "The scientific study of values," *Proceedings 7th Congress of Inter-American Society of Psychology*, Mexico, D. F., 1963.

h. "Notes on unstructured groups," *Human Relations Training News*, 1963, 7:1–4.

1964

a. "The superior person," *Trans-Action*, 1964, 1:10–13.

b. *Religion, Values and Peak-Experiences*, Columbus: Ohio State University Press, 1964; paperback ed., Viking Press, 1970. Reprinted fifteen times between 1970 and 1981.

c. "Synergy in the society and in the individual" (with L. Gross), *J. Individual Psy.*, 1964, 20:153–64; M1971a:199–211.

d. "Further notes on the psychology of being," *J. Hum. Psy.*, 1964, 4:45–58.

e. Preface to the Japanese translation of *Toward a Psychology of Being*, Tokyo: Seishin-Shobo, 1964.

1965

a. "Observing and reporting education experiments," *The Humanist*, 1965, 25:13.

b. Foreword to Andras Angyal, *Neurosis and Treatment: A Holistic Theory*, New York: Wiley, 1965, pp. v–vii.

c. "The need for creative people," *Personnel Administration*, 1965, 28:3–5,21–22; M1971a:96–101.

d. Critique and discussion in J. Money (Ed.), *Sex Research: New Developments*, New York: Holt, Rinehart and Winston, 1965, pp. 135–43,144–46.

e. "Humanistic science and transcendent experiences," *J. Hum. Psy.*, 1965, 5:219–27.

f. "Criteria for judging needs to be instinctoid," in M. R. Jones (Ed.), *Human Motivation: A Symposium*, Lincoln: University of Nebraska Press, 1965, pp. 33–47.

g. *Eupsychian Management: A Journal*, Homewood, Ill.: Irwin-Dorsey, 1965. A revised version of 1962h.

h. "Art judgment and the judgment of others: A preliminary study" (with R. Morant), *J. Clinical Psy.*, 1965, 21:389–91.

1966

a. "Isomorphic interrelationships between knower and known," in G. Kepes (Ed.), *Sign, Image, Symbol*, New York: Braziller, 1966; M1971a:155–67.

b. *The Psychology of Science: A Reconnaissance*, New York: Harper and Row, 1966.

c. "Toward a psychology of religious awareness," *Explorations*, 1966, 9:23–41.

d. "Comments on Dr. Frankl's paper," *J. Hum. Psy.*, 1966, 6:107–12.

1967

a. "Neurosis as a failure of personal growth," *Humanitas*, 1967, 3:153–69; M1971a:25–40.

b. "Synanon and Eupsychia," *J. Hum. Psy.*, 1967, 7:28–35; M1971a:226–36.

c. Preface to Japanese translation of *Eupsychian Management*; M1968e:220–22.

d. "A theory of metamotivation: The biological rooting of the value-life," *J. Hum. Psy.*, 1967, 7:93–127; M1971a:299–340.

e. "Dialogue on communication" (with E. M. Drews), in A. Hitchcock (Ed.), *Guidance and the Utilization of New Educational Media: Report of the 1962 Conference*, American Personnel and Guidance Association, Washington, D.C.: APGA, pp. 1–47,63–68.

f. Foreword to Japanese translation of *Motivation and Personality*, Tokyo: Sangyo Noritsu Tanki Daigatu, 1967.

g. "Self-actualizing and beyond," in J. F. T. Bugental (Ed.), *Challenges of Humanistic Psychology*, New York: McGraw-Hill, 1967; M1971a:41–53.

1968

a. "Music, education and peak-experiences," *Music Educators J.*, 1968, 54:72–75,163–71; M1971a:168–79.

b. "The farther reaches of human nature," *J. Transpersonal Psy.*, 1968, 1:1–9.

c. "Human potentialities and the healthy society," in Herbert Otto (Ed.), *Human Potentialities*, St. Louis, Mo.: Green, 1968, pp. 64–79.

d. "The new science of man," in papers on *The Human Potential*, New York: Twentieth Century Fund, 1968.

e. *Toward a Psychology of Being*, 2d ed., Princeton, N.J.: Nostrand, 1968.

f. "Conversation with Abraham H. Maslow," *Psy. Today*, 1968, 2:34–37,54–57.

g. "Towards the study of violence," in Ng Larry (Ed.), *Alternatives to Violence*, New York: Time-Life, 1968.

h. "Some educational implications of the humanistic psychologies," *Harv. Educ. Rev.*, 1968, 38:685–96; M1971a:180–95.

i. "Goals of humanistic education," *Esalen Papers*, Big Sur, Calif.: Esalen, 1968.

j. *Maslow and Self-Actualization*, Santa Ana, Calif.: Psychological Films, 1968. Film.

k. "Some fundamental questions that face the normative social psychologist," *J. Hum. Psy.*, 1968, 8:143–54; M1971a:212–25.

l. "Eupsychian Network," mimeographed; M1968e:237–40.

1969

a. "Theory Z," *J. Transpersonal Psy.*, 1969, 1:31–47; M1971a:280–95.

b. "Various meanings of transcendence," *J. Transpersonal Psy.*, 1969, 1:56–66; M1971a:269–279.

c. "A holistic approach to creativity," in C. W. Taylor (Ed.), *A Climate for Creativity*, Salt Lake City, Utah: Seventh National Research Conference on Creativity, 1969; M1971a:72–80.

d. Editor of *The Healthy Personality: Readings*, (with Hung-Min Chiang), New York: Nostrand, Reinhold, 1969. Includes in pp. 35–36 an abridged form of M1967d.

e. "Notice biographique et bibliographique," *Revue de Psychologie Appliquée*, 1969, 18:167–73.

f. "Toward a humanistic biology," *Amer. Psychologist*, 1969, 24:724–25; M1971a:3–24.

g. "Humanistic education vs. professional education," *New Directions in Teaching*, 1969, 2:6–8; *J. Hum. Psy.*, 1979, 19:14–15.

1970

a. *Motivation and Personality*, rev. ed., New York: Harper and Row, 1970.

b. "Humanistic education vs. professional education: Further comments," *New Directions in Teaching*, 1970, 2:3–10; *J. Hum. Psy.*, 1979, 19:17–25.

c. "Abraham H. Maslow: A bibliography," *J. Hum. Psy.*, 1970, 10:98–110.

1971

a. *Farther Reaches of Human Nature*, New York: Viking, 1971.

b. *Humanistic Psychology: Interview with Maslow, Murphy and Rogers*, Willard B. Frick (Ed.), Columbus, Ohio: Merrill, 1971, pp. 19–49.

1972

a. *Abraham H. Maslow: A Memorial Volume*, Monterey, Calif.: Brooks/Cole, 1972.

1973

a. *Dominance, Self-Esteem, Self-Actualization: Germinal Papers of A. H. Maslow*, Richard J. Lowry (Ed.), Monterey, Calif.: Brooks/Cole, 1973.

1979

a. *The Journals of A. H. Maslow*, Vols. 1 and 2, Richard J. Lowry (Ed.), Monterey, Calif.: Brooks/Cole, 1979.

C. CARL R. ROGERS

1930

a. "Intelligence as a factor in camping activities," *Camping Magazine*, 1930, 3(3):8–11.

1931

a. *Measuring Personality Adjustment in Children Nine to Thirteen*, New York: Teachers College, Columbia University, Bureau of Publications, 1931.

b. *A Test of Personality Adjustment*, New York: Association Press, 1931.

c. "We pay for the Smiths" (with M. E. Rappaport), *Survey Graphic*, 1931, 19:508–509, 527,533,535.

1933

a. "A good foster home: Its achievements and limitations," *Mental Hygiene*, 1933, 17:21–40.

1936

a. "Social workers and legislation," *Quarterly Bulletin New York State Conference on Social Work*, Syracuse: 1936, 7(3):3–9.

1937

a. "The clinical psychologist's approach to personality problems," *The Family*, 1937, 18:233–43.

b. "Three surveys of treatment measures used with children," *Amer. J. Orthopsychiat.*, 1937, 7:48–57.

1938

a. "A diagnostic study of Rochester youth," *Quarterly Bulletin New York State Conference on Social Work*, Syracuse: 1938, pp. 48–54.

1939

a. "Authority and case work—Are they compatible?" *Quarterly Bulletin New York State Conference on Social Work*, Albany: 1939, pp. 16–24.

b. *The Clinical Treatment of the Problem Child*, Boston: Houghton Mifflin, 1939.

c. "Needed emphases in the training of clinical psychologists," *J. Consult. Psy.*, 1939, 3:141–43.

1940

a. "The processes of therapy," *J. Consult. Psy.*, 1940, 4:161–64.

1941

a. "Psychology in clinical practice," in J. S. Gray (Ed.), *Psychology in Use*, New York: American Book Co., 1941, pp. 114–67.

b. "The clinical significance of problem syndromes" (with C. C. Bennett), *Amer. J. Orthopsychiat.*, 1941, 11:210–21.

1942

a. *Counseling and Psychotherapy*, Boston: Houghton Mifflin, 1942.

b. "Mental health findings in three elementary schools," *Educ. Research Bull.*, 1942, 21:69–79.

c. "The psychologist's contributions to parent, child, and community problems," *J. Consult. Psy.*, 1942, 6:8–18.

d. "A study of the mental health problems in three representative elementary schools," in T. C. Holy and G. L. Walker, *A Study of Health and Physical Education in Columbus Public Schools*, Columbus: Ohio State University, Bur. of Educ. Res. Monogr. No. 25, 1942, pp. 130–61.

e. "The use of electrically recorded interviews in improving psychotherapeutic techniques," *Amer. J. Orthopsychiat.*, 1942, 12:429–34.

1943

a. "Therapy in guidance clinics," *J. Abnorm. Soc. Psy.*, 1943, 38:284–89.

1944

a. *Adjustment after Combat*, Army Air Forces Flexible Gunnery School, Fort Myers, Fla:, 1944.

b. "The development of insight in a counseling relationship," *J. Consult. Psy.*, 1944, 8:331–41.

c. "The psychological adjustments of discharged service personnel," *Psychol. Bull.*, 1944, 41:689–96.

1945

a. "Counseling," *Rev. of Educ. Res.*, 1945, 15:155–63.

b. "A Counseling Viewpoint for the USO Worker," *USO Program Services Bulletin*, 1945.

c. "Dealing with Individuals in USO," *USO Program Services Bulletin*, 1945.

d. "The nondirective method as a technique for social research," *Amer. J. Sociol.*, 1945, 50:279–83.

e. "A teacher-therapist deals with a handicapped child" (with V. M. Axline), *J. Abnorm. Soc. Psy.*, 1945, 40:119–42.

f. "Current trends in counseling, a symposium" (with R. Dicks and S. B. Wortis), *Marriage & Family Living*, 1945, 7(4).

g. "Wartime issues in family counseling," *Marriage & Family Living*, 1945, 7:68,84.

h. "War challenges family relationships," *Marriage & Family Living*, 1945, 7:86–87.

1946

a. *Counseling with Returned Servicemen* (with J. L. Wallen), New York: McGraw-Hill, 1946.

b. "Psychometric tests and client-centered counseling," *Educ. Psy. Measmt.*, 1946, 6:139–44.

c. "Recent research in nondirective therapy and its implications," *Amer. J. Orthopsychiat.* 1946, 16:581–88.

d. "Significant aspects of client-centered therapy," *Amer. Psychol.*, 1946, 1:415–22.

e. "Counseling of emotional blocking in an aviator" (with G. A. Muench), *J. Abnorm. Soc. Psy.*, 1946, 41:207–16.

1947

a. "The case of Mary Jane Tilden," in W. U. Snyder (Ed.), *Casebook of Nondirective Counseling*, Boston: Houghton Mifflin, 1947, pp. 129–203.

b. "Psychotherapy," in W. Dennis (Ed.), *Current Trends in Psychotherapy*, Pittsburgh: University of Pittsburgh Press, 1947, pp. 109–37.

c. "Some observations on the organization of personality," *Amer. Psychol.*, 1947, 2:358–68.

1948

a. *Dealing with Social Tensions: A Presentation of Client-Centered Counseling as a Means of Handling Interpersonal Conflict*, New York: Hinds, Hayden, and Eldredge, 1948.

b. "Divergent trends in methods of improving adjustment," *Harv. Educ. Rev.*, 1948, 18:209–19; *Pastoral Psychol.*, 1952, 3(28):11–18.

c. "Research in psychotherapy: Round table," *Amer. J. Orthopsychiat.*, 1948, 18:96–100.

d. "Some implications of client-centered counseling for college personnel work," *Educ. Psy. Measmt.*, 1948, 8:540–49; *College & University*, 1948–1949, 24:59–67.

e. "The role of self-understanding in the prediction of behavior" (with B. L. Kell and H. McNeil), *J. Consult. Psy.*, 1948, 12:174–86.

1949

a. "The attitude and orientation of the counselor in client-centered therapy," *J. Consult. Psy.*, 1949, 13:82–94.

b. "A coordinated research in psychotherapy: A non-objective introduction," *J. Consult. Psy.*, 1949, 13:149–53.

1950

a. "A current formulation of client-centered therapy," *Social Services Rev.*, 1950, 24:442–50.

b. "The significance of the self-regarding attitudes and perceptions," in M. L. Reymert (Ed.), *Feelings & Emotions*, New York: McGraw-Hill, 1950, pp. 374–82.

c. "What is to be our basic professional relationship?" Annals of Allergy, 1950, pp. 234–39.

d. "A basic orientation for counseling" (with R. Becker), *Pastoral Psychol.*, 1950, 1(1):26–34.

e. "ABEPP policies and procedures" (with D. G. Marquis and E. R. Hilgard), *Amer. Psychol.*, 1950, 5:407–8.

1951

a. *Client-Centered Therapy: Its Current Practice, Implications, and Theory*, Boston: Houghton Mifflin, 1951.

b. "Client-centered therapy: A helping process," *The University of Chicago Round Table*, 1951, 698:12–21.

c. "Perceptual reorganization in client-centered therapy," in R. R. Blake and G. V. Ramsey (Eds.), *Perceptions: An Approach to Personality*, New York: Ronald Press, 1951, pp. 307–27.

d. "Studies in client-centered psychotherapy. III: The case of Mrs. Oak–A research analysis," *Psy. Serv. Center J.*, 1951, 3:47–65; R1954e:259–348.

e. "Through the eyes of a client," *Pastoral Psychol.* 1951, 2(16):32–40; (17):45–50; (18):26–32.

f. "Where are we going in clinical psychology?" *J. Consult. Psy.*, 1951, 15:171–77.

g. "Studies in client-centered psychotherapy. I: Developing a program of research in psychotherapy" (with T. Gordon, D. L. Grumman, and J. Seeman), *Psy. Serv. Center J.*, 1951, 3:3–28; R1954e:12–34.

1952

a. "Client-centered psychotherapy," *Sci. Amer.*, 1952, 187:66–74.

b. "Communication: Its blocking & facilitation," *Northwestern Univ. Information*, 1952, 20:9–15; R1961a:329–37.

c. "A personal formulation of client-centered therapy," *Marriage & Family Living*, 1952, 14:341–61.

d. *Client-Centered Therapy: Parts I & II*, 16 mm. motion picture with sound (with R. H. Segel), State College, Pa.: Psychological Cinema Register, 1952.

e. "Barriers and gateways to communication" (with F. J. Roethlisberger), *Harvard Business Rev.*, July-Aug. 1952, pp. 23–34.

1953

a. "The interest in the practice of psychotherapy," *Amer. Psychol.*, 1953, 8:48–50.

b. "A research program in client-centered therapy," *Res. Publ. Ass. Nerv. Ment. Dis.*, 1953, 31:106–13.

c. "Some directions and end points in therapy," in O. H. Mowrer (Ed.), *Psychotherapy: Theory & Research*, New York: Ronald Press, 1953, pp. 44–68; R1961a:73–106.

d. "Removing the obstacles to good employee communications" (with G. W. Brooks, R. S. Driver, W. V. Merrihue, P. Pigors, and A. J. Rinella), *Management Record*, 1953, 15(1):9–11,32–40.

e. *Counseling as I See It*, Transcript of a Talk at the Guidance and Counseling Department of San Francisco State College.

1954

a. "Becoming a person," *Oberlin College Nellie Heldt Lecture Series*, Oberlin: Oberlin Printing Co., 1954; R1961a:31–38,107–24.

b. "The case of Mr. Bebb: The analysis of a failure case," in R1954e:349–409.

c. "Changes in the maturity of behavior as related to therapy," in R1954e:215–37.

d. "An overview of the research and some questions for the future," in R1954e:413–34.

e. Editor of *Psychotherapy & Personality Change* (with R. F. Dymond), Chicago: University of Chicago Press, 1954.

f. "Towards a theory of creativity," *ETC: A Review of General Semantics*, 1954, 11:249–60; R1961a:347–59.

1955

a. "A personal view of some issues facing psychologists," *Amer. Psychol.*, 1955, 10:247–49.

b. "Personality change in psychotherapy," *The International J. Social Psychiatry*, 1955, 1:31–41; R1961a:225–42.

c. "Persons or science? A philosophical question," *Amer. Psychol.*, 1955, 10:267–78; *Cross Currents*, 1953, 3(4):289–306.

d. *Psychotherapy Begins: The Case of Mr. Lin*, 16 mm. motion picture with sound, State College, Pa.: Psychological Cinema Register, 1955.

e. *Psychotherapy in Process: The Case of Miss Mun*, 16 mm. motion picture with sound, State College, Pa.: Psychological Cinema Register, 1955.

1956

a. "Client-centered therapy: A current view," in F. Fromm-Reichmann and J. L. Moreno (Eds.), *Progress in Psychotherapy*, New York: Grune and Stratton, 1956, pp. 199–209.

b. "A counseling approach to human problems," *Amer. J. Nursing*, 1956, 56:994–97.

c. "Implications of recent advances in the prediction and control of behavior," *Teachers Coll. Rec.*, 1956, 57:316–22.

d. "Intellectualized psychotherapy," Review of George Kelly, *The Psychology of Personal Constructs, Contemp. Psy.*, 1956, 1:357–58.

e. Review of Reinhold Niebuhr, *The Self and the Dramas of History, Chicago Theological Seminary Register*, 1956, 46:13–14; *Pastoral Psychol.*, 1958, 9(85):15–17.

f. "Some issues concerning the control of human behavior" (Symposium with B. F. Skinner), *Science*, 1956, 124(3231):1057–66; R. I. Evans, *Carl Rogers: The Man and His Ideas*, New York: Dutton, 1975, pp. xiv–lxxxviii.

g. "What it means to become a person," in C. E. Moustakas (Ed.), *The Self*, New York: Harper, 1956, pp. 195–211.

h. "Behavior theories and a counseling case" (with E. J. Shoben, O. H. Mowrer, G. A. Kimble, and J. G. Miller), *J. Counsel. Psy.*, 1956, 3:107–24.

1957

a. "The necessary and sufficient conditions of therapeutic personality change," *J. Consult. Psy.*, 1957, 21(2):95–103.

b. "A note on the nature of man," *J. Counsel. Psy.*, 1957, 4:199–203; *Pastoral Psychol.*, 1960, 11(104):23–26.

c. "Personal thoughts on teaching and learning," *Merrill-Palmer Quart.*, 1957, 3:241–43.

d. "A therapist's view of the good life," *The Humanist*, 1957, 17:291–300; R1961a:183–96.

e. "Training individuals to engage in the therapeutic process," in C. R. Strother (Ed.), *Psychology and Mental Health*, Washington, D.C.: APA, 1957, pp. 76–92.

f. *Active Listening* (with R. E. Farson), Chicago: University of Chicago, Industrial Relations Center, 1957.

g. *To Be That Self which One Truly Is—A Therapist's View of Personal Goals*, Transcript of a talk at the College of Wodstes on March 14, 1957.

1958

a. "A process conception of psychotherapy," *Amer. Psychol.*, 1958, 13:142–49.

b. "The characteristics of a helping relationship," *Personnel & Guidance J.*, 1958, 37:6–16; R1961a:39–58.

c. "Listening and understanding," *The Friend*, 1958, 116(40):1248–51.

1959

a. "Client-centered therapy," in S. Arieti (Ed.), *American Handbook of Psychiatry*, Vol. 3, New York: Basic Books, 1959, pp. 183–200. See also R1966a.

b. "Comments on cases," in S. Standal and R. Corsini (Eds.), *Critical Incidents in Psychotherapy*, Englewood Cliffs, N.J.: Prentice-Hall, 1959, pp. 56–59,73–75,168–72,227–28,308–10,345–47.

c. "The essence of psychotherapy: A client-centered view," *Annals of Psychotherapy*, 1959, 1:51–57.

d. "Lessons I have learned in counseling with individuals," in W. E. Dugan (Ed.), *Modern School Practices, Series 3, Counseling Points of View*, University of Minnesota Press, 1959, pp. 14–26.

e. "Counseling theory and techniques: A panel discussion," in W. E. Dugan (Ed.), *Modern School Practices, Series 3, Counseling Points of View*, University of Minnesota Press, 1959, pp. 27–47.

f. "Significant learning: In therapy and in education," *Educational Leadership*, 1959, 16:232–42.

g. "A tentative scale for the measurement of process in psychotherapy," in E. A. Rubinstein and M. B. Parloff (Eds.), *Research in Psychotherapy*, Washington, D.C.: APA, 1959, pp. 96–107.

h. "A theory of therapy, personality, and interpersonal relationships, as developed in the client-centered framework," in S. Koch (Ed.), *Psychology: A Study of a Science*, New York: McGraw-Hill, 1959, pp. 184–256.

i. "The way is to be," Review of Rollo May, et al., *Existence: A New Dimension in Psychiatry and Psychology, Contemp. Psy.*, 1959, 4:196–98.

j. *Psychotherapie en Menselyke Verhoudingen* (with G. Marian Kinget), Utrecht: Uitgeverij Het Spectrum, 1959; R1961a:243–69.

k. "Time-limited, client-centered psychotherapy: Two cases" (with M. Lewis and J.

Shlien), in A. Burton (Ed.), *Case Studies of Counseling and Psychotherapy*, Englewood Cliffs, N.J.: Prentice-Hall, 1959, pp. 309–52.

1960

a. "Dialogue between Martin Buber and Carl Rogers," *Psychologia*, 1960, 3(4):208–21.

b. *Psychotherapy: The Counselor*, and *Psychotherapy: The Client*, 16 mm. motion pictures with sound, Madison: Bureau of Audio Visual Aids, University of Wisconsin, 1960.

c. "Significant trends in the client-centered orientation," in D. Brower and L. E. Abt (Eds.), *Progress in Clinical Psychology*, Vol. IV, New York: Grune and Stratton, 1960, pp. 85–99.

d. "A therapist's view of personal goals," *Pendle Hill Pamphlet*, No. 108, Wallingford, Pa., 1960; R1961a:163–182.

e. "Development of a scale to measure process change in psychotherapy" (with A. Walker and R. Rablen), *J. Clinical Psy.*, 1960, 16(1):79–85.

1961

a. *On Becoming a Person*, Boston: Houghton Mifflin, 1961.

b. "The loneliness of contemporary man as seen in 'The case of Ellen West'," *Rev. Exist. Psy. & Psychiatry*, 1961, 1(2):94–101; R1980a:164–80.

c. "Panel presentation: The client-centered approach to certain questions regarding psychotherapy," *Annals of Psychotherapy*, 1961, 2:51–53.

d. "The place of the person in the new world of the behavioral sciences," *Personnel & Guidance J.*, 1961, 39(6):442–51.

e. "The process equation of psychotherapy," *Amer. J. Psychotherapy*, 1961, 15(1):27–45.

f. "A theory of psychotherapy with schizophrenics and a proposal for its empirical investigation," in J. G. Dawson, H. K. Stone, and N. P. Dellis (Eds.), *Psychotherapy with Schizophrenics*, Baton Rouge: Louisiana State University Press, 1961, pp. 3–19.

g. "Two divergent trends," in R. May (Ed.), *Existential Psychology*, New York: Random House, 1961, pp. 85–93.

h. "What we know about psychotherapy," *Pastoral Psychol.*, 1961, 12:31–38.

i. *Personality Adjustment Inventory*, New York: Association Press, 1961. (Slightly revised form of R1931b).

j. "The developing values of the growing person," *The Psychiatric Inst. Bull.* (University of Wisconsin), 1961, 1(13):1–15.

k. "Introduction to the symposium," *The Psychiatric Inst. Bull.* (University of Wisconsin), 1961, 1(10a):1–5.

l. "The significance or meaning of the study to date," *The Psychiatric Inst. Bull.* (University of Wisconsin), 1961, 1(10):1–5.

m. "Comments on cultural evolution as viewed by psychologists," *Daedalus*, 1961, 90:574–75.

1962

a. Comment (on article by F. L. Vance), *J. Counsel. Psy.*, 1962, 9:16–17.

b. "The interpersonal relationship: The core of guidance," *Harv. Educ. Rev.*, 1962, 32(4):416–29.

c. "Niebuhr on the nature of man" (with discussion by B. M. Loomer, W. M. Horton, and H. Hofmann), in S. Doniger (Ed.), *The Nature of Man*, New York: Harper, 1962, pp. 53–71.

d. "Some learnings from a study of psychotherapy with schizophrenics," *Pennsylvania Psychiatric Quart.*, Summer 1962, pp. 3–15; R1967j:181–92.

e. "A study of psychotherapeutic change in schizophrenic and normals: Design and instrumentation," *Psychiatric Research Reports* (American Psychiatric Association), 1962, 15:51–60.

f. "The therapeutic relationship: Recent theory & research," Lecture to the Los Angeles Society of Clinical Psychologists in Beverly Hills, Calif., January 19, 1962. Privately printed.

g. "Toward becoming a fully functioning person," in A. W. Combs (Ed.), *Perceiving, Behaving, Becoming, 1962 Yearbook, Association for Supervision and Curriculum Development*, Washington, D.C.: ASCD, 1962, pp. 21–31.

h. "Enseigner et apprendre," *Education Nationale*, 1962, 22:12–14.

1963

a. "The actualizing tendency in relation to 'motives' and to consciousness," in M. Jones (Ed.), *Nebraska Symposium on Motivation*, University of Nebraska, 1963, pp. 1–24.

b. "The concept of the fully functioning person," *Psychotherapy: Theory, Research, and Practice*, 1963, 1(1):17–26.

c. "Learning to be free," in S. M. Farber and R. H. Wilson (Eds.), *Conflict and Creativity: Control of the Mind*, Pt. 2, New York: McGraw-Hill, 1963, pp. 268–88.

d. "Learning to be free," (condensation of the item above), *Nat. Educ. Ass. J.*, March 1963.

e. "Psychotherapy today: Or, where do we go from here?" *Amer. J. Psychotherapy*, 1963, 17(1):5–16.

f. "La relation thérapeutique: Les bases de son efficacité," *Bulletin de Psychologie*, 1963, 17(1):1–9.

g. "Towards a science of the person," *J. Hum. Psy.*, 1963, 3(2):72–92.

1964

a. "Freedom and commitment," *The Humanist*, 1964, 24(2):37–40.

b. "Toward a modern approach to values: The valuing process in the mature person," *J. Abnorm. Soc. Psy.*, 1964, 68(2):160–67.

c. *What Psychology Has to Offer to Teacher Education*, La Jolla, Calif.: Western Behavioral Sciences Institute, 1964.

d. *Some Elements of Effective Interpersonal Communication*, La Jolla, Calif.: Western Behavioral Sciences Institute, 1964.

1965

a. "An afternoon with Carl Rogers," *Explorations*, 1965, 3:1–4.

b. "Can we meet the need for counseling? A suggested plan," *Marriage & Family* (Queensland, Australia), 1965, 2(5):4–6.

c. "Dealing with psychological tensions," *J. Appl. Behav. Sci.*, 1965, 1:6–24.

d. Foreword to H. Anderson, *Creativity in Childhood and Adolescence*, Palo Alto: Science and Behavior Books, 1965, pp. v–vii.

e. "A humanistic conception of man," in R. E. Farson (Ed.), *Science and Human Affairs*, Palo Alto: Science and Behavior Books, 1965, pp. 18–31.

f. "Psychology and teacher training," in D. B. Gowan and C. Richardson (Eds.), *Five Fields and Teacher Training*, Ithaca, N.Y.: Project One Publication, Cornell University, 1965, pp. 56–91.

g. "Some questions and challenges facing a humanistic psychology," *J. Hum. Psy.*, 1965, 5:1–5.

h. "The therapeutic relationship: Recent theory and research," *Australian J. of Psy.*, 1965, 17:95–108.

i. "The potential of the human individual: The capacity for becoming fully functioning," *J. of Education*, 1965, 22:1–14.

j. "Some thoughts regarding the current philosophy of the behavioral sciences," *J. Hum. Psy.*, 1965, 5(2):182–94.

k. "The basic encounter group and its process," Transcript of a lecture delivered at the Atlanta Psychiatric Clinic, September 1965.

l. Interview with C. A. Dallis in *The Development of Rogerian Thought and Its Implications for Counselor Education*, unpublished doctoral dissertation, University of Wisconsin–Madison, 1965.

1966

a. "Client-centered therapy," in S. Arieti (Ed.), *Supplement to American Handbook of Psychiatry*, Vol. 3, New York: Basic Books, 1966, pp. 185–200; the same as R1959a.

b. *Dialogue between Michael Polanyi and Carl Rogers*, San Diego: San Diego State College and Western Behavioral Sciences Institute, July 1966.

c. *Dialogue between Paul Tillich and Carl Rogers*, Pts. 1 and 2, San Diego: San Diego State College, 1966.

d. "To facilitate learning," in M. Provus (Ed.), *Innovations for Time to Teach*, Washington, D.C.: National Education Association, 1966, pp. 4–19.

1967

a. "Autobiography," in E. W. Boring and G. Lindzey (Eds.), *A History of Psychology in Autobiography*, Vol. 5, New York: Appleton-Century-Crofts, 1967.

b. "Carl Rogers speaks out on group and the lack of a human science," Interview, *Psy. Today*, 1967, 1:19–21,62–66.

c. "Client-centered therapy," in A. M. Freedman and H. I. Kaplan (Eds.), *Comprehensive Textbook of Psychiatry*, Baltimore: Williams & Wilkins, 1967, pp. 1225–28.

d. "The facilitation of significant learning," in L. Siegel (Ed.), *Contemporary Theories of Instruction*, San Francisco: Chandler Publishing, 1967, pp. 37–54.

e. "The interpersonal relationship in the facilitation of learning," in R. Leeper (Ed.), *Humanizing Education*, Washington, D.C.: National Education Association, Association for Supervision and Curriculum Development, 1967.

f. "A plan for self-directed change in an educational system," *Educational Leadership*, 1967, 24:717–31.

g. "The process of the basic encounter group," in J. F. T. Bugental (Ed.), *Challenges of Humanistic Psychology*, New York: McGraw-Hill, 1967, pp. 261–78.

h. "Panel discussion with E. M. Drews and A. H. Maslow," in A. A. Hitchcock (Ed.), *Guidance and the Utilization of New Educational Media: Report of the 1962 Conference*, Washington, D.C.: American Personnel & Guidance Association, 1967, pp. 49–78.

i. *The Therapeutic Relationship and Its Impact: A Study of Psychotherapy with Schizophrenics* (with E. T. Gendlin, D. J. Kiesler, and C. B. Truax), Madison: University of Wisconsin Press, 1967.

j. *Person to Person* (with B. Stevens, et al.), Moab, Utah: Real People Press, 1967.

1968

a. "The interpersonal relationship in the facilitation of learning," *The Virgil E. Herrick Memorial Lecture Series*, Columbus, Ohio: Merrill, 1968.

b. "Interpersonal relationships: USA 2000," *J. Appl. Behav. Sci.*, 1968, 4(3):265–80; R1972a:7–30.

c. "A practical plan for educational revolution," in R. R. Goulet (Ed.), *Educational Change: The Reality and the Promise* (A report on the National Seminars on Innovation, Honolulu, July 1967), New York: Citation Press, 1968, pp. 120–35.

d. Review of J. Kavanaugh, *A Modern Priest Looks at His Outdated Church, Psy, Today*, 1968, p. 13.

e. "To the Japanese reader," introduction to a series of eighteen volumes of Rogers's work translated into Japanese, Tokyo: Iwasaki Shoten Press, 1968.

f. *Man and the Science of Man*, with W. R. Coulson (Eds.), Columbus, Ohio: Merrill, 1968.

1969

a. *Freedom to Learn: A View of What Education Might Become*, Columbus, Ohio: Merrill, 1969.

b. "Being in relationship," in R1969a:217–20.

c. "Graduate education in psychology: A passionate statement," in R1969a:169–88.

d. "Community: The group," *Psy. Today*, 1969, 3(12):27–31,58–61.

e. "The increasing involvement of the psychologist in social problems: Some comments, positive and negative," *J. Appl. Behav. Sci.*, 1969, 5:3–7.

f. "The intensive group experience," in *Psychology Today: An Introduction*, Del Mar, Calif.: CRM Books, 1969, pp. 539–55.

g. *The Person of Tomorrow*, Sonoma State College Pamphlet, 1969; *Colorado J. of Educational Research*, 1972, 12(1):30–32.

h. "Self-directed change for educators: Experiments and implications," in E. Morphet and D. L. Jesser (Eds.), *Preparing Educators to Meet Emerging Needs*, New York: Citation Press, Scholastic Magazine, 1969.

i. "Some personal learnings about interpersonal relationships," *Word*, Nov. 1969, 7(2).

1970

a. *Carl Rogers on Encounter Groups*, New York: Harper & Row, 1970.

b. Foreword and "Looking back & ahead: A conversation with Carl Rogers," in J. T. Hart and T. M. Tomlinson (Eds.), *New Direction in Client-Centered Therapy*, Boston: Houghton Mifflin, 1970, pp. vii,502–34.

c. "Rogers can change," *Educate*, 1970, 3(3):19–23,33.

d. "Views of USIU," *AHP Newsletter*, Oct. 1970, 7(1).

1971

a. "Can schools grow persons?" Editorial, *Educational Leadership*, 1971, 29:215–17.

b. "Forget you are a teacher. Carl Rogers tells why," *Instructor* (Dansville, New York), 1971, 81:65–66.

c. Interview with Carl Rogers, in W. B. Frick (Ed.), *Humanistic Psychology: Interviews with Maslow, Murphy and Rogers*, Columbus, Ohio: Merrill, 1971.

d. "Psychological maladjustment vs. continuing growth," in *Developmental Psychology*, Del Mar, Calif.: CRM Books, 1971.

e. "Facilitating encounter groups," *Amer. J. Nursing*, 1971, 71(2):275–79.

1972

a. *Becoming Partners: Marriage and Its Alternatives*, New York: Delacorte, 1972.

b. "Bringing together ideas and feelings in learning," *Learning Today*, 1972, 5:32–43.

c. Comment on Brown and Tedeschi article, *J. Hum. Psy.*, 1972, 12(1):16–21.

d. "Introduction to 'My experience in encounter group'," by H. Tsuge, *Voices*, 1972, 8(2):69–77.

e. "A research program in client-centered therapy," *Psychiatric Treatment*, Vol. 31, Proceedings of the Association for Research in Nervous and Mental Diseases, Baltimore: Williams & Wilkins, 1953, pp. 106–113.

f. "Some social issues which concern me," *J. Hum. Psy.*, 1972, 12(2):45–60.

g. Foreword to L. N. Solomon and B. Berzon (Eds.), *New Perspectives on Encounter Groups*, San Francisco: Jossey-Bass, 1972.

1973

a. "Comments on Pitts article," *J. Hum. Psy.*, 1973, 13:83–84.

b. "An encounter with Carl Rogers," in C. W. Kemper (Ed.), *Res Publica* (Claremont Men's College), 1973, 1(1):41–51.

c. "The good life as an ever-changing process," Ninth of newspaper series, *America and the Future of Man*, published by the Regents of the University of California and distributed by Copley News Service.

d. "The interpersonal relationship that helps schizophrenics," Contribution to panel discussion, "Psychotherapy is Effective with Schizophrenics," APA Convention, Montreal, August 28, 1973.

e. "My philosophy of interpersonal relationships and how it grew," *J. Hum. Psy.*, 1973, 13(2):3–15.

f. "Some new challenges," *Amer. Psychologist*, 1973, 28(5):379–87; R1980a:233–59.

g. "To be fully alive," *Penney's Forum*, Spring/Summer 1973, 3.

h. "Client-centered therapy" (with B. Meador), in R. Corsini (Ed.), *Current Psychotherapies*, Itasca, Ill.: F. E. Peacock, 1973, ch. 4, pp. 119–65.

i. "Entretien avec Carl Rogers," by J. Mousseau, *Psychologie*, 1973, 6:57–65.

j. Foreword to the Japanese translation of *Carl Rogers on Encounter Groups*, Tokyo, 1973.

1974

a. "Can learning encompass both ideas and feelings?" *Education*, 1974, 95(2):103–14.

b. Foreword to H. Lyon, *It's Me and I'm Here*, New York: Delacorte, 1974, pp. xi–xiii.

c. Foreword to A. dePeretti, *Pensée et Verité de Carl Rogers*, Toulouse: Privat, 1974, pp. 20–27.

d. Foreword to the Japanese translation of *Person to Person*, 1974.

e. "In retrospect: Forty-six years," *Amer. Psychol.*, 1974, 29(2):115–23; R. I. Evans, *Carl Rogers: The Man and His Ideas*, New York: Dutton, 1975, pp. 119–46.

f. "Interview on 'growth'," in W. Oltmans (Ed.), *On Growth: The Crisis of Exploring*

Population and Resource Depletion, New York: G. P. Putman's Sons, 1974, pp. 197–205.

g. "The project at Immaculate Heart: An experiment in self-directed change," *Education*, 1974, 95(2):172–96.

h. "Questions I would ask myself if I were a teacher," *Education*, 1974, 95(2):134–39.

i. "Remarks on the future of client-centered therapy," in D. A. Wexler and L. N. Rice (Eds.), *Innovations in Client-Centered Therapy*, New York: John Wiley & Sons, 1974, pp. 7–13.

j. "The changing theory of client-centered therapy" (with J. K. Wood), in A. Burton (Ed.), *Operational Theories of Personality*, New York: Brunner/Mazel, 1974, pp. 211–58.

k. "The cavern," included in R1980a:214–19.

1975

a. "Client-centered psychotherapy," in A. M. Freedman, H. I. Kaplan, and B. J. Sadock (Eds.), *Comprehensive Textbook of Psychiatry*, Vol. 2, Baltimore: Williams & Wilkins, 1975, pp. 1831–43.

b. "The emerging person: A new revolution," in R. I. Evans (Ed.), *Carl Rogers: The Man and His Ideas*, New York: Dutton, 1975, pp. 147–76.

c. Interview in R. I. Evans (Ed.), *Carl Rogers: The Man and His Ideas*, New York: Dutton, 1975.

d. "Emphatic: An unappreciated way of being," *The Counseling Psychologist*, 1975, 5(2):2–10.

e. Foreword to To Thi Anh, *Eastern & Western Cultural Values*, Manila, Philippines: East Asian Pastoral Institute, 1975.

f. "An interview with Dr. Carl Rogers," *Practical Psy. for Physicians*, 1975, 2(8):16–24.

1976

a. "Beyond the watershed of education," *Teaching-Learning J.*, Winter/Spring 1976, pp. 43–49.

b. "A dialogue on education and the control of human behavior," a six-cassette album of a dialogue held in Duluth in 1962, edited by Gerald Gladstein, with a descriptive booklet, New York: Jeffrey, Norton, 1976.

1977

a. *Carl Rogers on Personal Power*, New York: Delacorte, 1977.

b. "Beyond the watershed: And where now?" *Educational Leadership*, 1977, 34(8):623–31.

c. "Ellen West–And loneliness," in C. R. Rogers and R. L. Rosenberg, *A Pessoa Como Centro*, Sao Paolo, Brazil: Editora Pedagogica e Universitaria Ltda., 1977.

d. "Freedom to be: A person-centered approach," *Studies of a Person* (Japanese), Tokyo: Department of Education, Japan Women's University, 1977, 3:5–18.

e. "Nancy mourns," in D. Nevill (Ed.), *Humanistic Psychology: New Frontiers*, New York: Gardner, 1977, pp. 111–16; R1980a:219–25.

f. "Personal power at work," *Psy. Today*, 1977, 10(11):60–62,93–94.

g. "The politics of education," *J. Hum. Psy.*, 1977, 1(1):6–22.

h. *Therapeut und Klient*, Munich, West Germany: Kindler-Munchen, 1977 (various papers translated from the English).

i. "Tribute to Professor Haruko Tsuge," *Studies of the Person* (Japanese), Tokyo: Department of Education, Japan Women's University, 1977.

j. *A Pessoa Como Centro* (with R. L. Rosenberg), Sao Paolo, Brazil: Editora Pedagogica e Universitaria Ltda., 1977. Translation of several of Rogers's papers with the exception of chapters 2 and 5.

k. "Person-centered personality theory," Chapter 5 in R. Corsini (Ed.), *Current Personality Theories*, Itasca, Ill.: Peacock, 1977, pp. 125–51.

l. Preface to R. Fairfield, *Person-Centered Graduate Education*, Elmhurst, Ill.: Hagle, 1977.

1978

a. "Do we need 'a' reality?" *Dawnpoint*, 1(2):6–9; R1980a:96–108.

b. "The formative tendency," *J. Hum. Psy.*, 1978, 18:23–26.

c. "From heart to heart: Some elements of effective personal communication," *Marriage Encounter*, 1978, 7(2):8–15; R1980a:5–26.

d. "The necessary and sufficient conditions of therapeutic personality change (1957)," Abstract and commentary, *Current Contents*, 1978, 18(27):14. (No. 27 of "Citation Classics.")

e. "Evolving aspects of the person-centered workshop" (with M. V. Bowen, J. Justyn, J. Kass, M. Miller, N. Rogers, and J. K. Wood), *Self and Society* (England), 1978, 6(2):43–49; *AHP Newsletter*, January 1979, 11–14.

f. Interview in *San Diego Union*, July 9, 1978.

1979

a. "Foundations of the person-centered approach," *Education*, 1979, 100(2):98–107.

b. "Groups in two cultures," *Personnel & Guidance J.*, 1979, 38(1):11–15.

c. "Some new directions: A personal view," in T. Hanna (Ed.), *Explorers of Humankind*, San Francisco: Harper & Row, 1979, pp. 123–35.

d. "Learning in large groups: The implications for the future" (with M. V. Bowen, M. Miller, and J. K. Wood), *Education*, 1979, 100(2):108–16.

e. Interview with Carl Rogers in *Le Monde*, September 23, 1979.

f. "My hopes for the workshop in Rome," Interview with A. Zucconi, *Pulsazione*, 1979.

1980

a. *A Way of Being*, Boston: Houghton Mifflin, 1980.

b. "Building person-centered communities: The implications for the future," in R1980a:181–206.

c. Interview in *The Relator*, 1980, 23(1).

d. "Client-centered psychotherapy," in H. I. Kaplan, B. J. Sadock, and A. M. Freedman (Eds.), *Comprehensive Textbook of Psychiatry*, Vol. 3, Baltimore: Williams & Wilkins, 1980, pp. 2153–68.

e. "Growing old—or older and growing," *J. Hum. Psy.*, 1980, 20(4):5–16; R1980a:70–95.

f. Interview in *Los Angeles Times*, July 31, 1980.

g. Introduction to Japanese translation of *Carl Rogers on Personal Power* (1977), 1980.

h. "The person," *AHP Newsletter*, May 1980, pp. 8–9.

i. "Statement in 'A call to action: A report on AHP's 12-hour political party'," *AHP Newsletter*, special issue, February 1980.

j. "The world of tomorrow & the person of tomorrow," in *A Way of Being*, 1980, ch. 15, pp. 338–56.

k. "Conceptions of a new world and a new person," Paper given at a conference on "Living Companies in a New Age" in Abo, Finland, Oct. 1980. Unpublished.

1981

a. Introduction to the Japanese translation of *Becoming Partners: Marriage and Its Alternatives* (1972), 1981.

b. Introduction to the German translation of a portion of *A Way of Being* (1980), 1981.

c. "Some unanswered questions," *Journey*, 1981, 1(1):1,4.

d. "The foundation of the person-centered approach," *Dialectics and Humanism*, 1981, 1:5–16.

e. "Notes on Rollo May," *AHP Perspectives*, 1981, 2(1).

f. "Education: A personal activity," *Educational Change and Development* (Sheffield, England), 1981, 3(3):1–12.

g. "Foreword–The formative tendency," in J. R. Royce and P. M. Leendert (Eds.), *Humanistic Psychology–Concepts and Criticisms*, New York: Plenum, 1981, pp. vii–x.

1982

a. "Freedom to learn for the 80's," *AHP Perspective*, October 1982, pp. 20–21.

b. "A psychologist looks at nuclear war: Its threat, its possible prevention," *J. Hum. Psy.*, 1982, 22(4):9–21.

c. "My politics," *Journey*, September 1982, 1(6).

d. *The Effective Teacher: A Person-Centered Development Guide* (with J. Elliott-Kemp), Sheffield, England: PAVIC, 1982.

e. "Zeitschrift fur personenzentriert Psychologie und Psychotherapy," *Sonderdruck*, Beltz, 75–77.

f. "Entrevista con Carl Rogers," *Anuario de Psicologia* (Departamento de Psicologia, Universidad de Barcelona), 1982, 27(2):111–15.

g. "Reply to Rollo May's letter to Carl Rogers," *J. Hum. Psy.*, 1982, 22(4):85–89.

1983

a. *Freedom to Learn for the 80's*, Columbus, Ohio: Merrill, 1983.

b. "A visit to Credo Mutwa," *Journey*, 1983, 2(4):1,4–5.

c. "Um novo mundo–uma nova pessoa," in A. Fonseca (Ed.), *Em Busca de Vida*, Sao Paolo, Brazil: Summurs, 1983.

d. "Carl Rogers speaks to Montessorians," *The NAMTA Quart.*, 1983, 8(4):11–15.

e. "Dialogos con Carl Rogers," *Revista de Psiquiatria & Psicologia Humanista*, May 1983, (4).

f. "I walk softly through life," *Voices*, 1983, 18(4):6–14.

g. Some translations from *On Becoming a Person* (1961) in *Nowiny Psychologiczne*, (Polish monograph) 1983, 6(7).

h. "I can't read," *Visualtek News*, Summer 1983.

1984

a. "Client-centered psychotherapy" (with R. Sanford), in H. I. Kaplan and B. J. Sadock (Eds.), *Comprehensive Textbook of Psychiatry*, Vol. 4, Baltimore: Williams & Wilkins, 1984, pp. 1374–88.

b. "Person-centered approach foundations," in R. Corsini (Ed.), *Encyclopedia of Psychology*, New York: Wiley & Sons, 1984.

c. "The new world person," *Odyssey* (S. Africa), 1984, 8(2):16–19.

d. "One alternative to nuclear planetary suicide" (with D. Ryback), *The Counseling Psychologist*, 1984, 12(2):3–12; *Peabody J. of Education*, 1984, 61(3):91–110.

e. "Gloria—A historical note," in R. Levant and J. Shlien (Eds.), *Client-Centered Therapy and the Person-Centered Approach*, New York: Praeger, 1984, 403–25.

f. "A way of meeting life," Interview in *The Laughing Man*, 1984, 5(2):22–23.

g. Interview in *Holistic Living News*, 1984–1985, 7(3).

1985

a. "Le développement de la personne," *Le Journal des Psychologies*, 1985 23:10–12.

b. "Toward a more human science of the person," *J. Hum. Psy.*, 1985, 25(4):7–24.

1986

a. "The rust workshop," *J. Hum. Psy.*, 1986, 26(3):23–45.

1987

a. "Comments on the issue of equality in psychotherapy," *J. Hum. Psy.*, 1987, 27(1):38–40.

D. ROLLO MAY

1938

a. *A Comparison of Modern Psychotherapy and Christian Theology with Respect to the Doctrine of Man*, unpublished bachelor of divinity thesis, Union Theological Seminary, 1938.

1939

a. *The Art of Counseling*, Nashville: Cokesbury, 1939; New York: Abingdon, 1967.

1940

a. *The Springs of Creative Living: A Study of Human Nature and God*, Nashville: Abingdon-Cokesbury, 1940.

1943

a. "Recent developments in psychology and their significance for religious education," *Religious Education*, 1943, 38:142–52.

b. *The Ministry of Counseling*, New York: YMCA (Army & Navy Dept.), 1943.

1944

a. "The present functioning of counseling," *Teachers Coll. Rec.*, 1944, 46:9–16.

1949

a. Review of Jurgen Ruesch and Gregory Bateson, *Communication, The Social Matrix of Psychiatry, N.Y. Times* (Sunday Book Review Section), 1949.

1950

a. *The Meaning of Anxiety*, New York: Ronald Press, 1950; rev. ed., New York: Norton, 1977.

b. "Historical roots of modern anxiety theories," in Paul H. Hoch and Joseph Zubin (Eds.), *Anxiety*, New York: Grune and Stratton, 1950; MY1967a:55–71.

c. "The work and training of the psychological therapist," *The Psychological Service Center J.*, 1950, 2:3–23; MY1939a:75–97,165–78.

d. "Toward an understanding of anxiety," *Pastoral Psychol.*, 1950, 1:25–31.

e. "Religion and anxiety," *Pastoral Psychol.*, 1950, 1:46–49.

1951

a. "Psychotherapy, religion, and the achievement of selfhood," in Amos N. Wilder (Ed.), *Liberal Learning and Religion*, New York: Harper & Brothers, 1951.

1952

a. "The man who was put in a cage," *Psychiatry: J. of the Study of Interpersonal Processes*, 1952, 15:469–72; MY1967a:161–67.

b. "Prevention vs. treatment," *Pastoral Psychol.*, 1952, 3:52–53.

1953

a. *Man's Search for Himself*, New York: Norton, 1953.

b. "Medicines of the mind," *Sat. Rev.* Aug. 15, 1953, pp. 15–17.

c. "Jean-Paul Sartre and psychoanalysis," Introduction to the translation of Jean-Paul Sartre, *Existential Psychoanalysis*, New York: Philosophical Library, 1953; MY1967a:138–46.

d. "Historical and philosophical presuppositions for understanding therapy," in O. H. Mowrer (Ed.), *Psychotherapy: Theory and Research*, New York: Ronald Press, 1953, pp. 9–43; MY1950a:3–19,20–51.

1954

a. "A psychologist looks at mental health in today's world," *Mental Hygiene*, 1954, 38:1–11; MY1953a:13–69.

b. "Psychology and legislation," *Amer. Psychol.*, 1954, 9:585–86.

1955

a. "The idea of God as affected by modern knowledge," *The Garvin Lecture*, Lancaster, Pennsylvania, December 12, 1955.

b. "Human integrity in the age of conformity," *Ideals and Realities in Modern Education*, Bank Street College of Education, 1955, pp. 38–46.

c. "A psychological approach to anti-intellectualism," *J. Soc. Issues*, 1955, 11:41–47.

d. "Our time and its crucial psychological problem," *Our Faith and Ourselves Today*, New York: YWCA, 1955.

e. "Anxiety and chronical illness," *Medical and Psychological Teamwork in the Case of the Chronically Ill*, Charles Thomas, 1955.

f. "Foreword: Psychotherapy and counseling," consulting editor of *The Annals of the New York Academy of Sciences*, 1955, 63(3):319–432.

g. "Questions for a science of man," Address on the Annual Award of the New York Society of Clinical Psychologists at the New York Academy of Sciences, 1955; MY1967a:182–200.

1956

a. "Take a new look at the Ten Commandments" (with I. Leighton), *Women's Home Companion*, April 1956, pp. 46–47.

b. "The bearing of science on man and his nature as seen by a psychologist," *J. Public Law*, 1956, 4(2):351–57.

c. "The work and training of the psychological therapist," in Maurice H. Krout (Ed.), *Psychology, Psychiatry and the Public Interest*, Minnesota University Press, 1956, pp. 161–85.

d. "Fear and anxiety: A psychologist's view," in Simon Noveck (Ed.), *Judaism and Psychiatry*, National Academy for Adult Jewish Studies, Basic Books, 1956, pp. 35–44.

e. "A psychologist as a legal witness," *Amer. Psychol.*, 1956, 11:50.

1957

a. "Anxiety and values," in Jules H. Masserman and Jacob L. Moreno (Eds.), *Progress in Psychotherapy: Anxiety and Therapy*, Vol. 2, New York: Grune and Stratton, 1957, pp. 82–90; MY1967a:72–83.

b. "The relation between psychotherapy and religion," in Johnson E. Fairchild (Ed.), *Personal Problems and Psychological Frontiers*, New York: Sheridan, 1957, pp. 168–87.

1958

a. Editor of *Existence: A New Dimension in Psychiatry and Psychology* (with Ernest Angel and Henri F. Ellenberger), New York: Basic Books, 1958.

b. "The origins and significance of the existential movement in psychology," in MY1958a:3–36.

c. "Contributions of existential psychotherapy," in MY1958a:37–91.

1959

a. "El analisis existencial y el panorama Americano," *La Revista de Psiquiatria y Psicologia Medica de Europa y America Latinas* (Barcelona, Spain), April 1959, 4(2); MY1967a:128–37.

b. "The existential approach," in Silvano Arieti (Ed.), *American Handbook of Psychology*, Vol. 2, New York: Basic Books, 1959, pp. 1348–61.

c. "The nature of creativity," *ETC: A Review of General Semantics*, 1959, 16:261–76; MY1953a:138–42.

d. "Existentialism not Freudian," *Contemp. Psy.*, 1959, 4:375.

e. "Toward the ontological basis of psychotherapy," *Existential Inquiries*, 1959, 1:5–7; MY1967a:87–110.

1960

a. Editor of *Symbolism in Religion and Literature*, New York: Braziller, 1960.

b. Editor of *Existential Psychology*, New York: Random, 1960.

c. "The significance of symbols," in MY1960a:11–49.

d. "Kierkegaard and Freud," *The New School Bulletin* (New School for Social Research), Feb. 15, 1960, 17(24).

e. "The emergence of existential psychology," in MY1960b:11–51.

f. "Existential bases of psychotherapy," in MY1960b:75–84.

1961

a. "The meaning of Oedipus myth," *Rev. Exist. Psy. & Psychiatry*, 1961, 1:44–52; MY1967b:11–20,21–30.

b. "Will, decision, and responsibility," *Rev. Exist. Psy. & Psychiatry*, 1961, 1:249–59; MY1967b:31–40.

c. "Phenomenology and the theory of the unconscious," *The J. of Philosophy*, 1961, 58:641.

d. "The context of psychotherapy," in Morris I. Stein (Ed.), *Contemporary Psychotherapies*, Glencoe, Ill.: Free Press, 1961; MY1967a:87–110.

e. "Existential psychiatry: An evaluation," *J. Relig. & Health*, 1961, 1:31–40.

1962

a. "Symposium on the value systems of psychologists, or what are psychologists trying to do?" (with Gregory A. Kimble, B. von Haller Gilmer, and E. Terry Prothro), *Psi Chi Newsletter*, Fall 1962, pp. 5–7.

b. "Modern man's image of himself," *The Chicago Theological Seminary Register*, 1962, 52:1–11; MY1967a:25–39.

c. "Existential psychology and human freedom," *The Chicago Theological Seminary Register*, 1962, 52:11–19.

d. "A conversation with Rollo May," in Alan B. Tulipan (Ed.), *The Outpatient Patient*, Psychiatric Outpatient Centers of America, 1962, pp. 3–22.

e. "Dangers in the relation of existentialism to psychotherapy," in Hendrik M. Ruitenbeck (Ed.), *Psychoanalysis and Existential Philosophy*, New York: Dutton, 1962, pp. 179–87; MY1967a:147–57.

1963

a. "What is our problem?" *Rev. Exist. Psy. & Psychiatry*, 1963, 3:109–12.

b. "Existential theory and therapy" (with Adrian Van Kaam), in J. H. Masserman (Ed.), *Current Psychiatric Therapies*, Vol. 3, New York: Grune and Stratton, 1963, pp. 74–81.

c. "The nature of creativity," in C. Merton Babcock (Ed.), *Focus*, New York: Houghton & Mifflin, 1963.

d. "The psychological bases of freedom," in Seymour M. Farber and Roger H. L. Wilson (Eds.), *Conflict and Creativity*, New York: McGraw-Hill, 1963, pp. 199–207.

e. "Freedom and responsibility re-examined," in Esther Lloyd's Jones and E. M. Westervelt (Eds.), *Behavioral Science and Guidance: Proposals and Perspectives*, New York: Teachers College, Columbia University, 1963; MY1967a:168–81.

f. "Social responsibilities of psychologists," Paper delivered at the annual convention of the American Psychological Association, 1963; MY1967a:201–21.

g. "Creativity and encounter," *Union Seminary Quart. Review*, 1963, 18:369–75; MY1967b:41–50.

1964

a. "Creativity and the unconscious," *Annals of Psychotherapy*, 1964, 1:29–36; MY1967b:41–50.

b. "On the phenomenological bases of psychotherapy," *Rev. Exist. Psy. & Psychiatry*, 1964, 4:22–36; MY1967a:111–27.

c. "A preface to love," in Isidor Schneider (Ed.), *The Meanings of Love*, New York: Braziller, 1964, pp. 279–84.

d. "Some comments on existential psychotherapy," in Maurice Friedman (Ed.), *The Worlds of Existentialism: A Critical Reader*, New York: Random, 1964, pp. 446–53.

1965

a. "Anxiety among students and its relation to education," *New England Association Review*, 1965, 13:16–20; MY1967a:40–52.

b. "Relation of existential to humanistic psychology," *Amer. Association for Hum. Psy. Newsletter*, January 1965.

c. "Intentionality, the heart of human will," *J. Hum. Psy.*, 1965, 5:55–70; MY1967b:31–40.

d. "Memorial talk at interment of Paul Tillich," *Rev. Exist. Psy. & Psychiatry*, 1965, 5:302–4.

1966

a. "The problem of will and intentionality in psychoanalysis," *Contemp. Psychoanalysis*, 1966, 3:55–70.

b. "Sleeping beauty," *Redbook*, September 1966, pp. 62–63.

c. "Antidotes for the new puritanism," *Sat. Rev.*, March 26, 1966, pp. 19–21,42–43.

d. Introduction to Howard E. Guderman, "The phenomenology of delusions," *Rev. Exist. Psy. & Psychiatry*, 1966, 6:196–97.

e. "Wish and intentionality," in W. Von Baeyer and K. M. Griffith (Eds.), *Conditio Humana*, Berlin: Springer, 1966, pp. 233–40; MY1967b:31–40.

1967

a. *Psychology and the Human Dilemma*, New York: Norton, 1967.

b. *Existential Psychotherapy*, Toronto: Canadian Broadcasting Company Publications, 1967.

c. "Myth and culture: Their death and transformation," *ARC Directions*, New York: Foundation for the Arts, Religion, and Culture, Summer 1967, pp. 1–5.

d. "Passion for form," *Rev. Exist. Psy. & Psychiatry*, 1967, 7:6–12.

e. "Frontiers of being human," *Sat. Rev.*, May 20, 1967, pp. 37–39.

f. "Introduction: Imagination and existence," *Rev. Exist. Psy. & Psychiatry*, 1967, 7:4–5.

g. "An interview with Mr. 'Humanist': Rollo May," by Mary H. Hall, *Psy. Today*, 1967, 1(5):24–29,72–73.

1968

a. *Dreams and Symbols: Man's Unconscious Language* (with Leopold Caligor), New York: Basic Books, 1968.

b. "Paul Tillich: In memoriam," *Pastoral Psychol.*, 1968, 19:7–10.

c. "The healing power of myths," *Amer. J. Psychiatry*, 1968, 124:64–69.

d. "Humanism and psychotherapy," *Pastoral Psychol.*, 1968, 9:11–17.

e. "The Delphic oracles as therapist," in Marianne L. Simmel (Ed.), *The Reach of Mind: Essays in Memory of Kurt Goldstein*, New York: Springer, 1968, pp. 211–18.

f. "Existentialism, psychotherapy and the problem of death," in Roger L. Shinn (Ed.),

Restless Adventure: Essays on Contemporary Expressions of Existentialism, New York: Scribners' Sons, 1968, pp. 182–217.

g. "The daimonic: Love and death," *Psy. Today*, June 1968, pp. 16–25.

1969

a. *Love and Will*, New York: Norton, 1969.

b. "A grown-up religion," *Face to Face*, March 1969, pp. 30–32.

c. "Reality beyond rationalism," in C. Kerry Smith (Ed.), *Agony and Promise: Current Issues in Higher Education*, San Francisco: Jossey-Bass, 1969, pp. 189–93.

d. "Love and will: Our schizoid world," *Psy. Today*, Aug. 1969, pp. 17–64; excerpts from MY1969a.

1970

a. "Yes begins with a no," *Time Magazine*, June 22, 1970, pp. 66–70.

b. "Psychotherapy and the daimonic," in Joseph Campbell (Ed.), *Myths, Dreams, and Religion*, New York: Dutton, 1970; excerpts from MY1969a.

c. "Finding yourself: The bread and butter question," *Mademoiselle*, May 1970, pp. 152,211.

d. "When love becomes the problem," in David Darst and Joseph Forgue (Eds.), *Sexuality on the Island Earth*, New York: Paulist Press, 1970, pp. 55–62; abridged from MY1969a.

1971

a. "Too much sex, too little joy?" *Reader's Digest*, May 1971, pp. 68–70.

b. "Letter to the editor, reply to Dempsey," *New York Times*, April 18, 1971, p. 100.

c. "Vietnam," *New York Times*, April 10, 1971, p. 4.

1972

a. *Power and Innocence: A Search for the Sources of Violence*, New York: Norton, 1972.

b. "The innocent murderers," *Psy. Today*, Dec. 1972, pp. 52–58.

c. "Rollo May writes . . . ," *Association for Hum. Psy. Newsletter*, Jan. 1972, 8(4):1–3.

1973

a. *Paulus: Reminiscences of a Friendship*, New York: Harper & Row, 1973.

b. "Macht und Ohnmacht," *Separatdruck aus G. Condrau: Medard Boss zum siebzigsten Geburtstag*, 1973.

c. "Response to Morell's 'Love & will: A feminist critique'," *J. Hum. Psy.*, 1973, 13(2):47–50.

d. "The function of myth in sickness and health," in Earl G. Witenberg (Ed.), *Interpersonal Explorations in Psychoanalysis: New Directions in Theory and Practice*, New York: Basic Books, 1973, pp. 335–42.

e. "Using power with love: A conversation with Rollo May," *J. Current Soc. Issues*, 1973, 11:12–18.

1974

a. "Values and the future," *The Merrill-Palmer Institute*, 1974.

b. "The fall of Nixon: What we must not forget," *Redbook*, Nov. 1974, pp. 92,166,168.

c. "Nietzsche's contribution to psychology," *Quarterly Symposium*, Syracuse: Syracuse University Press, 1974.

d. "Some notes on ethics in a technological age," International Symposium on Ethics in an Age of Pervasive Technology, William Alanson White Institute of Psychiatry, 1974.

e. "Rollo May and the courage to create," *Media and Method*, 1974, 10:15–16.

f. "Values, myths, and symbols," *Rev. Exist. Psy. & Psychiatry*, 1974, 13(3):267–73; *Amer. J. Psychiatry*, 1975, 132(7):703–6.

1975

a. *The Courage to Create*, New York: Norton, 1975.

b. "The illusion of immortality," American Health Foundation, New York, Sept. 29, 1975.

1976

a. "Introduction to the AHP Theory Conference," *Association for Hum. Psy. Newsletter*, March 1976, pp. 1–2.

b. "How to release your creativity," *House & Garden*, April 1976, pp. 88,151.

c. "Comment on Prof. Giorgi's paper," *Soc. Research*, 1976, 43:737–38.

d. "How to cope with rejection," *Harper's Bazaar*, July 1976, pp. 27–96.

e. "Gregory Bateson and humanistic psychology," *J. Hum. Psy.*, 1976, 16(4):33–49.

1977

a. *The Meaning of Anxiety*, rev. ed., New York: Norton, 1977.

b. "Reflections and commentary," in Clement Reeves (Ed.), *The Psychology of Rollo May*, San Francisco: Jossey-Bass, 1977, pp. 295–309.

c. "Freedom, determinism and the future," *Psychology: Amer. Psychological Association*, 1977, pp. 6–9.

d. "Values and valuing," *Voices*, 1977, 12:18–21.

1978

a. "Creative anxiety," *Harper's Bazaar*, April 1978, pp. 112–13.

b. "The paradoxes of freedom," *Ohio Northern University Alumnus Magazine*, Summer 1978, pp. 16–19.

c. "Response to Bulka's article," *J. Hum. Psy.*, 1978, 18:55.

d. "Foreword," in Ronald S. Valle and Mark King (Eds.), *Existential-Phenomenological Alternatives for Psychology*, New York: Oxford University Press, 1978, pp. vii–viii.

1979

a. "Statement about *The Courage to Create*," *American Way*, March 1979, pp. 86–87.

b. "The 'freedom of being' needs creative pauses," *Creative Living*, Winter 1979, p. 206.

c. "Ethics," *N.Y. Times Book Rev.*, Sept. 23, 1979, p. 39.

1980

a. "The destiny of America," *Association for Hum. Psy. Newsletter*, May 1980, pp. 22–23.

b. "Value conflicts and anxiety," in I. L. Kutash and L. B. Schlesinger (Eds.), *Handbook on Stress and Anxiety*, San Francisco: Jossey-Bass, 1980, pp. 241–48.

1981

a. *Freedom and Destiny*, New York: Norton, 1981.

b. "The therapist and the journey into hell," Address presented at the American Psychological Association Convention, Aug. 1981.

1982

a. "Open letter to Carl Rogers: On the problem of evil," *J. Hum. Psy.*, 1982, 22:10–21.

b. "Significant developments in psychology," *Psy. Today*, May 1982, 16:56–57.

c. "The fear of knowledge," Boulder, Colo.: Academy of Independent Scholars, 1982.

1983

a. *The Discovery of Being: Writings in Existential Psychology*, New York: Norton, 1983.

b. *My Quest for Beauty*, San Francisco: Saybrook Pub., 1985.

1987

a. "The therapist and the journey into hell," *AHP Perspective*, Feb. 1987, p. 4–6.

b. "Wonder and ethics in therapy," *AHP Perspective*, Fall 1987, pp. 10–11.

E. JAMES F. T. BUGENTAL

1942

a. *Interviewer's Manual*, Nashville: Tennessee Dept. of Personnel, 1942.

1946

a. "Some factors in veteran adjustment," *Phi Delta Kappan*, 1946, 27:147–51.

1947

a. *A Counselor's Test Manual* (with H. E. Edgerton, J. R. Berkshire, and F. P. Cassens), Columbus, Ohio: Author, 1947.

1948

a. "A clinical approach to the guidance of the superior adult," *Peabody J. of Education*, 1948, 25:268–82.

b. "Test preferences of guidance centers" (with J. R. Berkshire, F. P. Cassens, and H. E. Edgerton), *Occupations*, 1948, 26:337–43.

c. *An Investigation of the Relationship of the Conceptual Matrix to the Self-Concept*, unpublished doctoral dissertation, Ohio State University, 1948.

1950

a. "Investigation into the 'Self-concept': I. The W-A-Y Technique" (with S. L. Zelen), *J. Pers.*, 1950, 18:483–98.

b. Review of H. L. Hollingworth, *Psychology and Ethics, J. Pers.*, 1950, 19:116–18.

1951

a. Review of Harsh and Schrickel, *Personality: Development and Assessment, J. Pers.*, 1951, 19:355–56.

b. *Workbook* (with G. E. Mount, J. S. Helmick, and I. Maltzman), in W. Brown and H. Gilhousen (Eds.), *College Psychology*, New York: Prentice-Hall, 1951.

c. *Psychological Interviewing*, Los Angeles: Author, 1951. Revised and enlarged in 1963 and 1966.

1952

a. "A method for assessing self and not-self attitudes during the therapeutic series," *J. Consult. Psy.*, 1952, 16:435–39.

b. "University administration of psychological clinics" (with G.F.J. Lehner), *Amer. Psychol.*, 1952, 7:578–82.

1953

a. Editor of *A Report on the Western Training Laboratory in Group Development*, Los Angeles: UCLA Extension, 1953.

b. "Explicit analysis of topical concurrence in diagnostic interviewing," *J. Clinical Psy.*, 1953, 9:3–6.

1954

a. Discussion in J. A. Gengerelli and F. J. Kirkner (Eds.), *The Psychological Variables in Human Cancer*, Berkeley and Los Angeles: University of California Press, 1954, pp. 66–72.

b. "Explicit analysis: A design for the study and improvement of psychological interviewing," *Educ. Psy. Measmt.*, 1954, 14:552–65.

c. "Self-perceptions in stuttering" (with J. G. Sheehan and S. L. Zelen), *J. Clinical Psy.*, 1954, 10:70–72.

1955

a. "Investigations into the self-concept: II. Stability of reported self-identifications," *J. Clinical Psy.*, 1955, 11:41–46.

1957

a. "Refusal rates in relation to interview approach" (with E. Stark and C. Salmon), *Indian J. Psy.*, 1957, 32:119–24.

1959

a. "Some data on participants," in A. Roe, et al (Eds.), *Graduate Education in Psychology*, Washington, D.C.: APA, 1959, App. B, pp. 95–96.

1962

a. "Five paradigms for group psychotherapy," *Psychological Reports*, 1962, 10:607–10.

b. "A phenomenological hypothesis of neurotic determinants and their therapy," *Psychological Reports*, 1962, 10:527–30.

c. "Precognition of a fossil," *J. Hum. Psy.*, 1962, 2:38–46.

d. *Processes of Communication*, Los Angeles: Author, 1962. Revised and extended 1963, 1966, 1977, 1978, 1980, 1982.

e. "Psychologists in clinics" (with T. C. Greening), in W. B. Webb (Ed.), *The Profession of Psychology*, New York: Holt, Rinehart and Winston, 1962, pp. 74–107.

f. Review of F. K. Thorne, *Personality*, *Contemp. Psy.*, 1962, 7:273–74.

g. "Self-fragmentation as a resistance to self-actualization," *Rev. Exist. Psy. & Psychiatry*, 1962, 2:241–48.

1963

a. "Dyads, clans, & tribe: A new design for sensitivity training" (with R. Tannenbaum), *National Training Lab. Human Relations Training News*, 1963, 7:1–3.

b. *The Existential Orientation in Extensive Psychotherapy: Workshop in Clinical Psychology*, Los Angeles: Author, 1963; chs. 2,4,6,7,8,12 in B1965f.

c. "Humanistic psychology: A new break-through," *Amer. Psychol.*, 1963, 18:563–67.

d. "Sensitivity training and being motivation" (with R. Tannenbaum) *J. Hum. Psy.*, 1963, 3:76–85.

e. "Teamwork at the top," *Credit Union Executive*, 1963, 2:14–20.

1964

a. "The human frontier in the schools," in *Action Patterns for School Psychologists*, Los Angeles: California Association of School Psychologists & Psychometrists, 1964.

b. "Investigations into the self-concept: III. Instructions for the W-A-Y experiment," *Psychological Reports*, 1964, 15:643–50.

c. "The nature of the therapeutic task in extensive psychotherapy," *J. Existentialism*, 1964, 5(18):199–204.

d. "Personality tests: A last word," *Credit Union Executive*, 1964, 3(1):16–20.

e. "The person who is the psychotherapist," *J. Consult. Psy.*, 1964, 28:272–77.

f. "The person behind the ideas" (a regular column), *J. Hum. Psy.*, Spring (pp. 111–13) and Fall (pp. 181–83) 1965; Fall (pp. 236–38) 1966.

g. "Psychodiagnostics and request for certainty," *Psychiatry*, 1964, 27:73–77.

h. "The third force in psychology," *J. Hum. Psy.*, 1964, 4:19–26.

1965

a. "A critique of Peter Koestenbaum's 'The vitality of death'," *J. Existentialism*, 1965, 5:433–36.

b. "The existential crisis in intensive psychotherapy," *Psychotherapy: Theory, Research & Practice*, 1965, 2:16–20.

c. "Existential tragedy & the psychotherapeutic process," *Process*, 1965, 2(1):item no. 3.

d. "Introduction to the papers presented at the First Invitational Conference on Humanistic Psychology," *J. Hum. Psy.*, 1965, 5:180–81.

e. "Psychology's stake in the field of psychotherapy," *Bulletin Psychologists Interested in the Advancement of Psychotherapy*, 1965, 5(1):16–18.

f. *The Search for Authenticity: An Existential-Analytic Approach to Psychotherapy*, New York: Holt, Rinehart & Winston, 1965.

1966

a. "Humanistic psychology and the clinician," in L. E. Abt and B. F. Riess (Eds.), *Progress in Clinical Psychology*, Vol. 7, New York: Grune and Stratton, 1966.

b. Editor and Epilogue of "Symposium on Karl Buhler's contributions to psychology," *J. General Psy.*, 1966, 75:181–219.

1967

a. Editor of *Challenges of Humanistic Psychology*, New York: McGraw-Hill, 1967.

b. "The challenge that is man," in B1967a:5–11.

c. "Commitment and the psychotherapist," *Existential Psychiatry*, 1967, 6(23):285–92.

d. "The elastic clock," *Humanitas*, 1967, 3:5–21.

e. "The existential and the everyday," *Amer. J. Orthopsychiatry*, 1967, 37:628–30.

f. "Existential non-being and the need for inspiriting in psychotherapy," in P. Koestenbaum (Ed.), *Proceedings of San Jose State College Conference on Existential Philosophy and Psychotherapy*, San Jose, Calif., Nov. 18, 1967.

g. "Marathon meetings for therapy groups," *POCA Press* (Psychiatric Outpatient Centers of America), 1967, 5:4,10.

h. "Psychology and retreats: Frontier for experimentation" (with Gerard V. Haigh), in R. J. Magee (Ed.), *Call to Adventure*, Nashville: Abdington-Collesbury, 1967.

1968

a. "The humanistic ethic," *J. Hum. Psy.*, 1968, 7:11–25.

b. "Psychotherapy as a source of the therapist's own authenticity and inauthenticity," *Voices*, 1968, 4:13–23.

c. "Values and existential unity," in C. Buhler and F. Massarik (Eds.), *The Human Cause of Life*, New York: Springer, 1968, pp. 383–92.

1969

a. "Intentionality and ambivalence," in R. MacLeod (Ed.), *The Unfinished Business of William James*, Washington, D.C.: American Psychological Association, 1969, pp. 383–92.

b. "Someone needs to worry: The existential anxiety of responsibility and decision," *J. Contemp. Psychotherapy*, 1969, 2(1):41–53; A. G. Athos, J. Gabarro, and G. Holtz, *Interpersonal Behavior and Management*, Englewood Cliffs, NJ: Prentice-Hall, 1978, pp. 518–28.

c. "Agency: Satan unmasked," Review of D. Bakan, *The Duality of Human Existence*, *J. Contemp. Psychotherapy*, 1969, 14:347–48.

1970

a. "Changes in inner human experience and the future," in C. S. Wallia (Ed.), *Toward Century 21: Technology, Society and Human Values*, New York: Basic Books, 1970, pp. 283–95.

b. Review of H. Cox, *The Feast of Fools, Psy. Today*, 1970, 3(11):8,10.

c. Contributor to Warren H. Schmidt, *Organizational Frontiers and Human Values* Belmont, Calif.: Wadsworth, 1970.

1971

a. "The search for the hidden God," *Voices*, 1971, 7:33–37.

b. *The Human Possibility: An Essay toward a Psychological Response to the World Macroproblems*, Research Memorandum EPRC 6747–16, Menlo Park, Calif.: SRI International, 1971.

c. "The self: Process or illusion," in T. C. Greening (Ed.), *Existential Humanistic Psychology*, Belmont, Calif.: Brooks/Cole, 1971, pp. 57–71.

d. *The Humanistic Challenge of the Seventies* (Educational Policy Research Center), Menlo Park, Calif.: Stanford Research Institute, 1971.

1972

a. "Misconceptions of transpersonal psychotherapy: Comment on Ellis," *Voices*, 1972, 8:26–27.

b. Review of Maslow, *The Farther Reaches of Human Nature, Psy. Today*, 1972, 5(11):18–20.

1973

a. "Confronting the existential meaning of 'My Death' through group exercises," *Interpersonal Development*, 1973–74, 4:148–63.

1974

a. "The flight from finitude: Sadism, exhibitionism, and political madness," *Voices*, 1974, 10:40–46.

b. "Human diversity and human unity," in K.R.S. Iyengar (Ed.), *Sri Aurobindo: A Centenary Tribute*, Pondicherry, India: Sri Aurobindo Press, 1974, pp. 262–70.

1976

a. *The Search for Existential Identity: Patient-Therapist Dialogues in Humanistic Psychotherapy*, San Francisco: Jossey-Bass, 1976.

b. Toward a subjective psychology: Tribute to Charlotte Buhler," *Interpersonal Development*, 1976, 6:48–61.

c. "A primer for adult living," Review of V. Daniels and L. J. Horowitz, *Being and Caring*, Santa Rosa, Calif.: Press-Democrat, June 10, 1976.

1977

a. "The far side of despair," in D. Nevill (Ed.), *Humanistic Psychology: New Frontiers*, New York: Gardner Press, 1977, pp. 133–56.

1978

a. "The silence of the sky," in A. G. Athos, J. Gabarro, and J. Holtz (Eds.), *Interpersonal Behavior and Management*, Englewood Cliffs, N.J.: Prentice Hall, 1978, pp. 176–85.

b. *Psychotherapy and Process: The Fundamentals of an Existential-Humanistic Approach*, Reading, Mass.: Addison-Wesley, 1978.

c. "Existential-humanistic psychotherapy: Evoking the subjective potential," in R. Herink (Ed.), *Psychotherapy Handbook*, New York: Jason Aronson, 1978.

d. "It's easier to fight than to switch," *Association for Humanistic Psychology Newsletter*, March 1978, pp. 1,21–23.

e. *The Humanistic Perspective in Psychology* (with Ann Webster, Jeff Davidson, and Dorothy Smith), San Francisco: Humanistic Psychology Institute, 1978.

f. "Two poems: 'Trail-song' and 'A vision of ending'," *J. Hum. Psy.* 1978, 18:68.

1980

a. *Talking: The Fundamentals of Humanistic Professional Communication*, Santa Rosa, Calif.: Author, 1980.

1981

a. *The Search for Authenticity: An Existential-Analytic Approach to Psychology*, New York: Irvington, 1981. Enlarged edition of B1965f.

1982

a. *The Art of Psychotherapy: A Workbook and Readings Resource for Counselors and Psychotherapists*, Santa Rosa, Calif.: Author, 1982.

b. "We must mobilize concern for human destiny," *Forum for Correspondence and Contact*, 1982, 13:42–47.

c. Foreword in P. S. Rappaport, *Value for Value Psychotherapy: The Economic and Therapeutic Barter*, New York: Praeger, pp. v–viii.

1983

a. "Prescription for Survival," *Forum for Correspondence and Contact*, 1983, 13:32–34.

b. "The one absolute necessity in psychotherapy," *The Script*, 1983, 13:1–2.

1984

a. "A fate worse than death: The fear of changing," *Psychotherapy: Theory, Research & Practice*, 1984, 21:543–49.

b. "Dispiritedness: A new perspective on a familiar state," *J. Hum. Psy.*, 1984, 24:49–67.

1985

a. "Seek a wild God," *Association for Humanistic Psychology Perspective*, March 1985, p. 8.

1986

a. "Existential-Humanistic Psychotherapy," in I. L. Kutash and A. Wolf (Eds.), *Psychotherapist's Casebook*, San Francisco: Jossey-Bass, pp. 222–36.

b. "Resistance to and fear of change," in F. Flach (Ed.), *The Directions in Psychiatry Monograph Series*, Vol. 6. New York: Norton, 1986, pp. 58–67.

c. "A Hupersonian invention," *Redwood Psychological Association Newsletter*, May 1986, pp. 5–6.

1987

a. *The Art of the Psychotherapist*, New York: Norton, 1987.

b. Discussion of Thomas S. Szasz, "Justifying coercion through theology and therapy," in J. K. Zeig (Ed.), *The Evolution of Psychotherapy*, New York: Bruner/Mazel, pp. 424–26.

c. "The depth psychotherapist as artist," *New Jersey Journal of Professional Counseling*, 1987, 50:5–8.

1988

a. "What is 'Failure' is psychotherapy?" *Psychotherapy*, 1989, 25:532–35.

b. Foreword in R. Valle and S. Halling (Eds.), *Existential-Phenomenological Perspective in Psychology*, San Francisco: Jossey-Bass, 1988.

c. "My writing credo," *J. Hum. Psy.*, 1988, 28:63.

d. "Whatever happened to scholarly discourse? A Reply to B. F. Skinner," (with S. Krippner, et al.), *Amer. Psychologist*, 1988, 43:819.

e. *Humanistic Psychology* (interview with J. Mishlove), San Rafael, Calif.: Thinking Allowed Productions: 1988. Video.

f. "Testing the lows," in N. Saltzman (Ed.), "Symposium", *Journal of Integrative and Eclectic Psychotherapy*, 1988, 7:462–65.

Index

Adler, Alfred, 25, 49–50, 58 n.10, 113–14
Allport, Gordon, W.: APA presidential addresses (1939 and 1946), 34, 38, 40; and behaviorism, 34, 38, 40–41, 138–39; biography, 17–19; Distinguished-Scientific Contribution Award, 19; early upbringing, 17; and Eastern thought, 80; education, 17; ego, view of, 85; ethics, views on, 96, 101–4, 107–9, 147–49; and existentialism, 61–62, 141–43; and Freud, S. (*see* psychoanalysis); functional autonomy, concept of, 19, 49, 51, 54, 65, 85, 103; and Gestalt psychology, 77–78; and Goldstein, Kurt, 76; and humanistic psychology, 18; human nature, understanding of, 18–19, 43, 84–86, 123, 145–47; and Lewin, Kurt, 78; life work, 18–19; on the Lockean/Leibnitzian philosophical traditions, 3; method in psychology, views on the problem of, 70, 112, 115–17, 121–26, 144–45; and personality psychology, 76; phenomenology, views on, 69–71; post-doctoral fellowship in Germany, 17, 34, 115; and psychoanalysis, 47–48, 51–54, 58 n.6, 140–41; systematic eclecticism, 18, 85, 122–24; trait, concept of, 85; values, (*see* views on ethics). Works: *Becoming: Basic Consideration for a Psychology of Personality*, 18, 43; *Letters from Jenny*, 124; *The Nature of Personality*, 19; *The Nature of Prejudice*, 69; *Patterns and Growth*, 18, 80; *Personality: A Psychological Interpretation*, 18, 76, 78; *Personality and Social Encounter*, 19; *The Person in Psychology*, 19; "The Standpoint of Gestalt Psychology," 78; *Studies in Expressive Movement*, 116; *A Study of Values*, 76, 116

American Psychological Association (APA), 7–8, 12–13, 18, 19, 34, 136; Cincinnati Symposium on Existential Psychology (1964), 64, 127

Ansbacher, Heinz, 9, 49

Arons, Myrons, 13

Association for Humanistic Psychology (AHP): "American" dropped from AHP's title, 10, 12; and APA, 1, 7–8, 12–13, 136; and Bugental, James F. T., 10; and Buhler, Charlotte, 12; disaffiliation from Brandeis, 11; early membership, 1–2, 137; early membership drive, 11; educational concerns of,